HISTORY OF FLORIDA.

HISTORY of FLORIDA

⁂

FROM ITS DISCOVERY BY
PONCE DE LEON IN 1512 TO THE
CLOSE OF THE FLORIDA WAR IN 1842

⁂

George R. Fairbanks

HERITAGE BOOKS
2011

HERITAGE BOOKS
AN IMPRINT OF HERITAGE BOOKS, INC.

Books, CDs, and more—Worldwide

For our listing of thousands of titles see our website
at
www.HeritageBooks.com

A Facsimile Reprint
Published 2011 by
HERITAGE BOOKS, INC.
Publishing Division
100 Railroad Ave. #104
Westminster, Maryland 21157

Originally published:
Philadelphia, Pennsylvania
1871

Copyright © 2003 Heritage Books, Inc.

— Publisher's Notice —
In reprints such as this, it is often not possible to remove blemishes from the original. We feel the contents of this book warrant its reissue despite these blemishes and hope you will agree and read it with pleasure.

International Standard Book Numbers
Paperbound: 978-0-7884-2280-5
Clothbound: 978-0-7884-8856-6

TO THE MEMORY OF MY HONORED FRIEND,

ISAAC H. BRONSON,

THE FIRST JUDGE OF THE UNITED STATES DISTRICT COURT, NORTHERN DISTRICT
OF FLORIDA,

A CITIZEN

WHOSE PRIVATE LIFE AND PUBLIC VIRTUES SHED LUSTRE UPON THE
STATE OF HIS ADOPTION,

THIS VOLUME

IS RESPECTFULLY INSCRIBED

BY THE AUTHOR.

PREFACE.

APART from the interest attached to Florida from its having been the first portion of the United States occupied by Europeans, it is associated with some of the most interesting and romantic events in American history. Portions of its long and eventful history have been written in the Latin, French, Spanish, and English languages. As early as 1591, De Bry published, in the Latin language, an account of the settlement of the Huguenots and the destruction of their colony, illustrated by fifty well-executed engravings; and many later writers have treated of the history, climate, and natural productions of Florida, among whom may be mentioned La Vega, Fernandez, Biedma, Barcia, De Vaca, Herrera, Hakluyt, Roberts, Stark, Romans, De Brahm, Bartram, Vignoles, Forbes, and Darby; Williams published a very complete gazetteer in 1837; and to these should be added the valuable work of General Sprague, of the United States Army, "The History of the Florida War." Buckingham Smith, Esq., formerly Secretary of Legation to Spain, whose life has been devoted to the investigation of Spanish and Indian antiquities, has edited, with valuable critical and descriptive notes, several of the most interesting works upon Florida. But, although so much has been written in reference to Florida, hitherto no connected history of the State has been published; and it has been the object of the writer of this work to bring within a moderate compass a complete and authentic history of the State, from its discovery by Ponce de Leon to the close of the Florida War.

For obvious reasons, the events of the late civil war have not been incorporated in the present volume. They will, doubtless, at some future time, form the material of a chapter of no inconsiderable interest.

UNIVERSITY OF THE SOUTH, *Sewanee, Tenn.*, Jan. 1871.

CONTENTS.

CHAPTER I.
Discovery of Florida by Ponce de Leon — Expeditions of De Ayllon, Miruelo, Cordova, Alaminos, and Verazzano . . 13

CHAPTER II.
Expedition and Shipwreck of Panfilo de Narvaez, and Adventures of Cabeça de Vaca, the Discoverer of the Mississippi . 29

CHAPTER III.
Expedition of Hernando de Soto 48

CHAPTER IV.
Expedition of Hernando de Soto, continued 60

CHAPTER V.
Route of De Soto's Expedition through Florida 73

CHAPTER VI.
Other Expeditions to Florida — Occupation of Santa Maria by Tristan de Luna — Expedition to the Borders of Tennessee and the Province of Coca 77

CHAPTER VII.

Huguenot Settlements at Charles Fort under Ribaut, and at Fort Caroline under Laudonnière 92

CHAPTER VIII.

French Expedition of Ribaut to relieve Fort Caroline—Spanish Expedition of Menendez to expel the Huguenots—Capture of Fort Caroline by Menendez, and Massacre of the Garrison . 111

CHAPTER IX.

Shipwreck and Massacre of Ribaut and his Followers . . 121

CHAPTER X.

Situation of Matters at St. Augustine, and Explorations made by Menendez 133

CHAPTER XI.

Recapture of Fort Caroline, and the Notable Revenge of Dominic de Gourgues 142

CHAPTER XII.

Return of Menendez—Attack on St. Augustine by Sir Francis Drake—Missions to the Indians, and Massacre of the Mission Fathers—Attack on St. Augustine by Captain Davis—Establishment of a Spanish Settlement at Pensacola . . . 156

CHAPTER XIII.

Governor Moore's Attack on St. Augustine—Invasion of Moore, with the Creek Indians, of the Indian Missions and Spanish Posts in Middle Florida—Erection of a Fort at St. Mark's—Capture of Pensacola by the French—Recapture of Pensacola by the Spaniards—Recapture of Pensacola by the French—Transfer of Pensacola to Spain 171

CONTENTS.

CHAPTER XIV.

Attack on St. Augustine by Oglethorpe—Attack of Monteano on St. Simon's Island—Transfer of Florida to Great Britain . . 190

CHAPTER XV.

Policy of the English Government for the Settlement of Florida—Land-Grants—Dr. Turnbull's Colony of Greeks and Minorcans at Smyrna—Governor Grant's Administration—Governor Tonyn's Administration—First Colonial Assembly—Revolutionary War—Burning of Effigies of Hancock and Adams . . 210

CHAPTER XVI.

English Occupation, continued—Capture of Pensacola by De Galvez—Capture of New Providence by the English—Retransfer of Florida to Spain 228

CHAPTER XVII.

Condition of the Province after its Recession to Spain—Notice of McGillivray—Operations of Bowles—Patriot Rebellion—Operations of United States Troops in Florida—Indian Hostilities, between the Americans and King Payne the Seminole . . 244

CHAPTER XVIII.

Occupation of Pensacola by the English—English driven from Pensacola by General Jackson—Destruction of Negro Fort on Apalachicola by Colonel Clinch—Defeat of Florida Indians by General Jackson—Occupation of Pensacola by General Jackson—Treaty with Spain, ceding Florida to United States . . 260

CHAPTER XIX.

Organization of Territory of Florida—Condition of the Indians—Treaty of Fort Moultrie—Indian Agency—Treaty of Payne's Landing—Collisions between the Races 269

CHAPTER XX.

Hostile Disposition of the Indians—Murder of General Thompson, Indian Agent—Massacre of Major Dade's Command—Battle of the Withlacoochee—General Scott's Campaign . . 284

CHAPTER XXI.

Florida War, continued—General Jesup in Command—Indian Assault on Fort Mellon—Capitulation of Fort Dade—Flight of the Indians from Fort Brooke—Capture of King Philip, Coacoochee, and Osceola—Battle of Okechobee—Escape of Coacoochee—Surrender of Halleck-Hajo and others—Results of General Jesup's Operations—General Taylor appointed to the Command 303

CHAPTER XXII.

Florida War, continued, under General Taylor—Removal of Apalachee Indians—General Macomb's Treaty with the Indians—Proclamation that the War was ended—Resumption of Hostilities—Massacre of Colonel Harney's Detachment—Tragical Fate of Mrs. Montgomery—The Cuba Bloodhounds—Expedition of Colonel Worth to Okechobee—Recapture of Coacoochee . 318

CHAPTER XXIII.

Florida War, continued, under Command of General Worth—Interview between General Worth and Coacoochee at Tampa Bay—Surrender of Coacoochee's Band—Active Operations of General Worth in the Everglades—Surrender of various Bands—Close of the Florida War 335

HISTORY OF FLORIDA.

CHAPTER I.

Discovery of Florida by Ponce de Leon—Expeditions of De Ayllon, Miruelo, Cordova, Alaminos, and Verazzano.

1512—1525.

THE discovery of Florida is one of the romantic episodes of history. Columbus and his successors had, rather by chance than design, pursued a southerly line of exploration, which had led them to the discovery, in the first instance, of the West India Islands, and, subsequently, of the mainland of South America and a small part of Central America. Even the shores of the vast Pacific had been reached by Balboa before the southeastern portion of the United States had been discovered. This seems the more singular, as the pursuit of a westerly course from Spain would have brought an expedition in sight of land on the coasts of North America much sooner than the southwesterly course, which carried the navigators to the islands and shores of the Caribbean Sea.

It has been claimed that Sebastian Cabot, in the year 1497, sailing under a commission granted by Henry VII. of England, coasted along the shores of North America from 61° to the southern extremity of Florida. It is, however, very doubtful whether he went south of Cape Hatteras, in lat. 36°, the whole statement resting upon a passage in Peter Martyr, in which it is stated "that Cabot sailed so far toward the west that he had the island of Cuba on his left hand, in manner, in the same degree of longitude."*

This expression, in connection with the previous statement that he had sailed as far southward as the Straits of Gibraltar, would indicate Cape Hatteras as the southern limit of his voyage. At the period of these early voyages the name of Florida was applied to the whole coast, from the Chesapeake southwards.

The generally received opinion, however, confers the credit of the discovery of Florida upon Juan Ponce de Leon, in the year 1512. The origin of the expedition which resulted in the discovery, and the object of its prosecution by the romantic old cavalier, have associated Florida with the Fountain of Youth so long embalmed in ancient fable.

Juan Ponce de Leon was one of the companions of Columbus upon his second voyage, and subsequently remained on the island of Hispaniola as an officer of some reputation under Ovando. While thus employed he visited the island of Porto Rico, and eventually received a commission to conquer and colonize that island. After various turns of fortune, checkered with successes and adversities, he at length succeeded in accomplishing its subjugation, only to find himself, as was not infrequent in those days, superseded

---

* "Thus seeing such heapes of yce before him, he was enforced to turne his saile and follow the west, so coasting still by the shore that he was thereby brought so farre into the south by reason of the land bending so much southwards that it was thereby almost equal in latitude with the Straits of Herculaneum, having the North Pole elevate in a manner with the same degree. He sailed likewise in this tract so far toward the west that he had the island of Cuba on his left hand, in manner, in the same degree of longitude."—HAKLUYT, vol. iii.

by some newer favorite of the court. Thus deprived of his dignity as Adelantado of Porto Rico, the restless old soldier turned, naturally enough, to the setting on foot of some new expedition, which should redound to his honor and profit.

The explorations to the south and west had already engaged the attention of many others, and it was the fashion in those days to apportion limits, which would preclude all, except the duly commissioned parties, from visiting or exploring within certain degrees of latitude and longitude.

This arrangement was the more readily made, inasmuch as at the outset of the discoveries in the western seas Pope Alexander VI. had, by special grant, given to his Catholic Majesty of Spain—no diplomatic notes of protest being made by other powers, those most interested being ignorant of the concession—unlimited sway over all the countries, nations, and people lying to the westward of those previously assigned to the crown of Portugal.

While casting about in his mind as to what direction to give to his proposed enterprise, the veteran was informed by some of those purveyors of the marvelous who can always manage to supply the appetite of the credulous, that there was a famous land, lying to the northwest, which contained within its borders all the treasures of El Dorado, and, moreover, to its other wonders added that of possessing a stream the waters of which were gifted with the power of conferring upon those who should bathe themselves therein the freshness of youth and a renovation of all their faculties.

This enticing description appealed to Ponce de Leon by many considerations, among the most prominent of which was the natural craving for gold felt by him in common with all the adventurers; and, moreover, to one sensibly declining in years and strength, nothing could be more desirable than to obtain a fresh lease of youthful vigor and enjoyment; while to these potent reasons was added the expectation that the honor which would crown the happy discoverer of this wonderful land would exceed that of all his predecessors in the field of discovery.

The veteran officer had acquired some degree of wealth in his public employments, and was thus enabled, from his own means, to equip three vessels for his expedition. He easily obtained followers to accompany him, as credulity was not a rare quality, and the real wonders of the New World were apparently as strange as any that could be invented.

Departing from Porto Rico in the spring of 1512, Ponce de Leon directed his course, in the first instance, towards the supposed location of Bimini, an island which shared with the other unknown region the possession of one of these wonderful fountains, and was said to lie near at hand in the Lucayan group. A long cruise amid the Bahama cluster of rocks and islets gave no satisfactory result to his search for the fabled Bimini, and, like many other wonders, more seemed to be known about it at a distance than in the locality where it was said to exist.

Unable, after a long exploration, to find Bimini, he then determined to seek the more distant land which had tempted his covetousness and his ambition. It is highly probable that, in cruising among the Bahamas, he received information of the existence of land to the northwest of them, as the Strait of Florida is but some fifty miles in width, and the natives had, doubtless, some intercourse across the calm summer seas with their neighbors of the main. He first made land on the eastern coast of Florida on Sunday, the 27th of March, 1512, but did not set foot upon its shores until the 2d of April, in lat. 30° 8', at a point probably a short distance northerly of St. Augustine. The Indian name of the country is said to have been Cautio, but Ponce de Leon, following the custom of the times, by reason of having come upon the coast on Palm-Sunday—Pascua Florida, as it is called in Spanish—and probably delighted with the green verdure and flowing glades which opened upon his view, gave to his supposed island the name of FLORIDA. The usual ceremony of planting a cross and taking possession of the country in the name of the Spanish monarch, swearing allegiance to his throne, and throwing the royal banner to the breeze, was observed, and the country came thereby to be considered by their Catholic Majesties a Spanish province by right of discovery.

They remained on the coast some two months, exploring the interior to some extent, and visiting various portions of the shores of the supposed island. The inhabitants they found to be fierce and implacable, and the explorations made brought to light neither riches nor treasures of any kind; nor could the eager De Leon obtain any tidings of the fabled fountain which was to renew his youth. Finally, discouraged with the fruitless results of his expedition, he returned to Porto Rico, carrying with him nothing of value but the report of his discovery.

Whether the story of the Fountain of Youth, and of the golden treasures of the mainland, was a pure fable, or whether it was merely a poetic and exaggerated description of the country, may well admit of a doubt: I am inclined, however, to the belief that the latter is the more reasonable view of it.

While much of Florida is in one sense comparatively barren, yet the evergreen and luxuriant foliage which covers its soil and hangs in rich masses along the banks of its streams, the pleasant equability of its climate, a country affording in its rivers, its forests, and its productions, easy means for the support of life to a savage race—while the passion for display could be gratified by the gold and pearls obtained, with no great difficulty, from the streams and hills of Georgia—might well cause it to be accounted by the occasional visitors from the adjoining isles as indeed a rich and pleasant country, and even the fabled fountain might seem to find a realization in some of the remarkably beautiful springs which exist in various portions of the country. Who that has ever floated on the bright waters of Silver Spring, or the bosom of the Wakulla, has not felt his pulses thrill with delight at the almost unreal character of the scene?—the waters so pellucid that one seems suspended in mid-air; the shadows from the skies above rest in changing beauty in its depths; while the bright sunlight flecks the silvery rocks below with rays of dazzling brightness, and an azure tinge encircles every object and surrounds it with a halo of purplish light. It is not strange that they should be deemed to possess a renovating elixir, and to promise, to those who would dwell by their banks and disport in their waters, a restoration of youthful vigor and energy.

Ponce de Leon, on leaving Florida, again searched for the renowned island Bimini, but with no better success than before, and thence returned to Porto Rico, putting the best face on the matter, and determined to gain whatever credit might attach to his discovery of a new region of country; doubtless to enhance its importance, he made a flattering report of its riches and value. The purpose of his expedition had in the mean time become widely known, and the wits of the Spanish court rallied him not a little upon his pursuit of the Fountain of Youth.

He sought for, and obtained, however, from the crown, the title and privileges, whatever they might be worth, of Adelantado of Florida, agreeing to transport thither three hundred men, and to conquer and colonize it for his Majesty. He was to commence his enterprise within one year, and to explore the country within three years. He did not appear, however, to be in any haste to revisit it, and accepted the command of an expedition against the Cauto Indians, in which he was unsuccessful.

In the mean time, in the year 1516, Diego Miruelo, a pilot, sailed from Cuba with a single vessel, and, directing his course to Florida, obtained from some of the natives he encountered, pieces of gold, but without much exploration returned to Cuba, where he gave most glowing accounts of the richness of that country and its neighboring islands, and excited the wish among a large number of persons to undertake an expedition to its shores.

In the following year an expedition landed in Florida from a vessel commanded by Fernandez de Cordova. Bernal Diaz, afterwards so well known in connection with the conquest of Mexico, accompanied this party. Although they placed sentinels upon their landing, and took every precaution against surprise, they were unexpectedly attacked by a large body of natives, who wounded six and killed one of their number. The attack was made so vigorously that the Spaniards escaped with difficulty to their vessel, and were glad to return to Cuba, where their leader died of his wounds.

One Anton de Alaminos was of this party, and, upon his arrival in Cuba, undertook to make a full report of what he had observed upon the coasts of New Spain and Florida, to the governor of Jamaica, Don Francisco de Garay, giving a glowing account of the extent and riches of those regions.

De Garay gave such encouragement to Alaminos that he went with three vessels to the coast of Florida, landed twice upon its shores, and was each time forced by the Indians to re-embark, and, pursuing his voyage, coasted the Mexican Gulf as far as the river Panuco. His patron, assured of the truth of the representations he had made, applied to the Spanish crown for the Adelantadoship and government of the country. As no further action was had by De Garay, it is presumable that he did not succeed in his application.

Lucas Vasquez de Ayllon, an officer of some distinction, holding several profitable employments in Hispaniola, and, as a consequence, very rich, formed a company on joint venture, in 1520, with six of his neighbors, having for its principal object the procuring slaves from among the Caribs, to work the mines of that island. The capture of these Caribs was an ingenious device of the settlers to replenish their supply of labor, which their hard usage of the natives had much diminished. The remonstrances and efforts of Las Casas had induced the Spanish court to issue decrees calculated to insure better treatment; but it was found that the inhabitants of some of the islands were entirely impracticable, and the story was started that these Caribs were cannibals, and they were thus placed beyond the pale of humanity; so that it was not difficult to exclude them from the benefit of the humane laws framed to repress the rapacity and cruelty of the colonists. Of course, if it was deemed necessary to obtain labor, nothing was easier than to discover an island of Caribs.

De Ayllon made his preparations for a descent upon the inhabitants of the Lucayan Isles, a quiet and inoffensive people, among whom Columbus had first landed, and from whom he had received every mark of unsophisticated kindness; but they happened to be near at hand, and some one could be found to declare that they were Caribs and cannibals, if it was the interest of others to have it so.

For the purpose of this expedition, De Ayllon fitted out two vessels, and made sail for these islands. Unsuccessful in entrapping the natives, and driven off by severe weather, he passed to the northward, and came to the land of Chicora, on the coast of South Carolina.

Of this wonderful land, two remarkable things are related with much gravity by the ancient chronicler. They say he reports that the royal personages of Xapida, a neighboring province, were giants, made so artificially. The mode in which this was accomplished was as follows: While in tender infancy, certain Indian masters of the art took the young prince and princess, and softened their bones like wax, with plasters made of certain herbs, until they left them lifeless in appearance. The nurse who suckled the children was fed with very nutritious food. After some days, the professors in charge of the matter returned and stretched the bones of the infants, and did the same with the nurse, until they had arrived at such a stage of progress as would enable them to increase more than any others in stature, according to their experience in such matters. Others say, upon the authority of the Indians, that they grew so large because they were fed upon such rare and efficacious herbs that their growth was forced. This wonderful art may be considered as one of those lost of old, and these rare and curious plants are no longer known, even to the weird sisters.

Another remarkable thing, which De Ayllon learned upon this expedition, was the existence of a race of beings with a caudal appendage, similar to that of the equine race, which was whisked about with great vigor. The diet of these singular beings was raw fish.

Subsequent explorers seem never to have encountered these races, unless Gulliver's visit to the Houyhnhnms be considered as authentic history. Such are the mixed creations of the imagination, interspersed with realities, which characterize the relations of the early voyagers.

De Ayllon landed at various points, and received only

kindness at the hands of the natives. By gifts and protestations of friendship, he enticed some one hundred and thirty of them on board his vessels, and set sail for Hispaniola.

So sudden and treacherous an act struck his captives with amazement, and aroused their fierce indignation; no kindness or attention could reconcile them to their fate, and no artifice could divert the minds of the proud and high-spirited sons of Chicora from their grief and proud despair. They were of a different race and spirit from the natives of the Antilles, and would not submit to the restraints sought to be placed upon them. They were of an unconquerable spirit, and their successors upon the soil of Chicora, the gallant sons of Carolina, have vindicated their claim to be considered their descendants, in their spirit of independence and bold assertion of their rights and liberties.

One of the two vessels foundered at sea, and went down with all on board. The other arrived in Hispaniola; but De Ayllon was severely censured for the artifices used to entrap the people of Chicora; and the final history and result of the expedition are thus briefly and pointedly told: *"y los Indios no sirvieron de nada, porque casi todos murieron de enejo y tristeca."* (These Indians profited them nothing, because they all died of care and grief.)

Some years had now elapsed since the veteran Juan Ponce de Leon had obtained the title and privileges of Adelantado of Florida and Bimini; but, discouraged by the reception which he had met with at the hands of the warlike Floridians, and by the ill success which he had encountered in his attempts to chastise the Caribs, he had remained inactive in his alcaldeship of the town of Porto Rico, yet not unobservant of the reports brought by the various expeditions which had, in the mean while, visited the shores of Florida. The voyages of Miruelos and Alaminos in the Gulf of Mexico, and of De Ayllon on the Atlantic coast, had proved that Florida was not, as he had supposed, an island, but a continent of illimitable extent, and of greater richness and value than his own observation had led him to believe.

His ambition and his avarice were again aroused, and he looked forward with renewed hope, not to finding his Fountain of Youth, but to founding an empire which should give to his name an enduring celebrity. During the year 1521 he concluded his arrangements for another expedition to Florida: Cortez had commenced his wonderful enterprise of effecting the conquest of Mexico two years previously, and the reports of his exploits had doubtless reached the sturdy Ponce de Leon and infused into his veins new ardor to undertake a similar enterprise. He fitted out two vessels at his own expense, and absorbed his entire fortune in his outfit. He reached Florida, after severe storms at sea, and landed on the nearest shore, eager to anticipate all others in planting his standard on the soil of his Adelantadoship. Doubtless his first act, upon landing, was to cause his notary to make proclamation of his sovereignty and right to the allegiance of the natives, as their governor-general, and to require their obedience, as was the custom of the great captains in those days. The answer of his liege subjects on this occasion was of a most unsatisfactory character, for they attacked his forces with the utmost fierceness and impetuosity, killing great numbers of the Spaniards, and wounding the governor himself severely, forcing them to retreat precipitately to their ships and to leave their coasts.

Ponce de Leon, grievously wounded and sick at heart, and doubtless depressed at the apparent ill fortune which seemed to attend all the enterprises of his declining years, and, perhaps, believing, with the superstitious feeling of his countrymen, that some malignant fate overshadowed his destiny, rankling with pain of both head and heart, succumbed to the adverse winds of fortune, abandoned the shores of Florida, and the prospective honors before him, and sailed to the neighboring coast of Cuba, where, after a few days, he died, regretted and honored by many who had known the bold and adventurous cavalier in his earlier years. This simple epitaph was inscribed on his monument :—*

> Mole sub hoc fortis
> Requiescunt ossa Leonis
> Qui vicit factis
> Nomina magna suis.

Which was rendered into Spanish by Castellano, as follows :—

> Aquesto lugar estrecho
> Es sepulcro del varon
> Que en el nombre fue Leon
> Y mucho mas en el hecho.†

Ponce de Leon left a son named Louis, upon whom the emperor conferred the Adelantadoship and honors of his father. It does not appear, however, that he ever made any use of his privileges, or attempted to carry out the designs of his father; and he is heard of no more in connection with the history of Florida.

Of all the historic names associated with its long history, De Soto alone perhaps excepted, the name of Ponce de Leon stands out more prominently than any other: the romantic character of his expedition has won for him a

---

* Irving's Spanish Voyages of Discovery.

† In this sepulchre rest the bones of a man who was a Lion by name and still more by nature.

name and a remembrance which the real importance of anything he attempted or accomplished, in that or any other quarter, would have failed to give him—so true it is that the folly or credulity of mankind often makes more impression upon the public mind than distinguished virtues.

In the mean time, De Ayllon, not discouraged by the profitless results of his abduction of the natives of Chicora, and trusting, by renewed effort, to make an advantageous lodgment upon that coast, proceeded first to Spain, taking with him one of the natives of Chicora, named Francisco, a captive whom he had instructed in the faith and language of the Spaniards. Having presented himself at court, De Ayllon related to the ministers of the crown the events of the voyage he had undertaken to Chicora, described the situation of the country, its fruits and productions, as well as the manners and customs of its inhabitants, and sought the privilege of its conquest and settlement. This was granted, with the additional honor of being created a Knight of the Order of St. Iago.

The agreement entered into between the king and De Ayllon contained, however, a special article, which forbade the subjection of the natives, or the granting of *repartimientos*, which, up to that period, had been usually given, and had been deemed a necessary privilege granted to the Royal Adelantados and conquerors. This clause was probably due to the untiring efforts of Las Casas to ameliorate the condition of the poor natives, and may also have had some reference to the previous foray of De Ayllon upon the people of Chicora. It is an interesting fact in this connection that a greater amount of consideration was accorded to the natives of the mainland of our own section of country, than to the people of the islands which the Spaniards had occupied. By the tenor of the Royal

Assiento with De Ayllon, the natives of Florida were to be treated as freedmen and vassals, and to receive compensation for their labor.

Owing to delays in making his preparations, it was not until 1524 that De Ayllon was enabled, in conformity with his agreement, to dispatch two vessels to begin the exploration of that portion of the mainland embraced within his contract, which was from the 35th to the 37th degree of N. latitude. These vessels soon returned, bringing specimens of gold, silver, and pearls, and with so favorable a report of the country which they had visited, that De Ayllon determined to set out at once and take possession of his province of Chicora. He refitted the two vessels which had just returned, and, adding a third, again set sail, and safely reached his destination. Choosing a favorable point for landing, with the view of establishing a settlement, he disembarked, and was received by the natives with affected cordiality and pleasure, and this was carried to such an extent as to disarm him of all suspicion. He at once concluded that his design would readily be accomplished, and congratulated himself upon the ease and dexterity with which he had glided into his government. For the purpose of exploring the country, he dispatched a party of two hundred men to visit a town a day's journey from the coast. This party was hospitably entertained and feasted by the natives for four days, and all precautions on the part of the Spaniards being laid aside, they were suddenly set upon, and the whole company destroyed, not one being left to carry to De Ayllon the news of the disaster. A vigorous attack was then made upon those who had remained in charge of the ships, who, getting on board with much difficulty, made sail.

It is said that De Ayllon himself perished in this massacre, and shared in the terrible retribution which was visited upon the expedition, on account of the duplicity and treachery of which De Ayllon had been guilty upon his first expedition. The son of De Ayllon sought of the crown the rights and privileges of his father, which were granted to him; but, being unable to equip an expedition, he died in Spain, it is said, of melancholy, in consequence of his disappointment.

About this period, Juan Verazzano, an Italian navigator in the French service, came upon the coast of North America in about latitude 35°, landed at various points as he coasted northward, enjoying the most friendly intercourse with the natives, and coasted as far north as Cape Cod. He returned thence to France, and gave a brief account of his voyage and of the manners, customs, and appearance of the different tribes of Indians whom he from time to time encountered at different points on the coast. He made a second voyage to America, and was never again heard of, having perished probably at sea.*

Public attention in Spain and the islands was now directed for many years to the progress of events in Mexico, where Cortez was prosecuting his successful career of conquest, surpassing in the brilliancy of his deeds all that had hitherto been accomplished upon the shores of America, and giving a new stimulus to the love for adventure in all classes.

From the success of Cortez, it seemed probable to the public mind that in the interior of both North and South America regions existed of great fertility, and abounding in gold, silver, and pearls, only requiring the stout arm and brave heart of a Cortez to give to whomsoever should discover them the like rewards.

An expedition for the conquest and settlement of Florida

---

* Hakluyt, vol. iii. p. 295.

was about to be undertaken upon a much larger scale, and under fairer auspices, than those which had preceded it.

It was hoped that a new empire would be conquered, north and east of Mexico, in an indefinitely located region described as lying between the River of Palms (near Tampico) and the limits of Florida, which latter was, in those days, a general designation of the countries bordering upon the Atlantic.

This long shore-line, from the Capes of Labrador southward to the Gulf of Mexico, was claimed at a subsequent period by two different parties, with about equal justice. The discovery of Florida by Ponce de Leon was considered by the Spanish crown as establishing their prior claim and right of dominion over the whole coast, while the English fell back upon the voyage of Cabot in 1497, and the view he obtained of the coast, as establishing theirs. Subsequently France, as a third party, interposed the much stronger claim of actual occupation to much of the country.

CHAPTER II.

Expedition and Shipwreck of Panfilo de Narvaez, and Adventures of Cabeça de Vaca, the Discoverer of the Mississippi.

1527.

THOSE familiar with the history of the conquest of Mexico will recollect that after the successful march of Cortez upon the city of Mexico, and his occupation of the capital of the Aztec Empire, Velasquez, the governor of Cuba, under whose orders he had originally commenced the enterprise, became jealous of the success and position of Cortez, and sent his lieutenant, Panfilo de Narvaez, to supersede the daring adventurer.

The gallant and astute conqueror of Mexico felt no disposition to have his laurels thus plucked from him, and although Narvaez had brought with him a force of nine hundred Spaniards and one thousand Indians of Cuba, while Cortez had less than three hundred at his command, yet he determined, by a sudden and bold attack, to seize his rival and frustrate his intentions. His plan, favored by a stormy night, during which his opponents slept in fancied security, was entirely successful. Narvaez was taken prisoner, having lost an eye in the mêlée, and his forces submitted willingly, for the most part, to the leadership of the gallant Hernan Cortez.

Narvaez appears to have been a leader of some military capacity, although negligent and lax in his discipline. He possessed undoubted courage, but this quality was rendered nugatory by an overweening confidence in his own powers, which made him deaf to the suggestions of others more sagacious than himself. He was altogether deficient in that prudent and calculating foresight demanded in a leader who has to travel out of the beaten track, face unforeseen obstacles and an active and enterprising foe.

Disappointed and crestfallen, after his release by Cortez, Narvaez returned to Spain, and endeavored to obtain redress at court, but his sagacious opponent had already rendered his own version of the affair, and had vindicated himself from the charge of disloyalty to the crown, while the lustre and interest attached to the report of his memorable adventures in the subjugation of the Mexican capital effaced all the detractions which had been so industriously sent home by his rival.

Failing to enlist any sympathy in his complaints against Cortez, Narvaez next turned his attention to getting up some new expedition, and asked the authority of the crown to undertake the conquest of Florida, with the title of Adelantado of all the regions which he might discover and conquer within certain limits. Hitherto the march of the Spanish explorers in America had, with few exceptions, been unchecked, and the path of discovery had become the road to successful conquest. Mexico, Panama, and the Spanish Main, as well as most of the islands in the Caribbean Sea, had submitted to the Spanish rule, and a mere handful of Spaniards had sufficed to rout thousands of defenseless natives. The native was consequently despised, and successful resistance was never anticipated.

Duly commissioned to conquer and govern the provinces of the mainland, extending from the River of Palms (near Tampico) to Cape Florida, Narvaez left the port of San Lucar, in Spain, on the 17th of June, 1527, with five vessels, carrying six hundred men. He stopped at Hispaniola, with the purpose of refitting and provisioning his vessels. While thus delayed, one hundred and forty of his men withdrew from the enterprise, preferring to remain in St. Domingo. After a sojourn of forty-five days, the vessels sailed to the port of St. Iago, in Cuba, and there made arrangements for procuring provisions, which he found he could obtain at Trinidad, a port a hundred leagues to the west. He dispatched two of his vessels to that point, where they were overtaken by a hurricane, and totally destroyed, with all on board, some seventy souls. Owing to this disaster, he was compelled to defer his expedition until the spring. He purchased other vessels to supply the place of those which had been wrecked, and found some additional followers to accompany him.

He finally embarked in April, 1528, with a company of four hundred men-at-arms and eighty horses, under the pilotage of Miruelo, before mentioned, who claimed to be familiar with the coast. They made land on the 12th of April, and on Holy Thursday, the 14th of April, they anchored near the shore, in the mouth of a bay which is conjectured to have been Clear Water Bay,* just north of that now known as Tampa Bay, but a long time known by its Spanish designation of the Bay of Espiritu Santo. The expedition had unwittingly passed the entrance of the larger bay, and supposed themselves to be still south of it. This error led to most fatal consequences.

At the head of the bay in which they had anchored they saw Indian houses, one of which is said to have been very large, and of sufficient capacity to hold more than three hundred persons. On Good-Friday, a day of bad omen for the expedition, the governor took formal possession of

---

* Buckingham Smith's Notes to Letter of De Soto, 1854.

the country in the name of his Catholic Majesty, and assumed the government of the province.

The natives received them with a bold fearlessness, yet not in an unfriendly manner, but at once made signs to them to go back to their ships. Upon a consultation of the principal officers, and, as De Vaca* says, against his decided opposition, it was determined to march along the coast to the large bay which their pilot had spoken of, and that the vessels should coast along to the bay and await them there. It was an unwise determination; but they had barely escaped shipwreck on their voyage, were weary of the sea, and anxious to try their fortunes on land. An exploring party had met some of the natives wearing gold ornaments. Inquiring by signs of the Indians as to where they obtained this precious metal, they pointed northward, and gave the name of Abalachie, and indicated that there was an abundance of it to be had there, and that it was a province a long way off. The Indians told them truly, and meant the head-waters of the Apalachee River, in the gold regions of Upper Georgia; but as the name of Apalachee attached to the whole course of the river, and there were Apalachian villages near the Gulf coast, they were misled by their Indian guides, whom they forced to accompany them. In an exploration, before starting, they had come to the shore of the Bay of Espiritu Santo, but were not aware that it was the bay of which they were in search.

One hundred men remained on board the vessels, which were placed under the command of one Caravallo. The remainder, numbering some three hundred, with forty horses, which remained out of the eighty put on board, constituted the land expedition. They seem to have

---

* Cabeça de Vaca, Relacion, p 31, Valladolid, 1555, Paris, 1837.

brought but a scanty supply of provisions with them, as the allowance on which they commenced their march amounted to but two pounds of bread and half a pound of meat to each man. On this scanty provision they marched fifteen days, without seeing a village, a house, or a single living soul. They then came to a river, which was probably the Withlacoochee, on the banks of which they were met by twelve hundred Indians, who conducted them to their village, which was near by.

A party was sent to the seashore, which they were told was not far distant, to look out for the ships; they found a shoal, marshy, and sandy shore, but no appearance of the bay or their ships, and returned next day. Uncertain as to any point where they could meet their vessels, they determined to proceed to Apalachee, where they might find the treasures they were in quest of. Resuming their march, they came to a river of considerable size and rapid current, which they crossed with difficulty. This was doubtless the Suwanee, and it is likely they crossed it some distance from the coast. After passing this river, they encountered much opposition from the Indians, and their guides led them through a most difficult country, much obstructed with the trunks of fallen trees of large size. They had occasionally in their march found fields of maize, but were now seven or eight days at a time without seeing any signs of cultivation. As no mention is made of crossing the Santa Fé River, they must have passed over the Natural Bridge, or at some point below its junction with the Suwanee. From the Suwanee they marched seven days, and reached the neighborhood of what was represented to them as the Apalachee they were in quest of. Narvaez and his companions seemed to have anticipated that this famed Apalachee was almost a second Mexico, where they were to receive the reward of all the privations and sufferings they had previously endured; but, much to their disappointment, they found only a petty Indian town, of some forty small cabins, made of thatch and built close to the ground.

The country through which they had passed is described as level, the soil sandy but firm, the trees large, and consisting of gum, cedar, oak, pine, and palms, with much fallen timber, and with numerous lakes. Maize was cultivated by the natives, and the country was said to abound in deer, rabbits, hares, bears, *lions*, and *kangaroos*.* The lions and kangaroos must have been exterminated since then, as none have been found by subsequent explorers. Falcons, gerfalcons, sparrow-hawks, merlins, and other birds are mentioned. By the name of falcon and gerfalcon they probably meant the chicken-hawk.

The town of Apalachee visited by them, it is supposed, was not the principal Indian town, but a small village of the Apalachees. De Soto's expedition took up their quarters in a village called *Anhayea*, which is said to have contained two hundred and fifty houses,† and the location of which is believed to have been near Tallahassee, and the existence of numerous towns of fifty or sixty houses is spoken of.

The town called Apalachee by De Vaca‡ was situated on a lake, and there was another village across the lake, which was possibly Miccasukie Lake.

The Spaniards remained at this Indian town of Apalachee for about a month, a grievous infliction, no doubt, upon the natives, who kept up a continued state of warfare, and discouraged them greatly as to the nature and re-

---

* Cabeça de Vaca.
† L'Inca, Hist. de Florida, p. 74.
‡ Cabeça de Vaca, p. 50.

sources of the country, telling them that there were few people in it, and that it was poor and sterile; but that nine days' journey towards the sea there was a town called Auté or Hauté, abounding in corn, squashes, and gourds, and well supplied with fish, being near the sea.

Narvaez exhibited no enterprise in exploring the country around him, but remained supinely in Apalachee with his whole force of three hundred men, without an effort to penetrate farther or to verify the accuracy of the accounts the Indians gave him. He was really in the midst of a rich, populous, and abundant country, but was incompetent for the position of a leader.

Following the interested advice of the Indians, he set out for Auté. His march was contested at every step by the Indians, who, from behind trees and ambuscades, discharged showers of arrows, and eluded all pursuit. Some of the Spaniards were willing to make oath that the force with which the Indians discharged their arrows was so great, that they had seen red oaks, as thick as the calf of a man's leg, shot through and through; and the narrator adds that this is nothing wonderful, for he himself had seen an arrow driven into an elm a span in depth. He says, further, that these Apalachee Indians were of such great stature, that at a distance they appeared to be *giants*, men of fine proportions, very tall, and of very great strength, and discharged their arrows with great force from bows eight feet in length, with entire precision at a distance of two hundred yards.

After nine days of constant molestation, the forces of Narvaez reached Auté, but the inhabitants, doubtless apprised of their approach, had abandoned their village and burned their dwellings. They had on their journey passed a river which they called Magdalena, and which was probably the Choctawhatchee.

Auté was one day's journey from an entrance to the sea, and has been by some supposed to have been located near St. Mark's; but the probabilities are that it was near the Bay of Apalachicola.*

Finding the town destroyed, and neither corn nor pumpkins, they were consoled by being able to procure an abundance of fish and oysters, but they were not allowed to rest in peace; whenever they went out they were waylaid, and could not leave their camp without danger. The wearied Spaniards, with insufficient food, kept in constant apprehension by the assaults of the natives, and unaccustomed to the country, were subjected to the miasma of the lowlands about them, now, in August, becoming noxious, and soon began to be prostrated by fevers.

The alluring hopes which had led them on to Apalachee, and thence to Auté, had now no further basis to rest upon. The gold and abundance which was to reward them at Apalachee had not been found, and the plenty which was to await them at Auté had vanished. Their dreams of the conquest and spoils of a barbarous and wealthy people like that of Mexico and Peru were miserably dissipated; they had now no further hope than self-preservation, or desire except to leave the country. Their vessels they had never heard of; sickness was daily thinning their ranks and lessening their ability to proceed farther, or even to defend themselves where they were. Theirs was indeed a pitiful case, destitute alike of resources for remaining in, or means of leaving, these fatal shores.

The reflections of Narvaez, as he wearily and wistfully looked over the expanse of sea stretching towards Cuba and the Spanish possessions, must have been painful indeed, as he recalled with bitterness the bright hopes with which

---

* De Vaca, p. 66.

he had set out from Cuba, empówered, as the lieutenant of the powerful Governor Velasquez, to wrest from Cortez the wealth and magnificence of Mexico, and vested with almost vice-regal powers, to play the sovereign of a great empire; then his inglorious defeat, and the renewed hopes with which he set out with a larger force to establish in Florida, as he believed, a government more than equal to that of Mexico; and now to find himself a wanderer, cut off from even the knowledge of his countrymen, hemmed in by cruel and relentless foes, faint with sickness and discouraged by disappointment, a miserable, defeated, and helpless man.

Utterly dispirited, he called a council of his followers, to consider how they could escape from the country before they all perished of disease and hunger. Their determination, as indeed they could have come to no other, was to construct boats, and endeavor to reach the coasts of Cuba or Mexico. This seemed almost a hopeless undertaking; they had no ship-carpenters, nor any materials to build with, but they had the energy of desperation and the incital of hope. A smith of the company said he could make bellows from deer-skins, and would forge the necessary bolts, nails, etc. from their swords, arms, and equipments.* This he immediately put into execution. Others cut timber and hewed it into shape; others gathered palmettos and made a substitute for tow for the caulking of the seams. Such was the diligence of despair, that, with but one single carpenter, they completed within six weeks five boats one hundred and thirty feet in length. They made cordage from the fibre of the palmetto, and from the tails and manes of the horses; the sails they made from their

---

* Cabeça de Vaca, p. 66.

clothing, and out of the hides of their horses they made bottles to carry water.

During their stay at Auté, they lost ten men, who were killed while seeking provisions, and forty had died from disease, leaving two hundred and forty to embark in the boats. They embarked on the 22d of September, 1528, having killed their remaining horses to furnish themselves with meat. Narvaez commanded the first boat; the second was in charge of Enriquez, the Controller, and Juan Suarez, the Commissary; in the third went Captains Castillo and Dorantes; in the fourth, Captains Tellez and Penalosa; and in the fifth, Cabeça de Vaca, each boat carrying about forty-eight men.

After the provisions and clothing had been put on board, their gunwales, it is said, were not more than six inches out of water, and they were so crowded they could hardly move. "So much," says the narrator,[*] "can necessity do, which drove us to hazard our lives in this manner, running into a sea so turbulent, with not a single one of the party having a knowledge of navigation."

It was indeed a most desperate undertaking for these two hundred and forty famished, sick, and down-hearted men, to launch upon an unknown and, at that season, stormy sea, with no knowledge of navigation, and scantily provisioned, in wretched, hastily-built boats, loaded down to the gunwales, and open to every swell of the sea. How different from their disembarkation a few months before, in the Bay of the True Cross, when, with banners displayed, and the sound of trumpets, they formally took possession of the country from which it was now their chief anxiety to escape!

They named the bay upon which they launched their

---

[*] Cabeça de Vaca, p. 68.

boats, the Bay of Cavallos, and their embarkation was probably from the head of the Bay of Apalachicola, as the boats were some days in reaching the Gulf of Mexico, and the water is said to have been shallow. When De Soto's expedition visited the country, eleven years afterwards, the Indians conducted them to the spot, where they saw the traces of Narvaez's camp, the forge used in making the spikes, scraps of iron, and the bones of the horses, and their guide pointed out to them where the ten Spaniards had been killed in the neighborhood of Auté.*

For several days the boats kept within the sound, and went out to sea at a pass which was probably that now known as Indian Pass, formed by St. Vincent's Island and the main. They then sailed westward along the coast in quest of the River of Palms.

The question naturally suggests itself, as to the motive which induced them to go westwardly to seek a port more than a thousand miles distant, when it would seem to have been so much more rational to try to regain the shores of Cuba, not more than four or five hundred miles distant. The real reason lay in their ignorance of the true position of the port which they wished to reach. The River of Palms is located on the old maps in the neighborhood of Tampico, and Panuco was the most northerly of the settlements occupied by the Spaniards on the coast of Mexico. The position of Florida, in reference to Mexico, was long misapprehended, and Narvaez and his companions supposed, when they embarked in their boats, that they would not have far to proceed before reaching the Spanish settlements in Mexico. Upon several ancient maps in existence, the Bay of Apalachee is represented as about equidistant from the Capes of Florida and the Bay of

---

* Historia de L'Inca, lib. iii. chap. v.

Tampico, and De Narvaez and his companions supposed it would be safer to coast along to Panuco, rather than cross over to Cuba. It is subsequently mentioned that a party of four started by land for Panuco, which was believed to be near, and, later, Esquivel refused to join De Vaca in an effort to reach Mexico, because he had understood from the friars in the expedition that Panuco had been already passed. Panuco was, in fact, twelve hundred miles distant from the Bay of Apalachee. Had they turned to the south and east, they could have coasted along Florida, often protected by islands, and procured fish and oysters in abundance, and would have been, when they reached the Tortugas, in the track of vessels going to Mexico. The remnant of De Soto's expedition, with better fortune, coasted westwardly from the mouth of the Mississippi, until they reached in safety the Spanish settlements in Mexico.

After passing into the Gulf, Narvaez and his followers coasted westwardly along the shore, and soon began to suffer from hunger and thirst, and were in constant danger of shipwreck. They occasionally ran into the coves and creeks, and sometimes encountered Indians engaged in fishing. Entering St. Joseph's Bay, they landed, and were hospitably received by an Indian chief, but in the night were attacked by the Indians. In the mêlée, they took from the chief his blanket, which was made of the skins of the civet-marten; with this other chiefs were occasionally seen decorated. Afterwards they landed upon an island, which appears to have been the island of Santa Rosa. Here their boats got aground, and they nearly perished from cold and hunger. The natives of this place treated them with great kindness, supplying them with fish and a kind of root which was like a walnut in size and obtained from under the water with much labor.

De Vaca's party, attempting to get their boat off in

order to re-embark, lost three of their number, who were drowned by the boat capsizing, one of whom was Alonzo de Salis, the Assessor. The sympathy of the Indians was much excited on their behalf, and every assistance in their power was freely given. By this disaster they lost their boat and all their clothing, and suffered severely from the cold winds of November. The boat of Captains Dorantes and Castillo was also wrecked on this island. The Spaniards soon exhausted the small amount of provisions furnished by the Indians, and were reduced to such extremity that they lived on the bodies of such as died, and in a short time, of eighty souls who had come in the two boats, but fifteen remained alive.* The fate of those who were in the other three boats was equally disastrous. The boat of Enriquez the Controller and Juan Suarez was wrecked near Pensacola Bay, and they proceeded along the shore to the Perdido, across which they were carried by the governor's boat. Afterwards, the rest of his men having gone on shore, Narvaez persisted in remaining on board, having with him only the cockswain and a lad, and having on board neither provisions nor water. At midnight the wind arose off shore, and his boat, being anchored with only a stone, was driven to sea, and nothing more was ever heard of this renowned Captain-General and Adelantado of Florida, Panfilo de Narvaez.

The survivors of these two boats, some ninety in number, gradually died from hunger and starvation, the living subsisting upon the dried flesh of their comrades, endeavoring to prolong their own existence until they too succumbed to their fate.

The fifth and last boat, that of Captains Tellez and Pena-

---

* Considering the abundance of fish and oysters in that vicinity, this tatement is remarkable.

losa, continued on across Mobile Bay, and as far as Pass Christian, where they landed among a people called the Camones, and, according to the report given to De Vaca by the Indians, were all killed by the natives, having become so feeble that they could offer no resistance.*

Of the three hundred who started on the land march from the Bay of the True Cross with Narvaez, but four are known to have escaped. These were Cabeça de Vaca, the Treasurer, Captain Alonzo Castillo, Captain Andreas Dorantes, and Estevanico, an Arabian negro or Moor. Juan Ortiz, who was found among the Indians by De Soto, and was his interpreter, was decoyed on shore from one of the vessels after Narvaez had begun his march.

When Narvaez began his land march, he left three vessels in the bay, with one hundred men and ten women on board, and with a very small amount of stores. These vessels were to have sailed along the coast, as near the shore as possible, and to enter the best port they could find and there await Narvaez. They accordingly followed the coast for some distance without finding any harbor, and then sailed to the southward, and five or six leagues below where they had landed on their arrival they found a bay which penetrated into the land seven or eight leagues. Two of the vessels continued the search for Narvaez for nearly a year, and then sailed to Mexico.

It is a curious circumstance that a woman who was on board one of the vessels had, before they began their march, predicted to Narvaez all the misfortunes which befell the party; he assumed to place little faith in the revelation, but doubtless, in so credulous an age, was depressed and dispirited by it.†

The survivors, Cabeça de Vaca and the others, owed

---

* Cabeça de Vaca, p. 155. † Ibid., p. 296.

their preservation to an idea which the Indians entertained that they were skilled in the healing art, and they were soon installed as great medicine-men. They rather hesitated at first about assuming the responsibilities of a profession of which they were entirely ignorant; but the Indians insisted on their practicing, and their success exceeded their anticipations. De Vaca thus describes their *modus operandi*, and it may be considered quite as rational as many systems now in vogue. He says, the custom of the Indians was, upon finding themselves sick, to send for a physician, and after the cure they gave him not only everything they themselves owned, but sought among their relatives for more to add to the gift, in order to evince their gratitude.

The medicine-man was also privileged to have two wives instead of one. De Vaca's style of practice was, to "bless the sick, breathe upon them, recite a Paternoster and an Ave Maria, praying with all earnestness to God our Lord that he would give them health and influence them to do us some great good, in his mercy;" and he piously says that "He willed that all those for whom we supplicated should, directly after we made the sign of the cross over them, tell the others that they were sound and in health."*

Prior to his advancement to the dignity of a Great Medicine, De Vaca engaged in the business of an itinerant trader, carrying shells, conchs, etc. from the coast, and exchanging them for skins, ochre, flints for arrow-heads, and other articles. He went by day entirely without clothing, having a covering of deer-skins at night.

De Vaca remained six years among the coast Indians, whom he calls the Mariannes, busily obtaining such information as would enable him to find his way back to the

---

* Cabeça de Vaca, p. 162.

Spanish settlements. Of a tribe called the Yezagues, he says, "Their support is principally roots, which are very bitter, and require two days in roasting. Occasionally they kill deer, and at times obtain some fish, but the quantity is so small and the famine so great, that they eat spiders, the eggs of ants, worms, lizards, salamanders, snakes and vipers which are poisonous, and earth and wood;" and, says De Vaca, "if there were *stones* in that land, I verily believe they would eat *them.*" The men carried no burdens, but devolved all menial and severe labor upon the old men and the women: the latter worked hard. These Indians, he says, were great thieves, great liars, and great drunkards, from the use of a certain liquor. They were so accustomed to running that, without rest or fatigue, they could follow a deer from morning until night. In this way they killed many, for they pursued them until tired down, and sometimes *overtook* them in the chase. Their houses were of matting, placed upon four hoops; they carried them on their backs, and moved every three or four days in search of food. They planted nothing, but were a very merry people, considering the hunger they suffered, and, notwithstanding, never ceased to dance, or to observe their festivities. To them the happiest part of the year was the season of eating prickly pears, for then they had a season of plenty, and could eat their fill, passing their time in dancing and eating day and night. They peeled and dried them, packing them in baskets like figs.

Mosquitoes were of three sorts, and all of them abundant in every part of the country, and their bite poisoned and inflamed the body. The Indians used to set the plains and the woods within their reach on fire, to drive away the mosquitoes, and to drive out lizards; they also fired the woods to drive in the deer, and to attract the cattle to young grass.

It will be seen by this brief statement of Indian customs, as given by De Vaca, that some of the usages of the pine-barren regions of Florida are inherited from the original occupants of the soil. A singular custom is mentioned of one tribe, that they suckled their children until twelve years old, and the reason given was, that they might not suffer in times of scarcity of food.

At the end of six years, De Vaca, Castillo, Dorantes, and Estevanico, having become thoroughly versed in the language and customs of the Indians, and, we may suppose, by exposure and the use of pigments, coming closely to resemble them, determined to carry out their cherished purpose of reaching Panuco, in Mexico.

Leaving the Mariannes at a favorable moment, they came to a tribe called the Avavares, and, having effected some remarkable cures among them, the medicine-men acquired an extraordinary reputation, and were considered superior beings. As such, they were carried upon their journey in great state, by large detachments of Indians, and had every want supplied. At times they were accompanied by as many as two or three thousand of the natives. They at length came to a large river, where they saw an Indian with a sword-buckle, and learned that others had seen white men upon the river in boats, and with horses upon the land, and at some distance from them came upon traces of the presence of Europeans; shortly afterwards they encountered a party of Spaniards who had come out eastwardly from the Spanish settlements in Mexico.

Cabeça de Vaca and his companions, after their long sojourn of seven years among the Indians, at length reached the abodes of civilized men, and were received with the greatest sympathy by the Spanish authorities in Mexico. He was enabled to return to Spain, where, upon his arrival, he addressed to his Catholic Majesty an interesting narrative of his adventures, with observations upon the manners and customs of the countries through which he had passed.*

It appears that he desired to secure the privilege of returning to Florida and to have the appointment of governor; but other parties of greater position and influence were seeking those privileges, and the governorship of La Plata was given to De Vaca, who failed to give satisfaction in the administration of the government of that country, and was sent home in disgrace. His narrative of the expedition and shipwreck of Narvaez and of his own personal adventures is exceedingly interesting, as containing the observations of the first European who traversed the region now known as the Cotton States, and the first white man who beheld the Mississippi and crossed the

---

* The following cotemporary notice of his return is found in the Relation of De Soto's Expedition, by Alvarez Fernandez, usually called the Narrative of the Portuguese Gentleman:—

"When Dom Fernando had obtained the government, there came a gentleman from the Indies to the Court, named Cabeza de Vaca, which had been with the Governor Pamphilo de Narvaez, which died in Florida, who reported that Narvaez was cast away at sea, with all the company y^t went with him, and how he with four more escaped and arrived in Nueva España. Also he brought a relation in writing of that which he had seene in Florida; which said in some places, In such a place I have seene this, and the rest which here I saw I leave to conferre of between his Majestie and myselfe. Generally he reported the misery of the country and the troubles which he passed, and hee told some of his kinsfolke, which were desirous to go into the Indies, and urged him very much to tell them whether he had seene any rich country in Florida, that he might not tell them, because hee and another whose name was Orantes (who remained in Nueva España with purpose to return into Florida) for which intent he came into Spaine to beg the government thereof of the Emperor, had sworn not to discover some of the things which they had seene, because no man should prevent them in begging the same, and he informed them that it was the richest country of the world."

great Father of Waters. The discovery of the Mississippi has for a long time been erroneously attributed to De Soto; but Cabeça de Vaca and his companions had rested upon its banks years before De Soto set out on his expedition; and upon some high bluff by that wondrous stream should be erected a column bearing the simple inscription:—

ALVAR NUÑEZ CABEÇA DE VACA

IN HOC LOCO PRIMUS OMNIUM EUROPÆORUM FUIT,

A.D. MDXXXV.

CHAPTER III.

Expedition of Hernando de Soto.

1539.

THOSE who have had occasion to consult the relations of the early adventurers who attempted the conquest or colonization of Florida, cannot fail to have been struck with the fact that the country is eulogized by them all as a very rich and fertile country. Thus, in the English translation of the relation of the Portuguese Gentleman, by Hakluyt, it is said, "Wherein are truly observed the riches and fertilities of these parts, abounding with things necessary, pleasant, and profitable for the life of man." And in the same work it is said that Cabeça de Vaca reported, upon his return to Spain, "that it was the richest country of the world." Doubtless to most persons this will seem so absurd and exaggerated, as to cast discredit upon the veracity of the narrator.

But this flattering estimate of the country by the early explorers and voyagers may be explained upon grounds perfectly consistent with the idea of sincerity on their part. It must be recollected, in the first place, that the name of Florida then designated a vast extent of country, stretching from the Gulf of Mexico, northwestwardly, towards unknown regions. The divisions of the country, as marked upon the maps, were Florida at the south, extending to the north of the Chesapeake, and meeting New France. In speaking of Florida, therefore, in those days, reference was had to a much larger scope of country than is now designated by the name.

The main object of all expeditions at that day was the discovery of precious metals, and, coming from the Old World, men had no standard of comparison by which to measure the agricultural value of the New. The shores of Florida presented to their eyes a more grateful and pleasing prospect than the sands of the Tierra Caliente of Mexico, or the swampy, impassable mesquite groves of South America.

Let us suppose for a moment a vessel, long tempest-tossed upon the wild waste of waters, entering one of the harbors of Florida. As the shores are approached, there opens a gentle and placid bay, land-locked, and reflecting with glassy stillness the shadows of the evergreen and towering trees of the forest. The fleeting clouds of heaven pass over its polished surface, and changing points of beauty are being constantly developed. The white-winged water-fowl skim quietly along its surface; the waving moss droops from the hanging boughs; pleasant coves and sylvan retreats border its banks.

The appearances upon the land are equally flattering: the green grass, even in midwinter, gives a vernal beauty to the landscape.

The evergreen forests, filled with birds of song and beauty, the magnolia grandiflora, with its glistening leaves and splendid flowers, the tall palm-trees, with their leafy canopies, the stalwart live-oak, the mournful cypress, the brilliant dogwood and honeysuckle, all give an air of enchantment and beauty to the scene. The antlers of the noble buck, and the glossy plumage of the wild turkey of the forest, signal both food and noble pastime. An oriental and tropical richness and profusion of vegetable life seem to invite to enjoyment and ease.

The voyagers ascend the gentle current of the placid

rivers, and new beauties are met at every turn. They seem to float amid flowers and perfume; the drooping vines, trailing in the water, mingle with water-plants of various tints; everything is tinged with richness and beauty; and from some captured savage they hear always of the gold of some distant province, which animates their hopes and expectations.

Is it strange that such a country should, where everything was new and marvelous and exaggerated, impart, without much license of the imagination, a pleasant glow of beauty and richness to the narrations of those who for the first time landed on its coasts?

The progress of discovery and of conquest had gone on in the south with almost uninterrupted success; a great and unexplored region was known to exist at the north, and the imagination had full scope to create for itself new fields for the acquisition of glory and of wealth.

Panfilo de Narvaez had miserably perished, with all his noble men-at-arms and splendid equipment, and Cabeça de Vaca had returned to Spain, himself and three others the only survivors of this unfortunate expedition.

Hernando de Soto, it would seem, had already projected an expedition for the conquest of Florida.

There was at that period no cavalier who occupied a more exalted position at the Spanish court than Hernando de Soto. He was a native of the town of Villa Nueva de Baccarota, in the southern part of Spain, near Xerez, and was of a good family. At an early age, living near one of the ports, San Lucar, whence sailed the expeditions for discovery and conquest of the New World, he went out under Don Pedro Arias D'Avilas, then Governor of the West Indies, by whom he was shortly promoted to the command of a troop of horse, and in 1531 was dispatched with one hundred men and a supply of horses by Arias to join

Pizarro, then on his way to undertake the conquest of Peru.

He proved a most welcome and valuable auxiliary, and soon rose to be second in command to Pizarro himself. He shared the varying fortunes of the invaders, and acquired a large experience and great reputation as an accomplished and gallant leader. Daring, yet prudent, brilliant, yet cautious, he was always foremost and always successful. Under Pizarro, with a small force, he captured the Inca, and left two thousand slain upon the field. After the conquest was achieved, and foreseeing the rivalries and difficulties about to spring up between the leaders, he withdrew, with a splendid booty of 180,000 ducats, which had fallen to his share, and, with some valiant comrades, returned to Spain in 1536.

In addition to the permission to undertake the conquest of Florida, he received the government of the island of Cuba, and the title of Adelantado of Florida, and marquis of the lands he might conquer.

Florida was then a *terra incognita*. Expeditions had touched upon the shores, and Narvaez had gone inland a short distance, but of the great extent of country reaching from the Atlantic to the Pacific, and from the Gulf of Mexico to the Arctic seas, very little was known; the general impression, however, was that Florida was an island, and that a passage was to be found to the northward, similar to that around Cape Horn.

The prestige of De Soto's name and reputation, and the evidences of his preceding good fortune, shown in the immense treasures he had brought back with him, and which were lavished by him with a calculating and magnificent prodigality, attracted to his standard a splendid retinue of followers, burning for adventure, and still more anxious, it is presumable, to share in the ransom of any Incas or Emperors they might find in the "richest country in the world," to the certain conquest and subjugation of which they confidently looked forward. *"Possunt quia posse videntur"* (they are successful who believe they will be so) was the practical motto upon which the Spanish adventurers acted, and, believing themselves invincible, they really achieved prodigies of valor and manly prowess.

One of the most distinguished of the associates of De Soto in the expedition was Vasco de Porcallo, one of the proprietary lords of the island of Cuba, who, although somewhat advanced in years, felt the spirit of both honor and gain within him. It was of a steward of this cavalier that the somewhat whimsical story is related by Alonzo Fernandez, "that understanding that his slaves would destroy themselves, he went for them with a cudgel in his hand at the place where they were to meet, and told them that they could neither do nor think anything that he did not know before, and that he came thither to kill himself with them, to the end that if he had used them badly in this world he might use them worse in the world to come; and this was a means, it is said, that they changed their purpose, and turned home again, to do that which he commanded them."

De Soto first made a general rendezvous for his forces in Cuba, and recruited his command; while staying here, he sent two brigantines, with fifty men, to discover the ports of Florida, and from thence they brought two Indians taken upon the coast, "wherewith" (as well because they might be necessary as guides and for interpreters, as because they said by signs that there was much gold in Florida) "the governor and all the company received much contentment, and longed for the hour of their departure, thinking in himself this was the richest country that unto that day had been discovered."

De Soto left Cuba on the 18th of May, 1539, and landed at Tampa Bay on Whitsunday, the 25th of May, and the name of Espiritu Santo was given to the bay in honor of the day. The number disembarked was about one thousand men-at-arms with three hundred and fifty horses, a force far more respectable in numbers and quality, in equipment and appurtenances, than had ever gone forth in any previous expedition.

The fleet entered the bay, on the west coast of Florida, now called Tampa Bay, and landed, probably at Gadsden's Point, a few miles from an Indian town belonging to a chief called Hirrihigua, and which stood on the site of the present town of Tampa. The house of the chief was upon an artificial eminence, which still remains, after more than three hundred years, to awaken the interest of the antiquary and certify the truth of ancient chronicles. While at this place, the two Indians whom they had been training for guides and interpreters escaped, to the great disappointment of De Soto. From some captured women, however, he learned that a Spaniard, left by Narvaez, was in the keeping of a neighboring chief. This man was Juan Ortiz, whose history would have been of itself a most interesting one had he possessed the skill to write it, or had he escaped with his life to Spain to relate it.

After Narvaez landed, he had sent back to Cuba, to his wife, one of his smaller vessels, on board of which was this Juan Ortiz, to convey intelligence of his landing. She immediately sent additional supplies by the same vessel, and they arrived at the bay after Narvaez had entered upon his march. Observing a letter fixed in the cleft of a stick on shore, they asked some Indians whom they saw to bring it to them, which the savages refused, and made signs to come for it. Juan Ortiz, then a youth of eighteen, with a comrade, took the boat and went on shore, when they were immediately captured by the Indians, and taken to the chief, who was greatly enraged against the Spaniards on account of injuries he had received from Narvaez, and the companion of Ortiz was at once sacrificed upon his attempting resistance. The chief ordered Ortiz to be stretched out upon a staging of poles like a gridiron, and a fire to be built under him. He was of a young and interesting age, and when this cruel order was given, and the victim was about undergoing this torture, a scene ensued which deservedly arouses our sympathies and admiration, and recalls at once the better-known and more widely appreciated incident of Pocahontas. The cruel Hirrihigua had a beautiful daughter, about the same age as Ortiz, who, when she saw the dreadful fate to which the young Spaniard was doomed, was moved to that pity and compassion which, to the credit of her sex be it spoken, are always aroused in woman's breast by misfortune and suffering. Narvaez had been guilty, it seems, of acts of atrocious cruelty towards the mother of the chief, and the wrong had sunk deep and ineffaceably into his heart. Overcoming her own natural feelings of resentment against the race, and braving the anger of her father, this noble Indian maid threw herself at her father's feet and implored him to spare the life of the captive youth, urging upon him that this smooth-cheeked boy could do him no injury, and that it was more noble for a brave and lofty chief like himself to keep the youth a captive, than to sacrifice so mere a lad to his revenge.

The intercession of the noble girl was successful, and the young Spaniard was loosed and his wounds cared for by the gentle hands of her who had saved his life.

After some months his life was again in jeopardy, and he was about to be sacrificed to the supposed requirements of the Demon of Evil, when his fair deliverer again interposed, warned him of his peril, and advised him to flee to Mucoso, a neighboring chief; and at the dead hour of night she herself led him half a league upon his way, and, placing him in the path of safety, gave him her true woman's blessing and hopes for his welfare. He reached Mucoso, who received him well and protected him from that period until the arrival of De Soto, twelve years afterwards. It adds not a little to the romance of the story, to repeat, that the daughter of Hirrihigua was affianced to the chief Mucoso, and that, owing to the refusal of Mucoso to surrender Ortiz upon the repeated demands of Hirrihigua, the proposed alliance was refused by that chief, and his daughter sacrificed her love to her humanity, and Mucoso his bride to his sense of honor. Savages though they were, they gave an example of noble virtues seldom equaled in any society more polished or more refined.

A party of horse sent by De Soto met Ortiz on his way to their camp, where he was received with great rejoicings, and the first question addressed to him from the very depths of their hearts was whether he knew of any neighboring country rich in the precious metals.

Some of the cavaliers had participated in the ransom of the Inca of Peru, and had entered upon this expedition with similar expectations. The others, excited by the success of the followers of Pizarro, were greedy to search some land rich in gold. What they hoped from a country which they supposed to be the richest of any yet discovered, may be inferred from an examination of that chapter of the Conquest of Peru devoted to the recital of the almost fabulous amount of treasure obtained as the ransom of Atahualpa, which, it was said, filled with gold a room twenty-two feet long, seventeen feet wide, and nine feet high; an amount of treasure which perhaps it would not be rash to say could not be obtained in gold, if Florida even now, at the end of three hundred years, were pillaged anew.

A dim vision of some distant and ever-receding city, resplendent with magnificence, and like Cuzco, "where the roofs of the temples were plated with gold, while the walls were hung with tapestry, and the floors inlaid with tiles of the same precious metal," was ever before their eyes, and, like an ignis-fatuus, led them for weeks and months and years, ever disappointed and ever credulous to the last, disbelieving everything else told them by the savage races, and believing every promise of this.*

Juan Ortiz was of much less real value to them as a guide than they expected. He had been kept within the limits of a single tribe, and knew little or nothing of the country beyond. The excursions of the troops soon became discouraging. The vessels were sent back, and Porcallo, the lieutenant of De Soto, found the hardships too great, and,

---

* In vol. iii. of Hakluyt will be found the relations of Pedro Morales, whom Sir Francis Drake brought from St. Augustine, in Florida, in 1586, in which he says: "There is a great city sixteene or twentie dayes journey from St. Helena northwestward, which the Spaniards call *La Grand Copal*, which they thinke to bee very rich and exceeding great, and have been in sight of it some of them." (P. 361.) There is also a relation of Nicolas Burguignon, *alias* Haly, whom Sir Francis Drake brought from Florida.

"He further affirmeth that there is a citie northwestward from St. Helena in the mountains, which the Spaniards call *La Grand Copal*, and is very great and rich, and that in these mountains there is great store of christal, gold, and rubies and diamonds; and that a Spaniard brought from thence a diamond which was worth £5000. He saith also that to make passage unto these mountains it is needful to have store of hatchets to give unto the Indians, and store of pickaxes to break the mountains, *which shine so bright* in the day in some places that they cannot behold them, and therefore they travel unto them by night." Ibid., p. 361.

leaving the honor to the younger candidates for glory, he returned to Cuba.

They then commenced their march to the northward, and, having no great supply of provisions, were soon reduced to the necessity of depending upon the Indian fields; but, it is said, "they were sore vexed with hunger and evil ways, because the countries were very barren of maiz, low, and full of water, bogs, and thick woods. Wheresoever any town was found, there were some beets, and they that came first, and sodden with water and salt, did eat them without any other thing, and such as could not get them gathered stalks of maiz, which, because they were young, had no maiz in them. When they came to the river (the Withlacoochee, it is supposed) they found palmettos upon low palm-trees like those of Andalusia."

They went thence to Ocali, which is described as being a fertile region, and where they found abundance of corn, and other provisions, as well as plums, grapes, nuts, and acorns. After leaving Ocali, situated in the neighborhood, it is supposed, of the present town of that name, they entered the domain of a chief called Vitachuco, who gave them battle in every form, and exerted his utmost efforts to destroy them. Those who have read Irving's Conquest of Florida will recall the bloody contest which took place on a level plain between two lakes, and the somewhat marvelous fact stated, that some two hundred Indians plunged into the lake, and remained there swimming for twenty-four hours without touching foot to the ground. This circumstance the chronicler La Vega thinks remarkable, and hardly credible, but for the fact that his informants were all honorable men. Hardships, and a fierce resistance to their farther progress, soon made their journey painful and disastrous; but De Soto was too determined a leader and too good a soldier to feel other than his martial ardor excited by opposition, and he with prudent sagacity overcame all the obstacles in his path. His line of march lay parallel to the shores of the gulf, and he probably at this time reached the neighborhood of Tallahassee. A party whom he dispatched to the coast were shown by the Indians the remains of De Narvaez's encampment at Auté, and the bleaching skeletons of his horses.

De Soto's treatment of the Indians was probably better than that practiced by most of the discoverers, and in fact this was forced upon him as a matter of policy, for he found the natives of Florida far superior to the effeminate races of South and Central America, trained to combat, and filled with the most indomitable courage and perseverance. In some instances they may have been treated with cruelty by him as a measure of policy, to overawe and terrify them.

In one of the illustrations to De Bry, is a large plate, showing the cutting off of the hands of a number of chiefs by De Soto; and many instances of his severity are scattered through the Portuguese narrative.

It is said that "after the well-fought battle of Vitachuco, some of the youngest of the prisoners the governour gave to them which had good chaines and were careful to look to them that they got not away. All the rest he commanded to be put to death, and they being tied to a stake, in the midst of the market-place, the Indians of the Paracoussi did shoot them to death."

In another place, it is said that "they took an hundred men and women, of which, as well there as in other places where they made any inroades, the captain chose one or two for the governour, and divided the others to himself and the rest that went with him. They led these Indians in chaines, with yron collars about their neckes, and they served to carry their stuffe, and to grind their maiz, and for other services that such captives could do. Sometimes it happened that, going for wood or maiz with them, they killed the Christian that led them, and ran away with the chain. Others filed their chaines by night with a piece of stone, wherewith they cut them, and use it instead of yron. The women and young boys, when they were once an hundred leagues from their countrie, and had forgotten things, were let go loose, and so they served, and in a very short space they understood the language of the Christians.''

A very creditable circumstance is mentioned, in the accounts of the expedition, of the attachment of the Indians to their wives. On one occasion the Spaniards found two men and a woman gathering beans: the men might have escaped, but one of them, being husband to the woman, would not leave her, and they fought most bravely until they were slain, having wounded three horses.

Their style of dress is thus described: "They have mantles like blankets, made of the inner rind of the barks of trees (probably the cabbage-palmetto), and some were made of a kind of grass like nettles, which on being beaten becomes like flax." The grass referred to is evidently the bear-grass, which has a strong and flexible fibre, suitable for cordage or cloth, and is very abundant in Florida. The women covered themselves with these mantles; one was fastened on the shoulders, and worn with the right arm out; they wore another fastened at the waist, and extending down towards the feet. The men wore a similar mantle over the shoulders, and deer-skins around the loins. The deer-skins were well dressed, and so well colored that they resembled very fine cloth. They made their moccasins of the same material. It would appear from this that the Indian costume of 1539 was the same as that of 1839.

CHAPTER IV.

Expedition of Hernando de Soto, continued.

1540.

The Spaniards under De Soto, leaving Apalachee, in the country east of the Apalachicola, turned to the northeast, and came to a town called Yupaha, the sound of which is suggestive of the Alapaha, a tributary of the Suwanee. Here the following notable speech is put into the mouth of an Indian chief, which has a strong smack of Castilian diplomatic grandiloquence:

"Right high, right mightie and excellent lord, those things which seldome happen doe cause admiration: what then may the sight of your lordship and your people doe to me and mine whom we never saw? especially being mounted on such fierce beasts as your horses are, entering with such violence and fury into my country, without any knowledge of your coming. It was a thing so strange, and caused such fear and terror in our minds, that it was not in our power to stay and receive your lordship with the solemnities due to so high and renowned a prince as your lordship is," (a diplomatic way of saying they could not help running away;) "and, trusting in your greatness and singular virtues, I do not only hope to be freed from blame, but also to receive favours, and the first which I demand of your lordship is that you will use me, my country and subjects, as your own; and the second, that you will tell me who you are, and whence you come, and whither you go, and what you seek, that I the better may serve you thereto."

To this courteous speech the governor replied, "that he was very much obliged to him; that he was the son of the sun, and came from those parts where he is, and sought the greatest lord and richest province in it."

De Soto here "left a very high crosse of wood sett up in the middest of the market-place."

The populousness of the country he had now entered, upon the Altamaha, may be inferred from the fact mentioned that a chief sent him "two thousand Indians, with a present, to wit: many conies and partridges, bread of maize, two hens, and many dogs, which last, it is said, were esteemed as if they had been fat wethers; and when they came to any town and found thirty or forty dogs, he that could get one and kill it thought himself no small man; and he that killed it and gave not his captain one quarter, if he knew it, he frowned on him, and made him feele it on the watches."

In another tribe four Indians were taken, and none of them would confess anything but that they knew of no other habitation.

The governor commanded one of them to be burned, and presently another confessed, and gave the information they desired.

Feminine chieftainship is an unfrequent occurrence among savage tribes; but near the Atlantic coast in South Carolina De Soto came into the territories of an Indian queen, invested with youth, beauty, and loveliness, who is styled by the old chronicles "the Ladie of the countrie." Upon De Soto's approach, he was met by a lady ambassadress, sister of her Majesty, who delivered a courteous speech of welcome, "and within a little time the Ladie came out of the town in a chaire, whereon certain of the principal Indians brought her to the river. She entered into a barge, which had the sterne tilted over, and on the floor her mat ready laid, with two cushions upon it, one upon another, where she sat her down, and with her came her principal Indians, in other barges, which did wait upon her." She went to the place where the governor was, and at her coming she made this speech: "Excellent lord, I wish this coming of your lordships into these your countries to be most happy; although my power be not answerable to my will, and my services be not according to my desire, nor such as so high a prince as your lordships deserveth, yet such the good will is rather to be accepted than all the treasures of the world that without it can be offered; with most unfailable and manifest affection I offer you my person, lords, and subjects, and this small service."

After this courteous and graceful speech from the throne, to which it may be inferred that so gallant a cavalier as De Soto must have replied in equally complimentary style, the princess caused to be presented to the Adelantado rich presents of the clothes and skins of the country, and—far greater attraction for them—beautiful strings of pearls. Her Majesty, after some maiden coyness, took from her own neck a great cordon of pearls and cast it about the neck of the governor, entertaining him with very gracious speeches of love and courtesy, and as soon as he was lodged in the town she sent him another present, of not quite so delicate and refined a character, but no doubt considered by her of far greater value, namely, some hens.

Perceiving that they valued the pearls, she advised the governor to send and search certain graves that were in that town, and that he should find many. They sought the graves, and there found fourteen "measures" of pearls, weighing two hundred and ninety-two pounds, and little babies and birds made of them, reminding one of the recent excavations at Chiriqui.

The people were brown, well made and well proportioned, and more civil than any others that were seen in all the country of Florida, and all of them went shod and clothed.

The Spaniards, wearied with their long and fruitless travel, and worn down by their hardships, urged upon their leader that it was a good country to inhabit, and in a temperate climate, and that ships going and coming from Spain might touch there, and that it was a productive country.

But the governor, it is said, "since his intent was to seek another treasure like that of Atahualpa, Lord of Peru, was not contented with a good country, nor with pearls, though many of them were worth their weight in gold. And being a stern man, and of few words, though he was glad to sift and know the opinion of all men, yet after he had delivered his own he would not be contraried, and always did what he liked himself, and so it is said all men did condescend unto his will, and though it seems an errour to leave that country, yet there was none that would say anything against him after they knew his resolution."

The fair princess seems to have been ill requited for her hospitable reception of the Spaniards. Held as a hostage (for the good behavior of the Indians, it is to be presumed), De Soto insisted upon her accompanying him, which she did for many days, until one day, turning aside into the forest upon some slight pretext, she disappeared, not without suspicion of design, as there happened to be missing at the same time one of the Spaniards, who report said had joined the fair princess for weal or for woe, and had returned with her to her tribe. Upon this meagre incident, the romance-writer of the South, W. Gilmore Simms, has woven an ingenious and pleasant tale in his story of Andres Vasconselos.

The journey of De Soto was thence to the borders of the Tennessee, meeting no opposition in his march. By one tribe he was met with a present of seven hundred hens, and by another with twenty baskets of mulberries, and on one occasion three hundred dogs were brought to him.

Led on by the indefinite stories of the Indians, whose motive was probably to mislead him, he traveled through the upper parts of South Carolina, Georgia, and Alabama, until he changed his course to the southwest, and arrived at a town called Mauvilla.

The tribes through which they had passed in the upper country seem to have offered no opposition, and were probably of a more peaceable disposition than those along the gulf.

Mauvilla was the scene of a bitter and sanguinary conflict. The pearls and baggage which the Spaniards had borne thus far were left in the hands of the Indian slaves, who were suddenly surprised by the Mauvillians and carried into the town. De Soto, determined to strike a blow which should carry terror to the natives, attacked the place with great impetuosity, and set fire to the buildings, consuming alike the stores of the Indians and his own baggage, and—what they seem to have most regretted—their stores of pearls. The number of Indians slain in this encounter is stated to have been twenty-five hundred, while of the Spaniards eighteen men were killed and one hundred and fifty wounded.

After this battle De Soto learned that Francisco Maldonado, who had been sent by him from Apalachicola with the brigantines to look for a port to the westward, awaited him at the port of Ochuse—(Pensacola), six days' journey from Mauvilla. This Mauvilla is supposed to have been on the Alabama River, and the name of Mobile is derived from it.

It might naturally be that De Soto, having now traveled several hundred leagues through the country, and finding his hopes ever disappointed, would, at the end of these eighteen months of travel, gladly embrace the means of extrication afforded by this opportune arrival of his vessels.

But the pride of the noble cavalier would not permit him to turn back while a glimmering hope remained of accomplishing his designs. He instructed Juan Ortiz to keep Maldonado's arrival a secret, because, it is quaintly said, "he had not accomplished that which he determined to do, and because the pearls were burnt there which he meant to have sent to Cuba for a show, that the people hearing the news might be desirous to come to that country." He feared also "that if they should have news of him, without seeing from Florida either gold or silver or anything of value, the country would get such a name that no man would seek to go thither when he should have need of people; and so he determined to send no news of himself until he had found some rich country."

And thus he deliberately turned his face forever from the shores of his native land, and from all the wealth and distinction of his viceroyalty in Cuba, intent on carrying out to its full solution the problem of the wealth and riches of Florida.

Maldonado long awaited the arrival of De Soto at Ochuse, and at last, despairing of ever again meeting him, turned his sails sorrowfully to bear to the Lady Isabella the report of the probable fate which had befallen the expedition.

De Soto changed his course thence to the northwest, sore in body and sore in spirit, and was met at every step with demonstrations of enmity; the towns were burned over their heads, and night-attacks were frequent. In the province of Quinague he was waited upon by six principal chiefs, who made this remarkable declaration: "That they came to see what people they were, and that long ago they had been informed by their forefathers that a white people should subdue them, and that therefore they would return to their cacique, and bid him come presently and serve the governour."

The Spaniards were then near to the Father of Waters, which they called the Great River—Rio Grande. They described the river as "about half a league broad. If a man stood still on the other side, it could not be discerned whether he were a man or no. The river was of great depth, and of a strong current; the water was always muddy; there came down the river, continually, many trees and timber, which the force of the water and stream brought down. There was a great store of fish in it of sundrie sorts, and the most of it differing from the fresh-water fish of Spain." From the cottonwood-trees on its banks, De Soto constructed boats large enough to carry three horses at a time, and crossed over at night without interruption from the natives. He spent the summer and autumn in exploring the regions beyond the Mississippi, and wintered, it is supposed, upon the White River. He here concluded that in the spring he would go to the seacoast, and dispatch a vessel to Cuba and another to Mexico, with the view of sending to his wife, the Lady Isabella, who was in Cuba, intelligence of himself, and for another outfit to enable him further to prosecute his expedition. Up to this time he had lost two hundred and fifty men and one hundred and fifty horses.

About the middle of April he returned to the banks of the Mississippi, with the view of going to the coast, and at once began to make inquiries about the country, but could get little intelligence. He then sent out an expedition to the southward, but it could make no progress on account of the numerous creeks and canebrakes.

The gallant chief, who had so long borne up under every species of discouragement, who had ever responded with alacrity to the call to battle, who bore himself always as a prudent and brave commander, now began to sink into despondency; and visions of the past, and a certain homesickness, it may well be imagined, came upon him. A slow and wearing fever daily detracted from his strength, and he soon felt that the hour approached wherein he was to leave this present life. He called his followers around him to receive his parting words, and said to them, "that now he was to go to give an account before the presence of God of all his life past, and since it pleased God to take him in such a time, and that the time was come; that he knew his death drew near, and that he, His most unworthy servant, did yield to Him many thanks therefor; and desired all that were present and absent (whom he confessed himself to be much beholding unto for their singular virtues, love, and loyalty, which himself had well tried in the travels which they had suffered, which always in his mind he did hope to satisfy and reward when it should please God to give him rest with more prosperities of his estate) that they would pray to God for him, that for His mercy He would forgive him his sins and receive his soul into eternal glory, and that they would quit and free him of the charge which he had over them, and that they would pardon him for some wrongs which they might have received of him; and, to avoid some divisions which upon his death might fall out upon the choice of his successor, he requested them to elect a principal person and able to govern, of whom all should like well, and, when he was elected, they should swear before him to obey him; and that he would thank them very much in so doing, because the grief that he had would somewhat be assuaged, and the pain that he felt because he left them in so great confusion, in leaving them in a strange country where they knew not where they were."

Baltazar de Gallegos answered in the name of all the rest; and first of all, comforting him, "he set before his eyes how short the life of this world was, and with how many troubles and miseries it is accompanied, and how God showed him a singular favor which soonest left it, and many other things proper for the occasion; and besought that he would himself appoint his successor." He therefore named Luis Muscoza de Alvarado his captain-general. The next day, being the 21st of May, 1542, "departed out of this life the valorous, virtuous, and valiant Captain Don Fernando de Soto, Governour of Cuba and Adelantado of Florida," whom, says the chronicler, "fortune advanced as it useth to do others, that he might have the higher fall. He departed in such a place and such a time, and in his sickness he had but little comfort."

They attempted to conceal De Soto's death, but, the Indians suspecting the place of his burial, he was taken up at a late hour of a dark night, and, wrapped in his mantle, was conveyed by the dim light of the stars to the middle of the Mississippi, and buried beneath its stream, in sorrow and silence, with a low whispered De Profundis from noble and saddened hearts, who seemed to bury with their chief beneath those dark waters almost the last ray of hope, and to look forward to the future with heavy forebodings.

The choice of a successor made by De Soto was ratified without dissent by his followers. and their first and only aim was to escape as soon as possible from a country which had disappointed all their hopes, and given not even the barren rewards of honorable fame.

They endeavored, at first, to follow the supposed route of Cabeça de Vaca, and reach Mexico, then called New Spain, by land; but after traveling to the southwest for some time they became discouraged, and concluded to build boats and attempt to coast along the shore. Finding a suitable place, called Minoya, the governor commanded them "to gather all the chaines which they had to lead the Indians," and collect the timber and material necessary for building boats. They built seven large boats and floated down the Mississippi, and, after several encounters with the natives, reached the open sea, and coasted along to the westward until they reached the northern Spanish settlements at Panuco, where they were joyfully received and treated with great kindness. Many went on shore "and kissed the ground, and kneeling on their knees, and lifting up their hands and eyes to heaven, they all ceased not to give God thanks."

Of those constituting De Soto's expedition who came out of Florida, there arrived at Panuco three hundred and eleven persons, the only survivors of the thousand brave men who, four years before, had landed at the harbor of Espiritu Santo.

The main interest of this extraordinary expedition centres in the person of the gallant chief with whom it originated, and who staked his name, his fortune, and his life upon the success of the enterprise; and as long as the great Father of Waters shall roll in resistless flood towards the sea, so long will the name of De Soto be recalled in connection with this expedition, and the sad fate which terminated his life upon its borders will excite a throb of sympathy for one who, at the early age of forty-two, passed from this world, second to none of his day or age in the practice of all manly virtues and deeds of knightly prowess.

We can hardly trace this long journey of De Soto through a trackless wilderness without astonishment at the perseverance and hardihood which, under such circumstances, could traverse thousands of miles unprovided with means of subsistence, marching from tribe to tribe and country to country, wherever the information of the hour produced hope for the future.

Let us, for a moment, carry ourselves back in imagination three hundred and thirty-one years. From the beautiful pine-glades of Florida we see issuing forth the gallant troops of the Adelantado. Three hundred mounted men, on noble Andalusian steeds, richly caparisoned, lead the advance. These are all gentlemen and noble cavaliers, hidalgos of rank and scions of the noblest families of Spain, officered by brave captains, whose names are emblazoned for their valor under the banner of Pizarro. Following these come six hundred and fifty men-at-arms, on foot, in close and serried ranks, and in their midst several hundred of the natives, bearing the burdens of their masters. These are the slaves, native Indians, whom they have impressed into their service; many are led by chains, and others manacled, to prevent escape. When a sufficient number of some other tribe are taken to supply their place, these will be relieved and allowed to return to their homes, and the others substituted, to be again relieved in like manner. Riding behind the cavaliers appear twelve men in long, black soutaines, who are evidently non-combatants. These are the clericos, priests and friars, and in their train are those who bear the ornaments and plate for celebrating mass. At each encampment an altar is erected, draped with rich altar-cloths, and surmounted with a golden crucifix, while lofty candelabra throw their pale light upon the worshipers. The priests, in their gorgeous vestments, celebrate mass in the sight of the whole army, drawn up in hollow square; and, kneeling amid their Christian masters, the natives of the forest, in mute wonderment, bow their heads in adoration of the Christians' God.

So, day by day and week by week, proceeded the march. Wherever an Indian field was found, its harvest was gathered; and wherever an Indian store-house or granary was discovered, its contents were speedily appropriated. For three years and a half this long march proceeded, without reinforcements or additional supplies. This fact of itself speaks volumes for the energy and generalship of this distinguished leader.

With but a thousand men, De Soto conquered and overran a country containing hundreds of thousands of inhabitants, and for over three years subsisted his troops and maintained the discipline of his forces in a wild and trackless country, without, so far as we know, a single murmur of discontent being raised against him by his devoted followers.

For three hundred years the red and white races have fought for supremacy over the countries traversed by De Soto, and now, at the end of more than three hundred years, the descendants of the warlike chiefs of Hirrihigua, Vitachuco, and Ocali still possess, amid the grassy everglades and cypress swamps beyond the Espiritu Santo, the hunting-grounds and graves of their ancestors.

Three hundred and thirty years ago, the advent of the horses of the adventurers, which the Indians invested with supernatural proportions, first struck with terror the savage races of Florida, and seemed to be the terrible precursors and forerunners of the domination of the white race, "the children of the sun;" and now the iron horse of an advancing civilization is startling those same pine forests with its shrill scream, indicating the fulfillment of that manifest destiny which was to strike forever from the land of their forefathers the last remains of the aboriginal races.

CHAPTER V.

Route of De Soto's Expedition through Florida.

The long sojourn of De Soto in the region bordering upon the Gulf of Mexico and on the banks of the Mississippi, and the remarkable adventures which he encountered, enhanced by his personal character and prowess, have invested the expedition of this gallant adventurer with unusual interest, and it has long been an important subject of inquiry to ascertain the route pursued by him and the localities of the more important events of his journey, beginning upon the beautiful bay of Espiritu Santo and ending with the descent of the great Father of Waters.

The task of thus tracing the steps of De Soto is by no means devoid of difficulty. We have to encounter not only the uncertainties of connecting names with localities imperfectly described, but have to be governed in these descriptions by three separate accounts of the expedition, exhibiting very important differences and discrepancies. The most voluminous of these is that of Garcilasso de la Vega, commonly called L'Inca. The next in extent is the work of a gentleman of Elvas, who accompanied the expedition, and who is commonly called the Portuguese Gentleman. The third and briefest is the narration of Lewis de Biedma.

The point where De Soto landed is stated by all to have been at Espiritu Santo Bay, on the western coast of Florida, and now known as Tampa Bay, a beautiful sheet of water, some thirty-six miles in length, and the largest bay on the Gulf of Mexico. There are two heads to the bay, one opening northerly and the other easterly. De Narvaez probably landed near and visited the northerly or old Tampa portion of the bay. De Soto, it is likely, landed near Gadsden's Point, where the shoal water begins, and beyond which it was of insufficient depth to carry his vessels. Their first day's march was to the village of Hirrihigua, two leagues northeasterly, and the location of which, as described by L'Inca, corresponds to the present town of Tampa.* The village consisted, it is said, of several large houses, built of wood and thatched with palm-leaves. In an opposite part of the village, near the water, upon an artificial eminence so constructed as to serve as a fortress, stood the dwelling of the cacique or chief.

From Hirrihigua, proceeding in a northeast course, at the end of two days De Soto came to the village of Mucoso, the chief who had befriended Ortiz. This may have been Hichipucsassa. They next, at a distance of twenty-five leagues from Hirrihigua, reached a town they call Urribarracaxi, which was likely on the Withlacoochee, as they there crossed a river. They next reached a town they name Ocali, which was on the banks of a river. This location is uncertain, but has been supposed to indicate the neighborhood of the present town of Ocali and the Ocklawaha.

From Ocali they went to Vitachuco—from the description of the adjacent country, indicating a location near Wacahootee. After leaving Vitachuco, they reached a great river, too deep to ford, which must have been the Suwanee.† Crossing this river, they reached Osachile, which is said to have been ten leagues from Vitachuco.‡

---

* Irving's Conquest of Florida, p. 58.
† Ibid., p. 127.   ‡ Ibid., p. 128.

From Osachile they marched three days, and on the fourth came to the Great Morass.* Passing this, they entered a fruitful country covered with fields of grain and containing many villages. In four days after passing the Great Morass they came to the village of Anhayea. The line of march from Vitachuco west would carry them to the Suwanee, near Suwanee Old Town; thence, bearing too far to the west, they were involved in one of the great coast swamps, but thence going northwestwardly they entered the fertile region embraced in the present counties of Madison, Jefferson, and Leon, and their Anhayea is thought to have been in the vicinity of Tallahassee. From Anhayea two exploring parties were sent out, one north and one south. The party which went north returned reporting very favorably of a rich and well inhabited country. The party which went down towards the coast found a sterile country, full of ponds and swamps. These descriptions would correspond very well with the country north and south of Monticello or Tallahassee. The village of Auté was twelve leagues from Anhayea, and not far from the Bay of Apalachee. De Soto sent back to Espiritu Santo and had his vessels brought into this bay. Afterwards he sent vessels coasting westwardly. At a distance of seventy leagues they entered a beautiful and spacious bay, called by them Ochuse, which was evidently Pensacola Bay. They reported that it was land-locked and completely sheltered with bold shores, and large enough for a fleet to anchor in. De Soto does not appear to have crossed the Apalachicola or Chattahoochee River, but, having made an appointment for vessels to be sent from Cuba to meet him in the fall at Ochuse, he determined to proceed to a province to the northeast, abounding in gold, pearls, etc. Leaving Anhayea,

---

* Irving's Conquest of Florida, p. 130.

he traveled northeast, and at the end of three days came to Copachique; this was probably on the Savannah River. Two days farther travel brought them to Atapaha. This name so closely resembles Alapaha that it is reasonable to suppose they are the same, and that the town was on the river of that name, which, passing through a portion of Georgia, discharges itself into the Suwanee, in Hamilton County, Florida. Traveling still in the same direction, it is supposed they crossed successively the Altamaha and the Savannah River, and reached the region of Middle Georgia between Milledgeville and Augusta. They marched thence northwestwardly to the mineral regions of Upper Georgia, where they had been informed the gold which they saw in possession of the natives had been procured. De Soto then passed to the Etowah River, and visited a large Indian town situated at the confluence of the Coosa and Etowah, called Chiapa, the location now occupied by the present city of Rome, Georgia. He then passed southwardly through a rich and fertile country called Coosa, and eventually reached Maubila or Mauvilla, which was situated, it is supposed, at Choctaw Bluff. He here heard of the arrival of his vessels at Ochuse, on Pensacola Bay, and at first contemplated going to meet them, but, fearing that once near his vessels his men would insist on leaving the country, he determined to pursue his march westward. At Maubila he was not more than one hundred and fifty miles from Pensacola. His course was then northwestward to the Mississippi, and it is conjectured that he crossed a few miles below Memphis.

CHAPTER VI.

Other Expeditions to Florida—Occupation of Santa Maria by Tristan de Luna—Expedition to the Borders of Tennessee and the Province of Coca.

1543—1561.

WHILE De Soto was thus traversing Florida and the country east of the Mississippi, Mendoza, the Viceroy of Mexico, had fitted out an expedition to enter upon the route of De Vaca. It consisted of but thirty horsemen, under the command first of Juan de Caldivar, and afterwards of Coronado, who passed as far north as Missouri, and crossed several rivers, to which he gave names, but which are described with so little accuracy as to give but slender aid to their being now identified. Passing through a province called Quivira, they were informed of four white men having been there, whom they supposed must have been De Vaca and his comrades. After the return of Coronado, the zealous brothers of the order of St. Francis determined to visit Quivira, which, having undertaken with a small party, these worthy men fell martyrs to their Christian zeal, being murdered by the natives, with all of their party, except two men who escaped to Mexico by different routes. Upon the arrival of Don Luis Muscoza de Alvarado in Mexico with the remnant of De Soto's expedition, Mendoza, the Viceroy, endeavored to induce some of them to lead an expedition he was anxious to fit out for Florida; but they were unwilling again to enter upon this enterprise.

In the following year, 1544, Julian de Samano and Pedro de Ahumada, being satisfied that Florida abounded in pearls and fine furs, and believing that mines of gold, silver, and other metals could be opened, sought the privilege of conquering the country, but failed to obtain the desired permission.

A treasure-ship, on a voyage to Spain from New Mexico, was lost, on the eastern coast of Florida, in the year 1545, and of some two hundred persons on board who escaped to the land, all were sacrificed by the Indians except a few who were reduced to servitude. One of these made his way to Laudonnière twenty years afterwards, and several others escaped to Menendez.

The religious zeal of the Franciscans again induced an attempt to plant the cross on the shores of Florida. It is probable that had this attempt preceded the armed expeditions which had landed on these shores, they would have been received with the kindness which seems to have welcomed the first comers to the shores of America. But the natives had learned to associate all white men with the armed invaders of their soil, and they could make no distinction between the sword of the one and the cross of the other.

Four Franciscan brothers, Fra Luis Cancer de Bastro, of the order of St. Dominic, who had been in Mexico, and held the office of Provincial Vicar of Guatemala and Chiapas, Fra Gregorio de Betata, Fra Diego de Penalosa, Fra Juan Garcia, and one Donado, called Fuentes, sailed from Havana in the year 1549, and landed at Espiritu Santo Bay. Penalosa and Fuentes, attempting to penetrate into the country, were set upon at once and massacred by the natives. The others had remained on board their vessel in the harbor, and, while lying there, a Spaniard came off to them, named Juan Munoz, who was a page of Captain

Calderon, an officer of De Soto's expedition. He had been captured by the Indians, and held by them ten years, and now most gladly availed himself of this opportunity of escape. Fra Luis, the chief of the clerical party, was not discouraged by the fate of Penalosa and Fuentes, and, notwithstanding the earnest efforts of Munoz and others to dissuade him from the attempt, he determined to try his power of persuasion upon the hostile natives. His Christian zeal could not be restrained by the dictates of prudence, and, unwilling to give up the object of his journey thither without a final effort to reach the hearts of those people, he prepared to sacrifice his life, if necessary, in the attempt.

Accordingly, he insisted upon landing alone among the dusky throng of warriors who lined the shores of the Espiritu Santo. Scarcely had the zealous priest touched the beach before he fell beneath the war-clubs of the infuriated savages, a martyr to his zeal; and the shores of this most beautiful bay were reddened with the blood of one whose Christian devotion and unselfishness formed a marked contrast to the characters of those whose lust for gold had brought them to the New World.

The companions of Fra Luis de Cancer, deterred by his fate from making any further effort to Christianize the natives of Florida, abandoned the expedition, and set sail for Cuba.

Some three years afterwards, a Spanish plate fleet, which had left Vera Cruz with upwards of one thousand persons on board, was wrecked on the coast of Florida. Stopping, as usual, at Havana, the fleet had again set sail for Spain, when it was overtaken by one of those tremendous gales which prevail with such terrific effect in the southern seas, and driven before its resistless power. The whole fleet, with the exception of a single vessel, was cast upon the inhospitable shores of Florida, somewhere within the Gulf of

Mexico, probably very considerably to the west. Of the thousand persons on board, only three hundred reached the shore. They endeavored to reach Mexico by passing along the shores, making rafts to cross the mouths of the rivers, but, incessantly harassed by the Indians, and overcome by fatigue, they gradually decreased in numbers until all had perished except one Francis Marcos. He had been left by his companions, in a dying condition, buried in the sand, with only his face exposed; but, reviving sufficiently to exert himself a little further, he crawled along the coast until he was discovered and taken up by two friendly Indians, who carried him in a boat to Panuco. With the exception of the few who were in the vessel that escaped shipwreck, this Francis Marcos was the sole survivor of more than a thousand persons who had left the shores of New Spain full of joyful anticipations of a return to their native land, where they would become famous among their countrymen as those who had visited. far countries, performed great feats, seen wonderful things, and returned enriched with some of the treasures of Mexico.

Notwithstanding the many disasters that had befallen those who had approached the shores of Florida, and which seemed to promise to the future invaders only disappointment and death, there yet appeared to exist some great attraction for the adventurous, and a belief in the hidden treasures of this country induced renewed efforts for its conquest.

In 1556 a memorial was addressed to the emperor by the Viceroy of Mexico, and the Bishop of Cuba, to whose diocese Florida belonged, setting forth the great richness of Florida, and the immense benefits which would result to the cause of religion and to the empire from its acquisition.

In consequence of this memorial, orders were transmitted to the Viceroy of New Spain to prepare an expedition for the conquest and settlement of Florida, and it was said that such were the accounts given by those who had been in the expeditions of Narvaez and De Soto, of the exceeding richness of the country, that there was a widespread desire to engage in the enterprise.

The expedition, which was to leave Vera Cruz in the spring of 1559, was planned upon an extensive scale. It consisted of fifteen hundred soldiers, and a large number of friars and zealous preachers, burning for the conversion of the Indians, all under the command of Don Tristan de Luna and other officers of experience.

They sailed from Vera Cruz amid salvos of artillery and shouts of good will and kind wishes from the assembled multitude, and, gayly flinging their pennons to the breeze, they went forth with the most brilliant anticipations of success.

On the 14th of August the fleet cast anchor in a bay to which they gave the name of Santa Maria, and described as a spacious and convenient harbor. This was doubtless the Bay of Pensacola, which we find frequently mentioned afterwards in the Spanish relations as the Bay of Santa Maria.

Upon their arrival at this point, dispatch-vessels were sent to Mexico and Spain to announce their progress and confirm the opinions entertained of the value of the country. Reconnoitring expeditions were sent along the rivers, and preparations made for exploring the interior. On the 20th of August, six days after their arrival, there was a terrible gale, which wrecked the entire fleet, and destroyed a large portion of their provisions. Don Tristan de Luna encouraged his followers to persevere in their course, assuring them that supplies would soon reach them from the viceroy, and he directed an expedition to be fitted out, composed of four companies, to penetrate the country which was called the Province of Coca.

With the remainder of his men he established himself at the port, with the hope that some opportunity would offer by which he might inform the viceroy of their unfortunate condition.

The sergeant-major, with the four companies, traveled for forty days through an uninhabited country, until he arrived upon the banks of a river which he was unable to cross. Following along the banks of this river, which was undoubtedly the Alabama, they at length came upon an Indian village, from which, on the approach of the Spaniards, the inhabitants all fled. They found within the houses a considerable supply of corn, beans, and other vegetable products.

In examining the surrounding country they encountered some of the natives, whom they propitiated with beads and other trifling presents, and who, although they seemed surprised, made no attempt at escape. By means of an Indian interpreter, the Spaniards asked the name of the town and province, why it was deserted, and what country lay beyond it. They replied that the town was called Napicnoca; that it had been very large and well peopled, but that other strangers, like the Spaniards, had destroyed it, and forced the inhabitants to fly, except a few who remained to gather the harvest.*

The sergeant-major sent out several detachments to examine the adjacent country, but they were greatly discouraged on finding only vast deserts and solitudes. Returning to Napicnoca, sixteen men were sent back to Santa Maria to report the progress of the expedition.

In the mean time Don Tristan de Luna, who had with him at Santa Maria a force of over one thousand men, receiving no intelligence from the sergeant-major, and con-

---

* Undoubtedly the other strangers were De Soto and his party.

cluding from the time which had elapsed that the exploring party had been cut off by the natives, determined to remain no longer at the bay, where they were suffering from the want of provisions, their supplies being now exhausted.

While preparing to go into the interior, the sixteen men sent back by the sergeant-major arrived, and, learning from them that at Napicnoca were corn and other supplies, De Luna determined to proceed with his men to that town, some going by land and others by the river. Upon his arrival, Don Tristan named the place Santa Cruz de Napicnoca. The large number of persons to be provisioned soon consumed the supplies which the sergeant-major had gathered, and they were obliged to rely upon such chance food as they could obtain, living upon acorns, which they partially relieved of their bitterness by boiling them first in salt water and afterwards in fresh water. The women and young children, unable to eat the acorns, lived upon the tender leaves and young twigs of the forest trees. They were soon reduced to the last stage of hunger and despair, looking forward to death as their only relief, when they were told of the province of Coca, which had the reputation of being an abundant and rich province, of which they had before heard, but were ignorant of the route to reach it. This information was gladly received; some of the party, who had probably visited that province with De Soto, assuring them that if they could once reach there they would find an abundance of everything.

De Luna thereupon sent the sergeant-major, with two hundred men, to explore the route to Coca, two worthy friars accompanying the expedition. The sergeant-major, now hopeful for the future, moved northwardly, forced to rely for food upon the roots and branches of trees; seeming to have been too unskillful to obtain game. They were forced to eat even their thongs and straps, and seven of their number died of starvation and from eating poisonous shrubs. They found no habitations, and encountered none of the natives, and were so reduced as to be almost incapable of either advancing or returning to their comrades; but they still pushed on, until they at length entered a wooded country, abounding in chestnuts and hickory-nuts. Relieved of their sufferings, they now felt cheered to prosecute their journey, and, fifty days after leaving Napicnoca, they came to Indian settlements upon the banks of a river which the Indians called Olibahaki, and farther on they came to small towns.

Making friendly advances to the natives, they procured provisions of them in limited quantities, the natives manifesting much caution and distrust.

A miracle is reported to have occurred while they were in this settlement, which is illustrative of the veneration entertained by the Spaniards for the mysteries of their faith. A rude chapel had been erected, of boughs, for the purpose of celebrating mass, and while the priest was in the act of consecrating the Host, he perceived upon the edge of the chalice a disgusting and probably poisonous worm, so situated that an attempt to remove it would cause its fall within the chalice. Perplexed by so unfortunate a circumstance, the priest fell upon his knees and earnestly prayed that the worm might not be permitted to fall into the holy sacrament, and immediately the worm fell from the cup to the altar, devoid of life. The priest, regarding it as a miraculous answer to his prayer, made use of the occasion to urge upon the company constancy and conformity in their works, at all times, to the will of God.*

The sergeant-major remained quite as long as was accept-

---

* Barcia, Ensayo Cronologico, p. 34.

able to his host on the Olibahaki, and they soon devised a plan for relieving themselves of their guests, which was no less cunning than amusing. Dressing up one of their number *en grand seigneur*, with proper attendants, they sent him to the camp of the Spaniards to represent himself to them as an ambassador from the cacique of the province of Coca, empowered to extend to them an urgent invitation to visit that province, and offering to act as a guide. The Spaniards gladly accepted the invitation, made much of the supposed ambassador, and informed him that they would at once set out with him for Coca. They marched out with high expectations, but at the close of the first day's march their guide disappeared, leaving them to find their way to Coca as best they could.

Finding themselves duped, some counseled a return to Olibahaki, but the majority preferred to go on, and a few days afterwards reached the object of their search,—the far-famed province of Coca. The principal town of this province contained about thirty houses, and there were seven other towns belonging to this tribe. The land, in consequence of the want of cultivation, did not appear so productive as had been reported in Mexico by the survivors of De Soto's expedition. The neglect of the soil was attributed by the Indians to the fact that the people had fled from their habitations and fields, and been dispersed by the followers of De Soto.

The sergeant-major remained at Coca seven days, receiving every mark of attention from the natives. Learning that the people of Coca were at war with a neighboring tribe, the Spaniards proposed, in recompense for the kindness they had received, to assist their friends of Coca,—a proposal which the Indians gladly accepted. Meanwhile, the friars were not unmindful of the spiritual purposes of their mission, and sought to enlighten the minds and reach the hearts of the natives, portraying to them, to the best of their ability, the truths of the gospel; but with little success, the Indians, it is said, being more intent upon punishing their enemies than upon the salvation of their own souls. The expedition against the Napaches, by the aid of the Spaniards, proved successful, no loss being sustained on either side, and a satisfactory treaty being made between the tribes.

The sergeant-major proceeded to examine the country with a view to settlement, and in the mean time dispatched an officer with twelve men to report to the general, who, with eight hundred of his followers, had remained at Napicnoca.

De Luna, having remained at the latter place for some time, and receiving no intelligence from the sergeant-major, concluded to return to the Bay of Santa Maria. Some of his party during their stay at the Indian town had died of hunger, and others had become greatly enfeebled. Before leaving, he buried at the foot of a tree a vase containing a scroll, with directions for any of the Coca expedition who should return there; and on the tree he cut the words, *"Dig below."* The Spaniards arrived at Santa Maria after a journey of severe toils and sufferings. At their own request, the friars were permitted to set sail with two small vessels for Havana, and to proceed thence to New Spain to procure succor for their companions.

The twelve soldiers dispatched by the sergeant-major reached Napicnoca in twelve days, traversing in this space of time the distance which the Spaniards had taken seventy days to pass over upon their advance. Arriving at Napicnoca, the detachment were surprised to see no signs of the Spaniards who had been left there, but, entering the town, they observed the inscription upon the tree, and disinterred the vase containing instructions for them, and rejoiced to learn that their friends were still living. Then pushing on with all haste to Santa Maria, which was forty leagues distant, they reached there in three days, when they met with a joyful reception from their friends.

The party which had been sent by the sergeant-major delivered the letters with which he had intrusted them for the general; and to the inquiries eagerly made in the camp as to the character of the country which they had visited, they replied, making a very unfavorable report of the regions which they had passed through, enlarging upon the trials and sufferings they had undergone, and depreciating the province of Coca. These reports caused great discontent in the camp, and disposed a large number to advocate the instant abandonment of such a country.

Juan de Ceron, the master of the camp, and others of the principal officers, expressed their opinion openly, and De Luna, in calling his officers together to announce to them his determination to proceed to the province of Coca, was met by a stout opposition on the part of De Ceron and those who entertained his views. The general, in reply to those who had no faith in the value of Coca, charged them with a desire to avoid the labor and trials attending the march and settlement of the country, and said that they were influenced more by their indolence than other reasons, and issued his orders that all should prepare for the march to Coca. But the discontent had already extended to the larger part of the army, and, supported in their opposition by their officers, they set at defiance the authority of the general, and secretly sent word to the sergeant-major to return to Santa Maria. The messenger sent by them arrived safely at Coca, and informed the sergeant-major that the general commanded his return, as the army was about to leave the country. The Indians of Coca parted from the Spaniards with great regret, accompanying them two or three days' journey, and crying with great demonstrations of affection. The sergeant-major arrived at Santa Maria in the beginning of November, having been engaged some seven months in this exploration of the country.

Events often derive their importance from the skill with which they are narrated; and had this journey of the sergeant-major been sufficiently fortunate to have a chronicler like Cabeça de Vaca, doubtless it would have been regarded with as much interest as the expeditions of Narvaez and De Soto. The route pursued cannot be very well traced, the slight notices of natural objects and the unrecognizable names of towns giving no clue to identification. It is quite probable that the river encountered on their march to Napicnoca was the Alabama, and that the Indian town was somewhere near Camden. The twelve days' travel thence to Coca was through the pine-barrens and sand-hills of South Alabama, and the Olibahaki was the Coosa or Alabama. The province of Coca was the Coosa country in the northeastern part of Alabama.

Upon the return of the sergeant-major to the Bay of Santa Maria, the camp still remained divided. The general retained his purpose to remain in the country, and the disaffected were equally determined to depart from that region. All respect for authority was weakened, and the quarrel became so violent as to render useless the efforts of the priests to reconcile it. The general, jealous of his authority and indignant at the opposition of his officers, became daily more harsh and irritable.

In the mean time, the two vessels which had gone with the friars to procure relief reached Havana in safety, and thence proceeded to Vera Cruz, where they carried to the unwilling ears of the Viceroy their tale of the sufferings and disappointments which had attended the expedition.

He was loath to credit the information; but the high character of the envoy, Don Pedro de Feria, afterwards Bishop of Chiapa, gave no room to doubt the painful truth. It was a sad disappointment, after all the flattering accounts which had been brought to Mexico of the riches and fertility of the country, to be compelled to believe otherwise. The viceroy promptly sent off the two vessels loaded with provisions to Santa Maria.

This opportune relief produced no change in the condition of affairs at the camp of Don Tristan de Luna. Five long months they lingered on the shores of Santa Maria, each party inflexibly adhering to its resolution, so that the general could not proceed with his expedition, nor could the disaffected leave the hated shores. A reconciliation was finally effected, from the foot of the altar, by the skill and energy of Father Domingo.

At length there arrived at the port of Santa Maria, Don Angel de Villafane, who had been sent out by the Viceroy of Cuba as Governor of Florida, with instructions to make an examination of the shores of the gulf, which, in consequence of the continual storms, he had been unable to do. Upon his arrival, councils were held by the officers as to the course which it was advisable to pursue. The general and a few others desired to continue the enterprise, but the larger number preferred to abandon the country. Those who desired to leave embarked on the vessels of Don Angel de Villafane.

Don Tristan de Luna, with a few of his followers, remained at the Bay of Santa Maria, and communicated to the Viceroy of Mexico the events which had occurred, the obstacles he had encountered, and his views of the manner of remedying them; but the Viceroy, discouraged by the failures which had hitherto attended the expedition, and unwilling further to pursue it, recalled De Luna, and abandoned his efforts for the conquest of Florida.

Thus ended the most considerable and best-appointed expedition which had ever landed on the shores of Florida, and which, under better management, might have been measurably successful in planting a colony on the banks of the Coosa. Although no such terrible disaster attended this as had befallen the previous expeditions, yet the privations and sufferings which were undergone were well calculated to deter others from a renewal of the attempt.

The cavalier Don Tristan de Luna remained to the last, unwilling to turn his back upon a country the conquest of which had been assigned to him, and which he was satisfied was really valuable and productive. The clergy, who had in considerable numbers been attached to the expedition, added their voices to those who felt unwilling to remain, and De Luna was forced to abandon the beautiful Bay of Santa Maria, and leave the occupation of the country he had explored to be accomplished by succeeding generations.

It seems evident, upon comparing the narrative of the expedition of the sergeant-major of De Luna with the accounts of Cabeça de Vaca and De Soto, that the sergeant-major must have wandered through some barren portion of Lower Alabama, and failed to reach more than the outskirts of the numerous Indian settlements in the country bordering on the Coosa and the Tennessee Rivers, and which De Vaca and De Soto had rightly described as rich and fertile.

This expedition of De Luna possesses much interest, as establishing the fact that a settlement of Spaniards occupied the shores of the Bay of Pensacola in 1561, and that the whole of that region was known to them. Moreover, this was the last of the exploring expeditions which visited Florida, and occurred only a year prior to the landing of the French Huguenots, under Ribaut, on the eastern coast, and only antedated by four years the permanent settlement of Florida, effected by Pedro de Menendez. It is but just that among the historic names connected with the discovery and exploration of Florida should be remembered that of DON TRISTAN DE LUNA.

CHAPTER VII.

Huguenot Settlements at Charles Fort under Ribaut, and at Fort Caroline under Laudonnière.

1562—1564.

WE have hitherto accompanied through the wilds of Florida the cavaliers of Spain, who, with the sound of the trumpet and the battle-cry of St. Iago, carried devastation and slaughter in their march. They styled themselves Conquistadors; their purpose was conquest, and their principal object the acquisition of gold, silver, and pearls. A country which promised rich rewards to the patient and laborious pursuits of the agriculturist offered no inducements to them. They had been corrupted and engorged with the plunder of Mexico and the spoil of Peru. They sought not to create wealth, but to seize and appropriate it wherever found, and they had little regard to the amount of suffering they caused the unhappy natives of the land, if either by torture or destruction they could force the discovery of their treasures.

Their efforts in Florida had proved fruitless. Where they had looked for easy conquest and great reward they had found only privation and toils, and had met a race fierce and implacable, who lacked only the means of offensive warfare to sweep their invaders from their shores. Narvaez and his followers had perished ingloriously in their attempt to leave a land hostile at every step, and the miserable remnant of the force of De Soto, baffled in all their efforts, had barely escaped into Mexico. The fruitless expedition of De Luna had failed of its object, and the whole of the vast country, from Mexico to the Polar Seas and from the Atlantic to the Pacific, contained not a single settlement of the white race. The dreams of conquest were over, and the adventurers were well satisfied to leave in peace "the richest country of the world."

An entirely different class of persons now made their appearance upon the shores of Florida, the principal aim of whom was colonization and settlement. They were of a different race and had come from different motives.

The weak and vacillating Charles IX. was King of France, and the Admiral De Chastellan, better known as the famous Coligny, was at the head of the Protestant party. Civil war raged between the votaries of the two religious bodies between whom the kingdom was divided. The transatlantic discoveries and settlements of the Spaniards in Mexico, Peru, and the Spanish Main suggested to the astute mind of the admiral the idea of founding beyond the sea a new empire which might extend the possessions of France, and at the same time strengthen, and, in case of need, afford a refuge to, the Huguenots, if borne down in their contest at home.

An expedition was fitted out, and sailed in February, 1562, consisting of two good vessels, under Captain Jean Ribaut, an officer of much experience and considerable reputation. A prosperous voyage brought them directly to the coast of Florida, in the neighborhood of St. Augustine. Sailing to the northward, they discovered the entrance of the St. John's River, landed, and erected a monument of stone, on which was engraved the arms of France, it being placed, it is said, within the said river, and not far from the mouth thereof, upon a little sandy knap. They named the river the river *May*, because they entered it upon the first day of that month.

Re-embarking, they sailed to the northward, landing occasionally, and being received with kindness by the numerous Indians they encountered, to whom they gave presents of trifling value, such as looking-glasses and tin bracelets, with which they were much pleased.

After sailing about ninety leagues to the north, they entered the harbor of Port Royal, and anchored. For several days they made excursions up the adjoining rivers, making peaceable overtures to the Indians, with whom they were now upon terms of amity.

Ribaut finally concluded to plant his colony at this point, but it was a question as to what portion of his followers would be willing to remain alone upon these unknown shores.

He thereupon called his men together and made them a skillful oration, which is reported to us with all the fullness of a modern "Herald" report. Adorning and illustrating his speech by various references to classical antiquity, he closed by saying, "How much, then, ought so many worthy examples to move you to plant here, considering also that you shall be registered forever as the first that inhabited this strange country! I pray you therefore all to advise yourselves thereof, and to deliver your mind freely unto me, protesting that I will so well imprint your names in the king's ears and the other princes, that your renown shall hereafter thrive unquenchably through our realms of France." Such has ever been the peculiarity of the Gallic race; they appeal, not to the appetite for gain, not to the riches to be acquired, but, from Charlemagne to Napoleon III., honor to France and renown to themselves have been the incentives to performance of duty and great enterprise. Ribaut judged rightly of the effect of such an appeal to the hearts of Frenchmen. He had hardly ended his oration when the majority of the soldiers replied that a greater pleasure could never betide them, perceiving well the acceptable service which by this means they do unto their prince, besides that this thing should be for the increase of their honors; whereupon, it is said, Jean Ribaut, being as glad as might be to see his men so well willing, determined at once to search out a place most fit and convenient to be inhabited. The matter was a momentous one—an empire was to be founded, and a continent taken possession of; it was felt to be a great occasion, and the minds of the little band ran forward to the time when a New France, with its peopled cities, its rich and fertile fields, its coasts, whitened with the sails of commerce, would be in existence, and *they* remembered in those after-days as the first occupants of this vast country.

A small fort was erected upon a little island and named Charles Fort; twenty-five men were selected to remain, and placed under the command of Captain Albert. Supplies of ammunition and provisions were left, and with a parting salute of artillery, replied to from the fort, the vessels left the infant settlement, and the destinies of New France were centred in that little fort. The Indians were on terms of amity, and everything promised fair for the future.

Ribaut, satisfied with this beginning, returned to France, having been absent about four months.

The colony left at Charles Fort prospered for some time, and made various excursions among the Indians, by whom they were well received and lovingly entreated. Indeed, the French seemed to have a peculiar faculty of ingratiating themselves; and the whole history of their explorations, in every part of America, shows most uniform and remarkable success in conciliating and securing the affection of the savage tribes.

The secret consists most probably in the peculiarly adaptable and versatile talent of the French, enabling them to accommodate themselves with ease to any customs or usages, and putting them at once at home wherever they may happen to be placed. Another reason is, that they are skilled in the art of pantomime, the only language at all available upon first meeting with a tribe whose language is unknown. The Frenchman, with his varying gestures, his expressive shrug, his flexible features, his animated manner of expressing himself, would soon be on a good footing and smoking a pipe with the cacique, where the stately Don would be expressing his pleasure in pure Castilian and making gestures at the end of his lance, or the Englishman, with his phlegmatic temperament, would be attempting a direct negotiation. Whether as missionaries, explorers, or traders, the French have ever been foremost in the facility with which they have managed their red brethren. A very little additional aid to French colonization would have made the United States indeed a New France.

Captain Albert made an excursion to a country called the Ouade, probably the Savannah River, where the cacique, after supplying them with corn, it is said, gave them a certain number of exceeding fair pearls, two stones of fine crystal, and certain silver ore, and being inquired of where the ore and crystals came from, they answered that it came ten days' journey, and that the inhabitants there dig the same at the foot of certain high mountains, referring, it is quite evident, to the gold regions of Georgia.

It had been the intention of Ribaut, when he left the colony, to return immediately with a much larger force, and provided with everything necessary to establish a permanent settlement; but, when he returned to France, civil war was raging, and nothing could be done, and the existence of Captain Albert and Charles Fort was almost forgotten.

Anxiously did the little garrison await the promised return. Their provisions were becoming more scarce, and, day by day, they in vain scanned the horizon in the hope of descrying relief; but none came, and with disappointment came discontent.

Their captain became exacting and tyrannical and the men careless and disobedient. A difficulty arising with one Guerlache, a poor drummer, he was ordered to be hung by the captain, and this conclusive evidence of civilization was carried into effect; another he placed on an island to starve, and then it was determined to remove Albert by taking his life, which they soon did. Months had rolled past since Ribaut was to have returned. After the death of Albert they chose one Nicolas Barré as their captain; and finally, despairing of the return of Ribaut, they determined to attempt to get away. They had not a single ship-carpenter among them, but they managed to build a small pinnace, probably a mere shallop. They covered it with moss, made the cordage of palmettos, and the sails of their shirts and linen. In this miserable little affair, caulked with moss, and with such sails, this little band attempted to cross the stormy ocean which separated them from their native land. It would seem as though the first shock of a tempest would have buried them beneath the waves. They had not laid in sufficient provisions for their long voyage, and, although the calms they encountered were favorable to their safety, they were soon placed in danger of starvation. Listlessly floating upon the sea, becalmed for many days, they were reduced to terrible extremities, until at last they cast lots for the life of one of their number, and Leclerc was sacrificed, and his flesh divided equally—"a thing so pitiful," says the writer, "that my pen is loath to write it." Fortunately, they were soon after fallen in with by an English vessel and rescued. It seems wonderful that they should have escaped at all, for so crazy a craft never crossed the Atlantic.

After the truce between the contending parties in France, Coligny turned his attention to the occupation of Florida, and on the 22d of April, 1564, he dispatched thither three vessels, respectively, of one hundred and twenty, one hundred, and sixty tons burden, under command of René de Laudonnière, who had accompanied Ribaut in the first expedition.

This René seems to have been a clever young man, somewhat fussy and undecided, and considerably elevated by his first command. In person, if Le Moyne's pictures are correct, he was small and slight, with a pleasant countenance. The Indian chiefs are represented as towering a head and shoulders above him.

On Thursday, the 22d day of June, 1564, about three o'clock in the afternoon, Laudonnière says he came to the land, went on shore near a little river which is 30° distant from the equator, and ten leagues above Cape François, drawing towards the south, and about 30° above the river May. "After we had stricken sail and cast anchor athwart the river, I determined to go on shore to discover the same. Therefore being accompanied with Monsieur d'Ottigni and Monsieur d'Arlac, my ensigne, and a certain number of soldiers, I embarked myself about 3 or 4 of the clock in the evening, and arrived at the mouth of the river. I caused the channel to be sounded, which was found to be very shallow, although that further within the same the water was there found reasonably deep, which separated itself with two great arms, whereof one runneth toward the south and the other toward the north. Having thus searched the river, I went on land to speak with the Indians which waited for us on the shore, which, at our incoming on land, came before us crying with a loud voice their Indian language, Antipola, benassan, which is as much as to say, brother, friend, or some such thing. After they had seen very much of us they showed us their paracoussi, that is to say their king and governor, to whom I presented certain toyes, wherewith he was well pleased; and for mine own part I pray God continually for the great love which I have found in these savages, which were sorry for nothing but that the night approached and made us retire unto our ships. For though they endeavoured by all means to make us tarry with them, and showed by signals the desire they had to present us with some rare things, yet, nevertheless, for many and reasonable occasions, I would not stay on shore all night, but excusing myself for all their offers, I embarked myself again and returned toward my ships. Howbeit, before mine departure, I named their river the River of Dolphins, because that at mine arrival I saw there a great number of dolphins which were playing in the mouth thereof."

This account by Laudonnière himself, of his first landing on the coast of Florida, is given at length, for the reason that it is the harbor of St. Augustine which he describes; and the spot where that city is now built was the scene of the interview which he here relates. The two arms of the river, running to the north and south, are the North River and the Matanzas River, and the shallow water on the bar, and the gentle and pleasant courtesy which characterized the natives, may be said to be perpetuated to this day. In the volume of De Bry, relating to Florida, the first plate contains a striking picture of the River of Dolphins, a boat with Captain Laudonnière about landing, a large number of the natives on the shore. One group represents the paracoussi, seated upon a carpet of green leaves, surrounded with his people, awaiting the landing of the French, whose three vessels are at anchor. The palm, the pine, and the cedar are represented as growing on the shore.

On the next day they sailed for the mouth of the river May, the St. John's, where Laudonnière was shown by the Indians the column erected by Ribaut. After examining various localities, Laudonnière concluded to establish his settlement at the point now known as St. John's Bluff.

The reasons which induced a location upon the St. John, as given by Laudonnière himself, were that "to the southward there was nothing but a flat, marshy country, unfit to inhabit, and, from the report of those who were left at Charles Fort, the country thereabouts was not productive, while the means of subsistence seemed to abound on the river May; and upon their first visit they had seen gold and silver in the possession of the natives, a thing which put me in hope," he says, "of some happy discovery in time to come."

The poetic nature of the Frenchman, and his eye for natural beauty, was kindled as he explored the margin of the river; and to one place which pleased his fancy, at the request of his soldiers, he gave the name of the Vale of Laudonnière—his eye charmed with the green meadows and bright visions of spring.

Having fixed upon the spot upon which to erect the fort, he commanded the trumpet to sound, and assembled his men, to return thanks to God for their favorable and happy arrival. "Thus they sang hymns of praise to the Lord, supplicating that His holy grace might be continued to His poor servants, and aid them in all undertakings which they desired should redound to His glory and the advancement of our Holy Faith." They laid out their fort in the form of a triangle, and received some assistance from the Indians in its construction.

An expedition went up the river in boats, and at twenty

leagues' distance, probably about Mandarin, they came to an Indian town called Thimagua, and by the Indians of this tribe he was informed of nine other kings or caciques, named Cadecha, Chilili, Eclanan, Enacoppe, Calany, Anacharagua, Anitagua, Æquera, Mucoso. The last named will be recognized as the protector of Juan Ortiz, thirty years before. From time to time, boat expeditions were made to the tribes settled along the river, and they had frequent applications to assist the caciques in their wars against each other, and on several occasions did so, to strengthen themselves with their neighbors.

On the 29th of August, 1564, it is said "a lightning from heaven fell within half a league of our fort, more worthy to be wondered at and put in writing than any of the strange signs which have been seen in times past, and whereof histories have been written. For although the meadows were then green, and half covered with water, nevertheless the lightning, in one instant, consumed about five hundred acres, therewith, and burned, with the ardent heat thereof, all the souls which took their pasture in the meadows, which thing continued for three days space, which caused us not a little to muse, not being able to judge whereof the fire proceeded. For one while we thought the Indians had burned their houses and abandoned their places for fear of us. Another while we thought they had discovered some ships at sea, and that, according to their customs, they had kindled many fires here and there to signify that their country was inhabited; nevertheless, being not assured, I was upon the point to send some one by boats to discover the matter, when six Indians came to me from Paracoussi Allimicany, which, at their first entry, made me a long discourse, and a very long and ample oration (after they had presented me with certain baskets full of maize, of pumpkins, and of grapes) of the loving amity which Allimicany desired to continue with me, and that he looked from day to day where it would please me to employ him in my service. Therefore, considering the serviceable affection that he bore unto me, he found it very strange that I thus discharged mine ordinance against his dwelling, which had burnt up an infinite sight of green meadows, and consumed even down unto the water, and came so near unto his mansion that he thought he saw the fire in his house; wherefore he besought me most humbly to command my men that they would not shoot any more towards his lodgings, otherwise he would be constrained to abandon his country, and to retire himself unto some place farther off from us."

The French commander, seeing that the Indians thought this wonderful stroke of lightning had proceeded from their cannon, encouraged the idea, and informed them he was glad they were inclined to be peaceable; that he could easily have reached his house, some miles distant, if he had chosen, but that he only fired half-way to show them his power. All this the Indians believed, and the paracoussi would not come within twenty-five leagues of the fort for two months. "Two days afterward there followed such an excessive heat in the air, that the river became so hot that I think it was almost ready to seethe, for there died so great abundance of fish, and that of so many divers sorts, that in the mouth of the river only there were found dead enough to have laden fifty carts, whereof there issued a putrefaction in the air which bred many dangerous diseases amongst us, inasmuch as most of my men fell sick and almost ready to end their days. Yet, notwithstanding, it pleased our merciful God so far to provide by his Providence, that all our men got well."

In September one of the Frenchmen pretended that by the secret art of magic he had discovered a mine of gold and silver, far up within the river, and that their captain was intending to conceal it from them. Acting upon the credulity of others, he soon organized a conspiracy to make way with Laudonnière.

At this time Laudonnière sent a small vessel back to France, under the command of Captain Bourdett, and with him seven or eight of those whose fidelity he suspected. He was subsequently prostrated by fever, and the discontented in his garrison proceeded to an open conspiracy. They seized his person, and confined him upon a small vessel in the river for fifteen days.

For the purpose of explorations by water, Laudonnière had constructed two small vessels. These they seized, and taking from the fort whatever they required, they set out upon a freebooting expedition against the Spaniards, or anybody else they might meet. The vessels were separated, and each went on its course. One of them captured the first vessel they met, and abandoned their own; afterwards, cruising among the islands, they made another capture, and were finally most of them taken and destroyed. A small brigantine, escaping pursuit, returned to Fort Caroline, and Laudonnière had them tried by court-martial, and the four leaders were sentenced to be hung. It is related "that when they found their proximity to Fort Caroline, in a kind of mockery, they counterfeited judges; but they played not this prank until they had tippled well of the wine they had on board. One counterfeited the judge, another Captain Laudonnière; another, after he had heard the matter pleaded, concluded thus: 'Make you your causes as good as it pleases you, but if, when you come to the Fort Caroline, the captain causes you not to be hanged, I will never take him for an honest man.' Others thought that, his choler being past, he would easily forget the matter."

Being out of provisions, they were obliged, however,

to enter the river and submit to Laudonnière. The only modification of the sentence of death upon the four leaders was that, being soldiers, they should be first shot before being hung. Being led out to execution, one of them endeavored to excite a rescue; but they were all four shot, and then hanged upon gibbets at the mouth of the river. Thus early did this sad emblem of crime and human depravity succeed the planting of the sign of man's redemption upon our shores.

During this period, Laudonnière heard that two white men were living at a distance among the Indians. He at once sent word to the caciques of the neighboring tribes that he would give a large reward to have them brought to him. He soon obtained them. They were naked, wearing their hair long to their hips, in the Indian fashion. They were Spaniards by birth, but had been fifteen years among the Indians, having been wrecked upon the keys called the Martyrs. They said a considerable number were saved, and among them several women, who had married among the Indians and had families, so that possibly the descendants of these Spaniards may be among the Seminoles to this day. Among other excursions which were made, was one to the widow of King Hia-caia, whose domain seems to have been at St. Mary's. It is said "she courteously received our men, sent me back my barks full of beans and acornes, with certain baskets of cassina, wherewith they make their drinke. And the place where this widow dwelleth is the most plentiful of any that is in all the coast, and the most pleasant. It is thought that the queene is the most beautiful of all the Indians, and of whom they make the most account, yea, and her subjects honor her so much, that almost continually they carry her on their shoulders, and will not suffer her to go on foot." In De Bry there is an engraving made from a sketch of Jacques

Morgues,* who accompanied this deputation, representing her Majesty in her state procession. At the head appear two trumpeters blowing upon reeds. Then follow six chiefs bearing a canopied platform, on which is seated, shaded by a leafy canopy, her Majesty in the person of a beautiful female. Around her neck is a cordon of pearls; bracelets and anklets adorn the person, *et præterea nihil*. On each side walk other chiefs, holding large feather shades or fans; beautiful young girls bearing baskets of fruits and flowers follow next to the queen, and then warriors and her household guards.

An excursion to Lake George and the island at its mouth —now called Drayton Island—is thus mentioned:

"I sent my two barks to discover along the river, and up towards the head thereof, which went so far up that they were thirty leagues good beyond a place named Matthiaqua; and there they discovered the entrance of a lake, upon the one side whereof no land can be seen, according to the report of the Indians, which was the cause that my men went no further, but returned backe, and in coming home went to see the Island of Edelano, situated in the midst of the river, as faire a place as any that may be seen through the world, for, in the space of three leagues that it may contain in length and breadth, a man may see an exceeding rich country and marvellously peopled. At the coming out of the village of Edelano to go unto the river's side, a man must pass through an alley about three hundred paces long and fifty paces broad, on both sides whereof great trees are planted; the boughs thereof are tied like an arch, and meet together so artificially, that a man would think that it were an arbor made of purpose, as fair, I say, as any in all Christendom, although it be altogether natural."

---

* Sometimes called Le Moyne.

They had expected succor from France, by the end of April, 1545, at the uttermost, and had not been prudent in the saving of their provisions. They had latterly lived upon the provisions they obtained from the Indians, but as spring and summer came on they began to suffer from want, and, the season wearing on, they despaired of receiving help from home, and resolved to leave the country so soon as they could repair their vessels, or build another. They were now in great straits to keep from starvation, and besought the Indians to furnish them. But the natives now became very exacting, and soon exhausted the store of articles suitable for presents which the French had with them. At last, finding themselves unable to procure of the savages provisions to victual their vessels, they determined to abandon the peaceful policy which they had hitherto pursued towards the Indians, and, by capturing one of the leading chiefs, force a large amount of provisions for his ransom. They thereupon seized Olata Utina, a great chief, and held him prisoner, but they failed to procure the expected ransom, and embittered the Indians fruitlessly. Afterwards they obtained some relief from the new corn in he Indian fields near them, and the fair queen, before spoken of, gave them a liberal quantity. In the mean time they pushed forward with all diligence their preparations for leaving.

In August there appeared on the coast four vessels, being the fleet of Sir John Hawkins, returning from an expedition to the Spanish Main. They came in for a supply of water, and were received and entertained by Laudonnière with the best he had, even, he says, "killing certain sheep and poultry which he had hitherto carefully preserved to stock the country withal."

Sir John, seeing the distress they were in, generously offered to transport them all back to France, which Laudonnière declined, because, he says, he was "in doubt upon what occasion he made so large an offer, for I knew not how the case stood between the French and English; and though he promised me, on his faith, to put me on land, in France, before he would touch England, yet I stood in doubt least he should attempt somewhat in Florida in the name of his mistress. Therefore I flatly refused his offer." The garrison, however, hearing of the offer made by the English general, had no such scruples, and said they would go, unless he made some arrangement for their departure. Laudonnière finally effected the purchase of the smallest of the English vessels. The English commander acted very handsomely, leaving the French to put their own valuation upon the vessel, who judged it worth seven hundred crowns. In payment of this sum, he delivered them four pieces of artillery, one thousand of iron, and one thousand of powder.

Seeing the small amount of provisions the French had on hand, Sir John most generously supplied them with twenty barrels of meal, five pipes of beans, a hogshead of salt, one hundred pounds of wax, to make candles with; forasmuch, as it is said, he saw the French soldiers were barefoot, he took compassion upon them and gave them fifty pairs of shoes; besides this, he made presents to all the officers. As soon as Sir John had sailed, they made all diligence to get their stores ready for their departure, and by the 15th of August they had everything ready, and awaited fair winds.

It was with no pleasant feelings they prepared to leave a country to which they seemed to have become much attached. Laudonnière says, "There was none of us to whom it was not an extreme grief to leave a country wherein we had endured so great travails and necessities, to discover that which we must forsake through our own countryman's fault. I leave it your cogitation to think how near it went to our hearts to leave a place abounding in riches, as we were thoroughly enformed thereof in coming whereunto, and doing service unto our prince, we left our own country, wives, children, parents, and friends, and passed the perils of the sea, and were therein arrived, as in a plentiful treasure of all our hearts' desire."

The question naturally suggests itself, how did it happen that, in a country abounding in the means of subsistence, this colony should have been reduced to such distress? Theirs was no peculiar case; in every instance of an attempt at settlement within the limits of the United States the same thing occurred: after they had eaten up what they had brought with them and what they could obtain of the Indians, they invariably starved. They were generally either soldiers, or persons not accustomed to labor, and their idea of obtaining the means of subsistence was the commissary's store, or the market; the labor of their own hands in the field they never looked to, and did not seem to know how to avail themselves of the resources of hunting and fishing. At this very period the river which ran by Fort Caroline abounded in fish and oysters, and, when literally starving, the Indians caught fish before their eyes, and demanded such prices as they chose. The example of the Indian fields of maize was before them, and yet they planted not a seed.

In interesting juxtaposition with Laudonnière's own account of his troubles, and of the visit of the English fleet, we have the account of this visit from one of Sir John Hawkins's expedition, who, after speaking of the condition in which he found the French, says: "Notwithstanding the great want that the Frenchmen had, the ground doth yield victuals sufficient, if they would have taken pains to get the same; but they, being soldiers, desired to live by the sweat of other men's brows. The ground yieldeth naturally grapes in great store, for in the time the Frenchmen were there, they made twenty hogsheads of wine. Also it yieldeth roots, passing good; deeres marvellous good, with divers others beasts and fowl serviceable to the use of man. There be things wherewith a man may live, having maize wherewith to make bread, for maize maketh good savory bread and cakes, as fine as flour; also it maketh good meale, beaten and sodden with water, and eateth like pap wherewith we feed children, a good drink, nourishable, which the French did use to drink of in the morning, and it assuageth their thirst, so that they had no neede to drink all the day after.*

"The commodities of this land are more than are yet known to any man; for besides the land itself, whereof there is more than any Christian king is able to inhabit, it flourisheth with meadow pasture-ground, with woods of cedar and cyprus, and other sorts, as better cannot be in the world. They have for apothecary, herbs, roots, and gums great store, as storax liquida, turpentine, gum myrrhe, and frankincense.

"Of beasts in the country, besides deer, foxes, hares, pole-cats, conies, ounces, and leopards, I am not able certainly to say, but it is thought that there are lions and tigers, as well as unicorns; lions especially. Also venomous beasts, such as crocodiles, whereof there is a great

---

* "The Floridians, when they travel, have a kind of herbe dried, who, with a cane, and earthen cup in the end with fire and the dried herbs put together, doe suck throu a cane the smoke thereof, which smoke satisfieth their hunger, and therewith they live four or five days without meate or drinke; and this all the Frenchmen used for this purpose; yet doe they hold, withal, that it causeth them to reject from their stomachs, and spit out water and phlegm."

This wonderful weed, or dried herb, was, of course, tobacco; although, from a defect in the quality, probably, it does not now "keepe us from hunger three or four days at a time."

abundance; adders of great bigness, whereof our men killed some a yard and a half long. On these adders" (rattlesnakes, probably) "the Frenchmen did feed, to no little admiration of us, and affirmed the same to be a delicate meat." A tolerably accurate description of the different kinds of fish and birds is given, and the writer seems to have been particularly struck with the advantages of the country for raising cattle. "The houses of the Indians," he says, "are not many together, for in one house an hundred of them do lodge, they being made much like a great barn, and in strength not inferior to ours, for they have stanchions and rafters of whole trees, and are covered with palmetto leaves, having no place divided but one small room for their king and queen. In the midst of this house is a hearth, where they make great fires all night, and they sleep upon certain pieces of wood, hewn in for the bowing of their backs, and another place made high for their heads."

CHAPTER VIII.

French Expedition of Ribaut to relieve Fort Caroline—Spanish Expedition of Menendez to expel the Huguenots—Capture of Fort Caroline by Menendez, and Massacre of the Garrison.

1565.

THE settlement at Fort Caroline, although neglected by France, had not been forgotten by its illustrious patron; but the civil commotions which distracted the country had rendered it impossible to forward the succors which were so much needed. Reports had reached France from the little colony, bearing unfavorably upon Laudonnière, set on foot by those who had been in the conspiracy against him. Among other things, they had accused him of playing the viceroy, of living in great state, and of aggrandizing himself. As soon as the admiral was enabled to devote his attention to the subject, an expedition of considerable magnitude was set on foot, to be under the command of Captain Ribaut, who had been in command in the first voyage. A fleet of seven vessels, some of considerable size, was provided, and ample provision made for a permanent occupation of the country. Some six hundred and fifty persons were embarked, and among the adventurers were representatives from many of the first families of France. By some means, and, as is charged by many, in accordance with direct information from the French court, the expedition of Ribaut destined to succor and insure the permanent establishment of the French Huguenots in

America was made known to Philip II. There was at the Spanish court at that period, unemployed, a man of considerable distinction, Menendez by name, who had acquired a high reputation by the success of many naval expeditions in which he had been engaged. He had shortly before learned that a son who had sailed from Mexico on board a treasure-fleet bound for Spain, which had been wrecked upon the coast of Florida, was a captive among the savage tribes who inhabited its shores. This man, soured by some difficulties and annoyances he had encountered, sorrowing over a favorite son whose fate presented itself to his imagination as worse than death, and largely imbued with the spirit of the military propagation of the faith, was led to seek the command of an expedition to Florida. His own principal thought was undoubtedly the recovery of his son, but the leading consideration he placed before the king was the salvation of the souls of the tribes of Florida. The coast of Florida had already acquired a bad reputation, on account of the numerous shipwrecks which had occurred there, and it was thought that a more thorough examination and acquaintance with its shores, harbors, currents, and soundings would enable such disasters to be avoided for the future.

The Spanish crown had long claimed an exclusive right to Florida, and under this designation included all of the country in North America which had been or might be discovered. The existence of the settlement made in 1564 by the French, on the St. John's River, must have been well known to the Spanish court, and would naturally have been considered an aggression upon their rights, although they had never been able themselves to occupy or take possession of any portion of the immense country claimed by them. It added not a little, undoubtedly, to their sensitiveness relative to this settlement, that it was made by the Huguenots of France, who were regarded by the Spaniards as the most detestable of the human race and beyond the pale of humanity. In view of the misfortunes which had attended every expedition to the shores of Florida, it seems as though it would have been a hopeless effort to procure the means or the men for another enterprise in that direction, and so undoubtedly it would have been, but for the character of the man who undertook it and the religious motives which urged him, and which have so often proved that no stronger passion can control the human heart than religious zeal, even among those who conform to none of the obligations of a religious life.

Although the sad fate of Narvaez's and De Soto's expeditions must have been fresh in their minds, yet the name of Florida had not lost its charm, and the appeal of Menendez was responded to by greater numbers than he could provide transportation for. The number to be furnished at the expense of the crown was to have been five hundred men-at-arms, but only two hundred and forty-nine of the force were actually provided. Notwithstanding this, a force amounting to two thousand six hundred persons were embarked on board of thirty-four vessels of various sizes, the largest of which was of near one thousand tons, and carried over one thousand persons,—a large vessel and a very large complement of passengers for that day. Menendez had expended in the equipment of the expedition nearly a million of ducats, the crown having provided but a single ship, and had embarked in the expedition all of his own means and all that he could obtain either by loan or gift from his friends. Although he had made the religious welfare of the natives of Florida the principal object of his mission in his interviews with the king, the number of the clerical party provided was not commensurate with so extensive a work,—twenty-six priests, brothers, and monks being the entire number mentioned out of the two thousand six hundred and fifty who embarked. The agreement with the king had authorized Menendez to take with him five hundred slaves, the third part to be men for his own service and that of his people, in order that he might build, settle, and cultivate Florida with more facility, and plant corn and put up sugar-works; but so great was the anxiety of the people to accompany him, it is said, that he found it unnecessary to carry with him the five hundred slaves.

The expedition of Ribaut, which set sail from Dieppe on the 23d of May, 1565, consisted of five hundred men, besides some families of artisans who accompanied the expedition; the fleet numbered seven sail, some of which must have been of considerable size, as four of the vessels were obliged to anchor outside the bar of the river May, now known as the St. John's. For nearly a month after their getting to sea they were detained on the coasts of France by contrary winds, and, when fairly on their course, were two months in reaching Florida. Making first one of the Bahamas, they came upon the coast of Florida north of Cape Canaveral, and probably first landed at Mosquito, where they found a Spaniard, who had been wrecked upon the coast twenty years before, and who informed them, upon the report of the natives, that Laudonnière's colony was about fifty leagues northward. Coasting along, they sounded the bar of the River of Dolphins, at St. Augustine, and, proceeding farther north, entered the river May (St. John's) on the 29th of August, 1565.

The three smaller vessels only were able to enter the river, as has been already stated. For several days they were employed in landing the stores and provisions intended for the colony, and disembarking the most of the people, leaving on board the vessels outside the bar but little more than their ordinary crew.

Menendez had pushed forward his preparations with the greatest vigor, and was extremely anxious to reach Florida before the French should be enabled to fortify and intrench themselves. He made all possible dispatch, and, leaving a portion of his fleet to follow after him, set sail from Cadiz on the 1st of July, 1565, with about two-thirds of the whole number who were to join in the expedition. A severe tempest which they encountered after leaving the Canaries wrecked and dispersed a portion of the fleet, so that when the general arrived at Porto Rico, on the 9th of August, he had but a third part of his expedition under his command. He learned here that a dispatch-vessel, sent with orders to him from Spain, had been intercepted by the French, and intelligence of his movements probably conveyed to the French colony in Florida. Menendez at once decided to pursue his voyage with all expedition, without awaiting the coming up of his other vessels; and, refitting as well as he was able, he sailed northward, by an untried route, among the Lucayan Islands, and on the 28th of August, being the day devoted in the calendar of the Roman Church to the memory of St. Augustine, they came in sight of Florida and landed on her coast. Upon the same day the French fleet, under Ribaut, had cast anchor at the mouth of the St. John's River,—the two hostile fleets being thus within fifty miles of each other, and landing simultaneously at two neighboring points, each unconscious of the proximity of the other.

It adds not a little interest to this concurrence of events to recall the fact that on the 4th of the same month the English fleet, under the celebrated Sir John Hawkins, had anchored and landed at the St. John's, thus bringing into close proximity the fleets of the then three great maritime powers; although upon all the great continent lying north of the Gulf of Mexico neither of them possessed a single foot of ground, except that occupied by the feeble detachment of the French at Fort Caroline, which was preparing to return to France on the very day that Ribaut's fleet appeared. Another day's detention, and Ribaut probably might not have landed to occupy the deserted fort. Menendez would have found no heretical colony to extirpate, and would probably not then have remained, and the first chapter of the colonization and permanent settlement might have been deferred for a long period. The Spaniards, on landing, had learned from the Indians that the French were at twenty leagues' distance to the north, and, re-embarking eight leagues beyond, they arrived at the harbor of St. Augustine, to which, in honor of the day upon which they arrived on the coast, they gave the name which it has now borne for nearly three hundred years. Again coasting northward, on the 4th of September they descried the four large vessels of the French anchored at the mouth of the St. John's River.

A council of war was now held by the Spanish captains, and the opinions of a majority were in favor of withdrawing to Hispaniola and preparing a more powerful expedition to attack the French in the spring. The Adelantado could not, however, brook this timid counsel, and declared his intention of making an attack at once. Preparations were accordingly made, and about daybreak the Spanish vessels began to move up towards the French transports. These, distrusting the intentions of the Spaniards, hoisted sail and prepared to slip their cables. Confirmed in their suspicions by the actions of the Spaniards, the officers of Ribaut's fleet put to sea, and the Spaniards, perceiving this, fired upon them from their heavy guns, at too great a distance, however, to effect any injury. Pursuit was kept up all day, but they were unable to overtake the French vessels, and at nightfall they abandoned the pursuit, sailed to the southward, and cast anchor in the river Seloy, called by the French the River of Dolphins, now known as the port of St. Augustine, whither they were followed at a distance by one of the French vessels, in order to observe their further movements. There they were seen to disembark their forces, victuals, and munitions, three of their vessels entering the harbor and three remaining outside. Having made a reconnoissance, the French vessel returned, and reported to Ribaut that the Spaniards had landed and commenced fortifying themselves. That zealous officer at once conceived the idea of surprising them, and by the capture of their ships so far disabling them as to prevent any molestation of his colony on their part. Calling a council of his officers, he laid his views before them. Laudonnière and his other captains remonstrated against his enterprise, deeming it altogether too hazardous and uncertain in its results—Laudonnière, by his own account, especially opposing it because of the severe gales which prevailed along the coast at that season of the year. But to all of these objections Ribaut replied that he was instructed not to allow his colony to be encroached upon, and that the landing and fortifications commenced by the Spaniards indicated that hostile intentions were entertained.

He accordingly, on the 8th of September, re-embarked all of his effective force, and with them most of the able-bodied men of Laudonnière, to the number of thirty-eight, leaving him an invalid force with which to defend Fort Caroline. Ribaut did not anticipate an absence of more than two days, as the Spaniards were within fifteen leagues of him. He was, however, by a fatal mischance, two days too early or too late, for, sailing on the 10th of September, on that very day he encountered a terrible tempest, which drove him, helpless to resist, far down the coast. In the mean time, his rival, Menendez, was influenced by similar wishes to act promptly, and discussed with his captains an expedition by land to attack the Huguenots in their fort. His own force was estimated at six hundred, and he supposed the French garrison to be about the same number— perhaps a little stronger. Having secured guides, Menendez determined, against the advice of his officers, to undertake the expedition. The storm which now raged along the coast, accompanied with a deluge of rain, seemed to favor his design of surprising the French at a time and by a mode of attack which they could hardly anticipate. He felt almost confident, however, that the French fleet was at sea, and that even if it escaped shipwreck it would be hardly possible for it to regain the harbor for several days. On the 17th of September, Menendez set out at the head of five hundred men, to pursue a most difficult march over an almost impassable country, guided by two Indian chiefs who were enemies to the French. Their march was much impeded by the effects of the heavy rains, which had overflowed the streams and made the marshes almost impassable. They were three days in reaching the vicinity of Fort Caroline, and during the whole march were exposed to heavy rains. Many of the officers and men wished to return, and much dissatisfaction was felt, but the character and energy of their leader restrained them from deserting him.

In the mean time, Laudonnière had done his best to repair the injuries to his works which had been made preparatory to their abandonment, and endeavored to infuse some spirit into and restore some order to his invalid garrison. He was himself very ill, and had only sixteen or seventeen well men in the fort. Of Ribaut's men, whom he had left behind, there were some who had never drawn a sword—four being boys who kept Ribaut's dogs; one cook; a carpenter, Nicholas Chaleux, who wrote an account of his escape; a beer-brewer; an old cross-bow maker; two shoemakers; four or five men who had wives; a player on the virginals—in all, about fourscore and five or six, counting lackeys and women and children. Two captains of the watch were appointed, and a strict guard was kept up for several days. But the terrible tempest which prevailed relaxed their vigilance, they thinking it absurd to expect an attack at such a time. The night of the 19th of September was very stormy, and at dawn the sentinels were withdrawn under shelter, and the officer of the watch himself retired to his quarters.

At break of day the forces of Menendez reached the fort, and commenced the attack. A sudden rush, a quick alarm, a surprise, a feeble resistance by a bewildered garrison, and the fort was taken. Laudonnière, by his own account, tried to rally his men, and fought in person, as long as there was hope; but, finding himself recognized and pursued, he fled to the neighboring forest, and there fell in with other fugitives from the fort. With much difficulty they made their way through the sedge that lined the banks of the river, and, reaching some vessels that lay at its mouth, they escaped. In the first assault on the fort, many of the garrison were cut down, without regard to age or sex; a statement which may well be believed, in view of the more deliberate cruelty afterwards practiced. When we recall in how many instances religious rancor has carried men into the extremes of cruelty, it will not seem incredible that even women and children fell victims to the ferocious soldiery who accompanied Menendez. The Spanish account of the massacre admits that an indiscriminate slaughter took place until checked by an order from Menendez that no woman, child, or cripple, under the age of fifteen, should be injured,—by which it is said that seventy persons were saved. "The rest were killed." Some of the prisoners were hung upon the neighboring trees, and this inscription placed over them,—"NO POR FRANCESES, SINO POR LUTERANOS." ("Not as Frenchmen, but as Lutherans.")

Menendez changed the name of the fort to San Mateo, in honor of the apostle whose festival occurred on the day subsequent to its capture. The Spaniards also changed the name of the river May to San Mateo. Menendez repaired the fort, and made such arrangements as were necessary to fortify the post against an attack should Ribaut return; garrisoning it with three hundred men-at-arms under Gonzalez de Villareal. Before leaving, he had crosses erected in prominent situations, and marked out the site of a church, to be built of the timber which Laudonnière had prepared for building vessels.

Taking a small number of his men with him, he returned to St. Augustine, finding even greater difficulty than before in crossing the swamps and creeks. His arrival at St. Augustine was signalized by great rejoicings, and a solemn mass was celebrated, and a Te Deum sung, in commemoration of the victory.

CHAPTER IX.

Shipwreck and Massacre of Ribaut and his Followers.

1565.

RIBAUT'S unfortunate vessels, which had encountered the gale the night after leaving port, were driven down the coast at the mercy of the storm, which increased in violence, and, after ineffectual efforts to keep out to sea, they were driven ashore between Matanzas and Mosquito Inlet. Such is the character of the shelvy beach on the eastern coast of Florida that but little danger to life attends a shipwreck there. The low and sandy shore is devoid of rocks, and vessels are ofttimes driven high upon the land, and, at the fall of the tide, one may pass almost dry-shod from the stranded ship. But one person was lost from Ribaut's vessels, a Captain La Grange, who had opposed the expedition, and only at the last moment consented to share the perils of which he was the first victim. Of the occurrence of this fatal expedition of Ribaut we have no account from his own party, except that given by Le Moyne, as having been related to him by a sailor, a native of Dieppe, who escaped the massacre, having been left for dead. There are two detailed Spanish accounts extant, emanating from chaplains attached to Menendez's colony.

The information of the disaster that had befallen Ribaut's vessels was brought to St. Augustine by the Indians, who gave Menendez to understand, by signs, that a large number of persons were at an inlet, four leagues distant, which they were unable to cross. Menendez at once set out with a party of his men, and, arriving the same evening at Matanzas Inlet, he saw in the morning, on the opposite side of the inlet, quite a number of men with standards, one of whom swam across to Menendez and told him they were a portion of the French forces under Ribaut, whose vessels had all been wrecked, twenty leagues distant from each other, along the coast below. The first question of Menendez was, "Are they Catholics or Lutherans?" The reply was, " They are all of the New Sect," a fact known, of course, to Menendez; but the question was intended to justify the course he intended to pursue towards them. He allowed the man to return to his comrades, with a guarantee of protection for his captain and four or five of his followers, should they choose to cross over. The captain and four men came across, and held an interview with Menendez. The Spanish chaplain, De Solis, gives a minute account of the conversation, and says that the French captain informed Menendez that he was the commander of one of the vessels which had been wrecked; that he desired a boat to cross this river and one four leagues farther on, at St. Augustine, in order to reach the fort, twenty leagues beyond. To this Menendez replied at length, informing him of the capture of Fort Caroline and the slaughter of the garrison. The captain then desired to be furnished with a pilot and vessels to carry them to France, as there was no war existing between their respective sovereigns, who were friends and brothers. Menendez thereupon replied that this was true, and as Catholics or friends he would favor them, and feel that he was serving both kings in doing so; but as for those of the new sect, he considered them enemies, and would wage war upon them with fire and sword, and this he intended to do to all such as should come into those seas or countries where he governed as viceroy and captain-general for his sovereign; that he had come to plant the Holy Evangelist in this land, in order that the savages might be enlightened and brought to the knowledge of the Holy Catholic Faith of Christ our Lord, as declared by the Roman Church ("*la Iglesia Romana*"), and that if they desired to surrender their standards and arms, and yield themselves to his mercy, they could do so, "in order that he might do to them what should be directed him by the grace of God."*

This is the precise language attributed to Menendez by De Solis; and as in the course of his narrative he refers to charges of cruelty made at the time, and as he was writing an apology for the acts of his brother-in-law, it is not to be doubted that he would give such a statement of the transactions as would be most favorable to Menendez. The language attributed to Menendez by De Solis was certainly evasive, and by his allusion to their trusting to his mercy, and his intention of following divine guidance, the French were naturally deceived, as it seems very evident he intended they should be, into yielding themselves as prisoners into his hands. The French captain returned to his men, and reported the result of his conference with the Spanish leader. Among Ribaut's men were many of wealth and noble birth, who were willing to pay as much as fifty thousand ducats as a ransom for their lives; and the offer was made to Menendez, but he refused, in an evasive manner, to accept it. The French finally agreed to surrender their standards and all their arms, and cast themselves upon the clemency of Menendez. They were brought over ten at a time, and when the first party reached the shore, Menendez said to them, "As I have but a few men, and you are

---

* "Para que il haga de ellos lo que Dios le diere de gracia."—*Ensayo Cronologico*, p. 86.

numerous, it will be easy for you to revenge yourselves upon us for the destruction of your fort and people: it is necessary, therefore, that you should march, with your hands tied behind you, four leagues from here, to my camp.''

To this the French assented, and they were marched behind a clump of trees, where they could not be seen by their comrades, and their hands were strongly secured behind them; the same course being pursued with each succeeding party that came over, to the number, it is said, of two hundred and eight persons. Upon being questioned, eight of their number declared themselves to be Catholics, and were sent in a boat to St. Augustine; the others were ordered to march in that direction by land, probably along the beach of Anastasia Island; and orders were given by Menendez to the officers in charge of them, that when they reached a designated spot in the path, the prisoners should be killed.* The order was carried out, and Menendez and his men returned to St. Augustine the same night. The next day Menendez was informed by the same Indians who had brought the first report that a much larger party of Christians were at the same place. Menendez supposed that this must be Ribaut himself, and, taking one hundred and fifty soldiers with him, marched to the spot, where he saw, on the opposite bank, a considerable force, with standards displayed, who had constructed a raft for the purpose of crossing, but found much difficulty in managing it on account of the strength of the tide. One of the party had been allowed to swim over and obtain a boat, in which the sergeant-major crossed. Menendez informed this officer that he had destroyed the French fort and all its garrison, as well as a portion of those who had been shipwrecked, and caused the bodies of those slain on the previous day

---

* Barcia, Ensayo Cronologico.

to be pointed out to him. He directed the sergeant-major to guarantee Ribaut safe conduct, if he chose to come over and confer with him. Ribaut accordingly crossed with eight of his officers, held a long conference with the Spanish general, and was handsomely entertained by him. Menendez repeated to Ribaut the story of the capture of Fort Caroline, and he was allowed to converse with one of the garrison who accompanied Menendez. He, too, was shown the bodies of his cruelly murdered men.

To Ribaut's offer of a very large amount for the ransom of himself and party, Menendez turned a deaf ear, and would give no assurance as to the treatment he would receive. Ribaut returned to consult with his officers and men, and the next morning they gave themselves up as prisoners, to the number of one hundred and fifty, with all their arms, standards, etc. Two hundred of his party refused to surrender, and withdrew during the night. Ribaut and his comrades were carried across in parties of ten, as upon the former occasion, and the same pretense was urged to induce them to have their hands tied behind them. Ribaut himself, with the philosophy of a stoic and the firmness of a Christian, when he saw the fate that awaited him, began to sing the psalm *Domine, memento mei*, and, that finished, he said, "From earth we came, and to the earth we must return; that twenty years of life, more or less, did not matter, and the Adelantado might do unto them what he wished."

One would suppose that the noble, Christian, and serene deportment of Ribaut would have touched the chivalry of Menendez's nature, and that the spectacle of a gentleman, his equal in rank, reduced by shipwreck to suffering and helplessness, appealing to his generosity for aid and to his humanity for life, helpless, powerless, and prostrate, would have called forth some spark of sympathy from a heart yet sore under the loss of a son whom he believed to have been cast, like Ribaut, upon a savage coast, and who doubtless, like him, was bound by the chains of his enemies. But, alas! Menendez's was a nature full of deadly hatred, and it was now roused almost to a frenzy towards the unfortunate Frenchman. His apologist closes the drama with these words: *É mandando el Adelantado los matasen* (and the Adelantado directed them to be killed). The entire number, one hundred and fifty, were massacred at the same spot and in the same manner as their comrades who had gone before them.

The account given by the Dieppe sailor of the death of Ribaut is somewhat different. He says that, after the shipwreck, Ribaut sent a boat to the river May, and upon its arrival they discovered the Spanish flag floating over Fort Caroline. The messenger immediately returned and informed Ribaut, who was overwhelmed with distress at the intelligence, and sent a second time, directing his messenger to communicate with the Spaniards and find out what had become of the French garrison. Meeting some Spaniards, they were informed by them that the Spanish general, a most humane man, had sent all of the French garrison in a large vessel to France, well provisioned and equipped, and that he would treat Ribaut and his followers with like humanity. Upon this intelligence, Ribaut himself, distrustful of the Spanish clemency, called a council of his officers. Being on the verge of starvation, and hopeless of relief from any quarter, a majority were in favor of yielding themselves up to Menendez, and an envoy, one La Caille, was sent to obtain terms. He was taken before the Spanish commander, who pledged his faith by the most solemn assurances, by religious invocations and sacred oaths in the presence of his followers, and promised, without fraud, faithfully, and as a true man, that he would spare the lives of Ribaut and of all his people. La Caille returned with these assurances, which some received with great joy, while to others they carried but little hope. Yet all consented, in their desperation, to surrender, and came to the river, which was near the fort. Ribaut and Ottigny alone were taken into the fort. Here appearances soon indicated the fate that awaited them. Ribaut demanded an audience with Menendez, and Ottigny indignantly required a pledge of safety. To Ribaut no reply was given, and Ottigny received only contemptuous laughter. Ribaut again demanded to see Menendez, when a soldier asked him if he was not Ribaut, the French commander. He replied, "Yes." Then said the soldier, "When you issue orders to your men, do you not expect obedience?" "Certainly," replied Ribaut. "Thus," said the soldier, "do I desire to obey my commander. I have been directed to kill you." And thereupon he plunged his dagger to the heart of Ribaut, and immediately after Ottigny fell by the same hand. The rest were killed outside the fort, three musicians alone being spared.* The author of this account, whose name is not given by Le Moyne, was left for dead, but his wounds were not mortal, and he escaped during the night to the Indians, with whom he remained some months, but was finally given up to Menendez, who was doubtless not aware of his having belonged to Ribaut's party, and sent him to Havana, and thence to Spain; but on this voyage he was released by a French vessel, and so reached France.† Other accounts, cotemporaneous with the event, say that Ribaut was quartered and his dissevered body placed on the four angles of the fort, and that his beard was sent as a

---

* De Bry, Brevis Narratio—Secunda Pars, Florida, p. 29.

† This sailor and another, named Pompierre, mentioned in Ensayo Cronologico, p. 135.

trophy to Spain—a statement indignantly denied by Spanish authorities.

Besides this account, we find in De Bry a statement given in a supplicatory letter addressed to Charles IX., offered in the name of the widows, orphans, and relatives of those who were slaughtered by the Spaniards in this expedition.* This letter states that Menendez gave them his faith that if they would surrender they should receive no injury, but would be forwarded with vessels and provisions to enable them to return to France, but that they were tied, and led after the manner of brute beasts to the castle, where they were received with taunts and jeering mockery by the Spanish soldiers, subjected to abuse and insults, and then most cruelly massacred; that Ribaut, after being forced to witness the slaughter of his men, vainly appealing to the faith of Menendez, was struck down from behind, his body treated with the grossest indignity, his beard cut off and sent as a trophy to Spain, and his head quartered and stuck upon spears in the area of the fort. This letter, bearing date 1565, the same year in which the destruction of the Huguenot colony occurred, shows at least what were the accredited reports received in France. But these statements are denied by Spanish writers, whose representations of the course of Menendez, his pledges to Ribaut, and treatment of his body after he had been killed, are so utterly at variance that the historian has no means of deciding upon facts, and can only state the probabilities of the case, which on this point lean in favor of the Spaniards,—divesting Menendez's conduct of none of its enormity, but relieving the tragedy of some of the horrors with which the French records surround it. The atrocity of the deed struck all Europe with horror,

---

* Brevis Narratio, Epis. Supp.

even in that day; and the shocking story has been perpetuated over three hundred years, giving the name of Menendez a stain of infamy which time cannot wipe out.

Of those who accompanied Ribaut, two hundred refused to surrender, and, withdrawing to the southward, made preparations to construct vessels with which they might leave the coast. Some twenty days afterwards a party of Indians came in, and informed Menendez that at a distance of eight days' journey southward, near Canaveral, the French were building a fort and a ship. Menendez, after getting part of the garrison from San Mateo, sent vessels by sea, and marched himself by land with three hundred men, to attack the French, who, on the approach of the Spaniards, fled to the woods. A messenger was sent out, offering them protection, and telling them that they should have the same treatment as Spaniards if they would come in. One hundred and fifty surrendered, and, it is said, received kind treatment. Twenty others sent word that they would rather be devoured by the Indians than surrender to the Spaniards.* The fort was destroyed, the vessel burnt, and the cannon spiked. A small garrison was left at a fort the Spaniards built and called St. Lucia. The names of Canaveral and St. Lucia are still found on the eastern coast of Florida.

The Spanish forces returned to St. Augustine accompanied by their French prisoners, who were incorporated into the colony. Some of them eventually returned to France; others remained, renouncing their faith and accepting that of their captors.

---

* The subsequent history of these twenty is unknown. Those who desire to follow in the path of their probable adventures will find in "The Lily and the Totem" an interesting story, of which D'Erlach and his companions are the heroes.

Let us now return to Laudonnière and the few survivors of the massacre at Fort Caroline.

There were two small vessels remaining to the French, at the mouth of the river, and some eighteen or twenty of the fugitives, with Laudonnière, were received on board. On the 25th of September, these two vessels put out to sea, one commanded by Laudonnière, the other by Jean Ribaut, the son of the admiral. After a long voyage, and much suffering, Laudonnière arrived on the coast of Wales about the middle of November. He here left his vessel, and returned to France, where he was badly received by the court, and died in obscurity. The other vessel, under Captain Ribaut, had proceeded prosperously some five hundred leagues, when they fell in with a Spanish vessel, with which they had a severe encounter. The French claim the victory, having lost but one man, their cook; but they were unable to secure their prize. Pursuing their voyage, they reached Rochelle, where they were most kindly received and entertained.

Thus ended the efforts of the French to establish a colony on the southern coast of America. The Lilies of France had been trampled in the dust, and the flag of Spain waved over St. Augustine, San Mateo, and San Lucia.*

The destruction of the Huguenots excited the utmost gratification at the court of Spain; and the conduct of Menendez was approved and commended by his Catholic

---

* Laudonnière, after his return to France, wrote an account of the attempted settlement by the French, under the title of "L'Histoire des trois Voyages des François en la Floride," which was published in the year 1586, by M. Basanier, to which was added a relation of a fourth voyage, by De Gourgues.

Majesty, the bigoted Philip II.,* and even drew forth a letter of gratitude from the pontiff, Pius V.†

---

* "Of the great success that has attended your enterprise we have the most entire satisfaction; and as to the retribution you have visited upon the Lutheran pirates who sought to occupy the country, and to fortify themselves there in order to disseminate in it their wicked creed, and to prosecute there those wrongs and robberies which they have done, and were doing, against God's service and my own, we believe that you did it with every justification and propriety, and we consider ourselves to have been well served in your so doing."—*Ensayo Cronologico*, p. 115.

† *Letter of St. Pius V. to Pedro Menendez.*

"To our beloved son and nobleman, Pedro Menendez Aviles, Viceroy in the Province of Florida, in the Indies: Beloved son and nobleman, Grace and Benediction of our Lord be with you, Amen.—We greatly rejoice that our much-beloved, dear son in Christ, Philip, the most Catholic King, had appointed and honored you by the government of Florida, making you Adelantado of the country; for we had received such accounts of your person, and the excellencies of your virtues, your worth and dignity were so satisfactorily spoken of, that we believed, without doubt, that you would not only fulfill faithfully, and with care and diligence, the orders and instructions which had been delivered to you by so catholic a king; but we also fully trusted that you would with discretion do all that was requisite, and see carried forward the extension of our Holy Catholic Faith, and the gaining of souls for God. I would that you should well understand that the Indians should be governed in good faith and prudently, that those who may be weak in the faith, being newly converted, be strengthened and confirmed; and the idolaters may be converted and receive the faith of Christ, that the first may praise God, knowing the benefits of his divine mercy, and the others who are yet infidels, by the example and imitation of those who are already freed from blindness, may be led to the knowledge of the Faith. But there is no one thing that is more important for the conversion of the Indian idolaters, than to endeavor by every means that they shall not be scandalized by the vices and bad habits of those who pass from our Western shores to those parts. This is the key of this holy enterprise, in which are in-

The French court seem to have received the news of the destruction of their colony and the atrocious massacre of their countrymen with perfect indifference. This is believed to have arisen from the religious animosities that existed at that period, and which destroyed all sympathy between those of different faith. The sufferings of the Huguenots excited no pity in the hearts of the opposite party, to which the court of Charles IX. belonged. This must have excited great indignation among the people, and particularly among the Huguenots. The narratives of the survivors were published, and the widows and orphans of the slain sent up a memorial to the king, calling upon him for a speedy revenge upon the Spaniards for the acts of Menendez; but his Majesty made no response, and it was left to private individuals to resent the indignities to the flag and honor of France, and to avenge the wrongs of her people.

---

cluded all things requisite. Well understand, most noble man, that I declare to you that a great opportunity is offered to you in the carrying out and management of these matters, which shall redound on the one hand to the service of God, and on the other to the increase of the dignity of your king, esteemed of men, as well as loved and rewarded by God. Wherefore, we give you our Paternal and Apostolic Benediction. We seek and charge you to give entire faith to our brother, the Archbishop of Rossini, who in our name will signify our wishes in more ample words.

"Given in Rome, at St. Peter's, with the ring of the Fisherman, the 1st of August, 1569; the 3d year of our Pontificate."

CHAPTER X.

Situation of Matters at St. Augustine, and Explorations made by Menendez.

1566—1567.

ONE purpose of the expedition of Menendez was now accomplished. He had destroyed the French colony, and, for the present, at least, put an end to the efforts of that much-despised sect, the Lutheran, to establish itself in the New World. He needed now to strengthen his own position, and guard against any attempts the French might make to reoccupy the country which he was so anxious to secure to the Spanish crown. Unlike those who had preceded him, Menendez had, by accident and good fortune, placed his settlement at a peculiarly favorable point. The harbor, while affording ample accommodation for vessels bringing in supplies for the garrison, was inaccessible to those of a larger class, and he was thus effectually protected from the attack of any hostile fleet, and, being on a peninsula of moderate size, he could without much difficulty guard against attack from the Indians. A still more favorable feature in the location of Menendez's garrison was its great healthiness. Surrounded by salt marshes, free from all miasmatic exhalations, the balmy and pure sea-air preserved the colonists almost wholly from those fatal diseases which had swept away so many of the first settlers on this continent.

The old town of St. Augustine is built upon the precise

point that was occupied by Menendez. Its Indian name was Seloy, and the Spaniards found several habitations of considerable size which had been built by the natives. Satisfied that his position was a good one, Menendez proceeded to fortify it. A fort was constructed of logs at a point commanding the approaches by sea and by land, and made as effective as the limited means at hand would permit. Other buildings were erected, and the forms of civil as well as military government were instituted in the province. Among the buildings erected was, undoubtedly, one in which the rites of the Roman Church were celebrated, and we may probably say without hesitation that the first Roman Catholic church on the Atlantic coast of North America was erected at St. Augustine. Menendez did all in his power to advance the cause of religion wherever he gained a footing in the New World, and never forgot this feature in the object of conquest.

Having done all that he could for the comfort and security of his garrison, Menendez proceeded to strengthen Fort Mateo, formerly Fort Caroline, and erected further defenses nearer the mouth of the river. In the mean time he had caused explorations to be made into the interior, but with what result we are not informed.

The Spaniards were not left very long in undisturbed possession of their ground. The most powerful of the neighboring chiefs who were hostile to them soon came and waged war upon them. The soldiers of Menendez could not venture out of camp in any direction without being fired upon by their savage foe, and day after day, one after another of those who went out fishing or hunting, were cut off, until more than a hundred men and several officers fell victims. The Indians came up to the lines of the fort, and on one occasion succeeded in setting fire to a magazine and a great number of the thatched houses, causing great destruction of property and provisions, and much suffering. Menendez finally determined to ask aid from the Governor of Cuba, but none was granted him, and he was obliged to send a vessel to Campeachy. Up to this time he had in vain sought tidings of his lost son, and, while waiting the return of the vessel from Campeachy, he determined to make search himself on the part of the coast where he was reported to have been shipwrecked, and for this purpose took a vessel and sailed along the coast of South Florida. Landing at Cape Florida, he found there, at an Indian settlement, seven Spaniards who had been, with many others, wrecked on the coast some twenty years before, these alone surviving the cruelty and hardships to which all had been subjected. From these Spaniards the Indians had obtained the name of Carlos, which we find given to one of the tribes of South Florida. Hearing that their king, the greatest king in all the world, was called Carlos, the Indians adopted the name in their royal family, thinking thereby to attain to greater power and honor.

Releasing his countrymen from captivity, Menendez received them on board his vessel, and returned to St. Augustine, much depressed at the failure of all his efforts to recover his child. New trials and difficulties awaited him. Increasing distress at St. Augustine and Fort Mateo had created disaffection. Both garrisons mutinied, and determined to abandon the colony. The officers left in command were unable to control the mutineers at St. Augustine, who seized one of the vessels and sailed for the West Indies. Of the garrison at Fort Mateo, consisting of one hundred and fifty persons, all but twenty-one mutinied, and determined to leave the country. A vessel of seventy tons arriving with provisions, they seized upon it, intending to sail to the West Indies or Peru.

Menendez returned after the mutineers had embarked,

but had not yet sailed, and tried to arrest their movements and induce them to return to the garrison. But the greater number were obstinately determined to go, and of one hundred and thirty on board the vessel only thirty-five expressed their willingness to remain. These the mutineers placed on board a bateau, but before they could reach St Augustine they were fired upon by the Indians, and most of them killed. Those who escaped turned their course, hoping to reach Cuba, but were wrecked on Cape Florida, and remained among the Indians of Carlos.

Of the garrison at St. Augustine, over one hundred, at the head of whom was Juan de Vicente, forced Menendez to allow them to return to Porto Rico. Crowded upon a small vessel, they suffered much from heat and sickness, and during a long voyage many of them died.

Relieved of the disaffected portion of his command, Menendez restored what order he could; but his position was a most discouraging one, and under a less resolute leader the enterprise must have failed. Many of the deserters returned to Spain, and, by their unfavorable reports of the country, greatly abated the interest which Menendez had excited, and prevented other colonists from joining him. The Adelantado now undertook a voyage to the north, visiting and making overtures of peace to the chiefs along the coast of Georgia and South Carolina, and is supposed to have sailed as far north as the Chesapeake. The points especially mentioned are Guale, Avista, and St. Helena. At St. Helena he left a number of his men to erect a fort; and also at Avista and all the Indian settlements which he visited he insisted upon building forts. Returning south, Menendez ascended the San Mateo River, visiting several Indian tribes on its borders. It seems to have been supposed by Menendez that this river communicated with the sea at some point in the lower part of the peninsula, and the Indians told him of a lake, called Miami, that communicated with the sea and with this river. They may have alluded to that extensive savanna now known as the Everglades, which is more or less covered with water at all times, and in seasons of heavy rains may have afforded access by light canoes to the head-waters of the St. John's. One of the outlets to the Everglades, near Cape Florida, is now known as the Miami River, and we find the same name given to two rivers of Ohio, from which circumstance we may suppose it probable that the original inhabitants of these States, Ohio and Florida, had a common origin and language.

Menendez revisited his posts at St. Helena, Avista, and Guale, and took measures for their secure establishment; and at these and all other places which he visited he caused the cross to be planted, and left religious teachers, who were to instruct the natives. He seems to have been gratified with the willingness of most of them to receive instruction and become Christians. One of the chiefs, however, Satourioura, always stood aloof, and showed no good feeling for the Spaniards, who, notwithstanding this fact, ventured to visit his tribe. On one occasion, seventeen of them going out to the Indian houses, about two leagues from Fort Mateo, were fallen upon and eight of their number killed, the rest returning to camp covered with wounds. The distress for provisions continued, and Menendez was compelled to go himself to the West Indies to seek relief for his colonists.

During his absence a fleet of fifteen sail arrived, bringing heavy reinforcements, which were greatly needed, for, in addition to the loss sustained at Fort Mateo and St. Augustine by mutiny and desertion, the greater part of the garrison left at St. Helena had deserted. Seizing upon a transport, they made sail for Cuba, but were cast upon that fatal coast of North Florida, and there fell in with the wrecked mutineers from Fort Mateo, who most gladly welcomed this accession to their numbers.

About this time a vessel arrived off the coast with three Jesuit fathers of some distinction,—the first of their order who had visited this part of the New World,—all of the priests who had come over before being Franciscans. Father Martinez, having landed in a small boat, proceeded with the crew in search of the fort which was their point of destination, but, a sudden squall coming up, the vessel was driven out to sea, and the good priest and his boat's crew were left on shore defenseless and without provisions.

Falling in with a party of Indians, they were directed to Fort Mateo; but within half a league of the mouth of the river they were attacked by another party of savages, and Father Martinez and three of his men were slaughtered on the shores of St. George's Island.

When Menendez returned from Cuba he was much encouraged at finding the reinforcements which had arrived during his absence, and he proceeded at once to strengthen his garrisons at Fort Mateo and St. Helena. Leaving them in good condition, he started on an expedition to South Florida, wishing to visit all the tribes who occupied the lower part of the peninsula. The most southerly of these was that of Tequesta, and next were the tribes of Carlos, the most powerful of all the Indian tribes of this peninsula, and whose limits extended from one coast to the other. Within their domain, probably near Cape Florida, Menendez built a small fort and left a garrison. In reply to inquiries made here relative to Lake Miami and its connection with the San Mateo River, the Indians directed him to the country of the Tocobayo, fifty leagues to the north.

Before leaving Fort Mateo he had given orders that a

vessel should be sent up the San Mateo River to search for Lake Miami, and to meet him, if possible, on the north coast of Florida. Three vessels were accordingly sent; but, finding the course of the river very tortuous and its borders inhabited by numerous Indians, in whose good feeling they felt no confidence, the commanders determined to return to the fort. From the country of Carlos Menendez came to Tocobayo and obtained permission to erect a fort and leave some religious teachers to bring them to a knowledge of the true faith.

From Tocobayo three days' march brought him to Fort Mateo, from which we may suppose that the location of Tocobayo was about that of Cape Canaveral. The Adelantado is said to have met at Tocobayo more than fifteen hundred Indians, and at a council held there twenty-nine caciques were present.

At Fort Mateo Menendez found Juan Pardo, who had been sent out with one hundred and fifty men to explore the country to the west and see if there was any communication open with New Spain by means of rivers having their course in that direction. Pardo penetrated some one hundred and fifty leagues to the Apalachian Mountains, making friendly overtures to the caciques of the country, and building a fort in the territory of one named Coava. Leaving a garrison and religious teachers here, Pardo returned to Felipe.

Upon the river Mateo several caciques had rule, the most powerful of whom was Otima, whose territory was on the west bank of the river, near the Ocklawaha. To the north was the domain of Macaya, and to the south that of Ays. Satourioura, the bitter enemy of the Spaniards, occupied the country between St. Augustine and the San Mateo River, east and north, and so cut off all communication between the Spanish forts by land. The hostility of this chief could not be appeased, and his proximity to the two most important posts was peculiarly annoying to Menendez, who determined to attack Satourioura with all the available force he could command. Four detachments of seventy men each, one of them under the command of Menendez himself, marched out, hoping to surprise the Indian chief; but the wily savage was on the alert, and, after a fruitless effort, the Spaniards returned to their posts.

It seemed highly important, at this stage of affairs, that Menendez should visit Spain. He was aware that injurious reports had been circulated against him at home, and many complaints and accusations made before the Spanish court, all of which he believed it his duty to refute in person before his sovereign.

Within the eighteen months that had elapsed since his landing in Florida, Menendez had carefully examined the entire coast from Cape Florida to St. Helena, had built forts at St. Augustine, San Mateo, Avista, Guale, and St. Helena, and had established block-houses at Tequesta, Carlos, Tocobayo, and Coava, in all of which he had left garrisons and religious teachers. In most of this work Menendez had been personally engaged, while he was responsible for all; and mind and body now required change and relaxation.

Believing that the interest of the colony, as well as his own, would be advanced by his going to Spain, Menendez caused a small vessel of twenty tons to be built, and in the spring of 1567 he set sail in his frail bark, accompanied by thirty-eight persons, including the crew. Fair weather and favorable winds brought them rapidly on their way, and in seventeen days they reached the Azores, making, it was said, seventy-two leagues a day,—a statement hardly to be believed.

They arrived safely in Spain, and Menendez was received with great favor at court. But empty honors were not what the Adelantado wanted. He required prompt and substantial aid to enable him to carry on his enterprise; and this he found not easily to be obtained. He was kept in anxious suspense at court, chafing under unnecessary delay and the obstacles thrown in his way, all the while fearful that the French might avail themselves of his absence and make an attack upon his colony in retaliation for the massacres at Matanzas and Fort Caroline. Indeed, rumors of such designs had already reached him. Those who escaped those terrible massacres and returned home had scattered widely through France the bloody story of their countrymen's sufferings at the hands of the Spanish leader, and the indignation of the people grew stronger day by day as they witnessed the indifference of the French court. It was said that they intended to take the matter into their own hands, and that an avenger was about to appear.

CHAPTER XI.

Recapture of Fort Caroline, and the Notable Revenge of Dominic de Gourgues.

1567.

THE name of Dominic de Gourgues occupies a place secondary in interest to none, perhaps, in the history of Florida. Associated as he is with one of the most remarkable and dramatic incidents on record, we find a more than usual attraction in the character and circumstances of his early life.

This self-constituted champion of his country's wrongs and of the rights of humanity was a native of Marsan, in Guienne.* In those days all persons of gentle birth adopted the profession of arms, and Dominic entered the service of his king as a private soldier, deeming it honor enough to be allowed, even in this humble position, to serve France. Winning promotion on the field, he obtained the rank of captain, a place at that time of greater distinction than now. He was charged with the defense of a place near Sienna, with only thirty soldiers at his command, and, being attacked by a largely superior force, made a desperate resistance, but all his followers were slain, and he fell into the hands of the Spaniards.

To show their appreciation of his signal bravery, and, as the French chronicler with bitter sarcasm remarks, with

---

* " He was a brother of the Governor of Guienne."—*Ensayo Cronologico*, p. 133.

rare Spanish generosity, De Gourgues, instead of being put to death, was condemned to the galleys. The vessel upon which he was placed as a galley-slave was captured by the Turks, and he was carried to Rhodes and Constantinople, and had the good fortune afterwards to be recaptured, and, by the French commander at Malta, restored to his country. He did not remain long unemployed, but embarked with an expedition to Brazil and the South Seas, where he probably acquired a considerable fortune.

From this voyage Dominic returned in time to sympathize in the grief and indignation excited throughout France by the massacre of the Huguenots at Fort Caroline, and the fate of Ribaut and his shipwrecked companions. The treatment De Gourgues had received at the hands of the Spaniards, and the fetters of his galley-life, had left scars on his soul which nothing could efface, and it may well be supposed that this new tale of horrors stirred to its depths all the concentrated hatred of his nature. The spirit of retaliation was fully aroused, and he felt that the blood of his countrymen, no less than his own wrongs, cried for vengeance.

It has been seen that the destruction of the Huguenots in Florida was treated by the king and court of France with an indifference that greatly embittered the people, many of whom had religious sympathies with the sufferers, while others doubtless lost friends and relatives in the bloody massacre. Of the faith of De Gourgues we know nothing,* and are only told of his sympathy with his illtreated countrymen, and his determination to resent their wrongs. He seems to have deemed it unwise or unsafe to make his feelings public by asking aid of the king, and it

---

* The Spanish account says he was a terrible heretic—*Herege terrible.*—*Ensayo Cron.*, p. 133.

is not improbable that had he done so he would have met with strong opposition at court, and that his plans would have been communicated to the Spaniards. He more prudently concealed his intentions, and began his preparations professedly with the design of making a trip to the coast of Africa to procure slaves. Fortunately, the king's lieutenant in Guienne, Monsieur Montluc, was a friend of De Gourgues, and readily granted the necessary license for a voyage to Africa.

Dominic did not underrate the difficulties that lay before him. He had reason to believe that the Spaniards in Florida were strongly fortified, and that their consciousness of guilt, while probably making cowards of them all, would yet point out the necessity of being always on the alert and prepared for an attack from those they had so cruelly wronged. He felt the justice of his own cause, and trusted to this, and to his utter fearlessness of danger, rather than to the strength of any force he might possibly be able to command. His own resources were not large, for it was said of him "that in all his life he had sought to attain honor rather than wealth," and the sale of his estate did not bring him means sufficient to enable him to equip an expedition. He was compelled therefore, however reluctantly, to borrow money from his friends. With the assistance thus obtained, he was able to procure and fit out three vessels,—one of them quite small, and intended to be used only as a tender, with either sails or oars. De Gourgues then enlisted one hundred men (many of whom are said to have been gentlemen) and eighty-four mariners, who were expected in any emergency to take up arms as soldiers. By the 2d of August, 1567, he had all things in readiness to put to sea, but, being detained twenty days by a long and very severe gale, he could not commence his voyage until the 22d of the same month.

He at first proceeded to the coast of Africa, where he encountered another violent gale, and was attacked by three African chiefs, whom he repulsed. Turning westward, he made land at Dominica, and then touched at St. Domingo, where he repaired his vessels, but was not allowed to procure supplies or even to take in water.

It was not until after leaving St. Domingo, and on the point of sailing for Florida, that De Gourgues made known to his men his real place of destination and the object of his expedition.

He then addressed them most eloquently, depicting the wrongs their countrymen had received at the hands of the Spaniards, the indignity their nation and flag had suffered, and the shame that rested upon France for leaving so long unavenged an act so wicked and base as the murder of the Huguenots and the destruction of the French colony. He told them that the work that lay before them was to punish the Spaniards, and wipe out the stain that rested upon their own country, and explained, as fully as he could, his plans, and the means by which he hoped to attain success, expressing entire confidence in his men, and hoping, as he said, they would not disappoint the high expectations he had formed when he selected them from the many who had been eager to join in this expedition.

His words fell upon willing ears, and the hearts of his followers burned with anxiety to reach the shore and begin their work of revenge. A favorable wind soon brought them to the coast of Florida, and, passing near the mouth of the San Mateo River, they were descried from the forts at its entrance. The garrison, supposing they were Spanish vessels, fired a salute, which De Gourgues returned, in order to keep up the deception. A few leagues north of the San Mateo they entered the fine harbor of Fernandina, near the mouth of the St. Mary's River, called by the natives Tacatacouron, and, by the French, La Seine. At daybreak, the morning after their arrival, they beheld the shores of the harbor lined with savages in hostile array, ready to prevent their landing, for the Indians supposed them to be Spaniards. Fortunately, the trumpeter on board De Gourgues's vessel was well acquainted with the Indian language, having been out with Laudonnière, and he was sent on shore to give assurances of friendship, and to engage their services. The trumpeter was soon recognized by the Indians, and received with demonstrations of joy. Satourioura, the bitter foe of the Spaniards, was present, and welcomed De Gourgues as the friend of Laudonnière. The complaints of the Indians against the Spaniards were very bitter, and they expressed an impatient desire for revenge. Having explained, as far as was prudent, his plans to the Indians, De Gourgues started out on a reconnoitring expedition to the mouth of the San Mateo, in order to make himself thoroughly acquainted with the position of the Spanish forts and the strength of their garrisons; then, returning to his vessel, he awaited the assembling of the Indians, who, under their chiefs Olocatora and Satourioura, were to join him in the assault. They had promised to return in three days and bring their warriors with them, and, true to their word, they came in on the third day with thousands of dusky followers.

Satourioura brought with him a youth of sixteen or seventeen, by the name of Peter de Bré, who had escaped from Fort Caroline, and had been all this time with the Indians. The Spaniards had made many efforts to get possession of De Bré, but the Indians faithfully protected him and now allowed him to join De Gourgues. He proved most useful as an interpreter, and informed De Gourgues of the strength of the three forts on the river, which he said contained in all but four hundred men-at-arms. The French were rejoiced to find themselves supported by the Indians, and De Gourgues skillfully availed himself of their enmity towards the Spaniards, to further his own purposes. The attack was to be made upon the fort on the north side of the river; and, guided by Helicopali, one of the chiefs, the French arrived in the neighborhood of the fort just at dawn, but were obliged to wait until the ebb tide should enable them to reach the island on which it stood. At mid-day they passed over, and, the sentinel not being at his post, the French troops had nearly reached the fort before they were discovered. The Spaniards, though for three years they had been dreading this attack, were at last taken by surprise, and the cry which now reached their ears—"The French! the French!"—struck terror to every heart. The sentinel flew to his post and fired a culverin twice at the enemy, and was on the point of firing a third time when Olocatora leaped on the platform and transfixed him with a pike. Ignorant from what direction the French had come upon them, and probably only expecting an attack to be made by sea, the garrison rushed to the gates, hoping to escape, but were met by De Gourgues's men, and their entire number, sixty in all, either killed or captured. The inmates of the fort on the opposite side of the river, observing the contest, opened fire upon the French, who, being now in possession of the first fort, turned the captured guns upon their assailants, and returned their fire with good effect. In the mean time De Gourgues's vessels had come around to the mouth of the river and commenced an attack by sea, while the Indians, in large numbers, swam across the stream to the fort. The Spaniards, finding themselves thus surrounded, gave up all for lost, and endeavored to escape, hoping to reach Fort Mateo by passing through the woods along the shores of the river. But De Gourgues, suspecting their purpose, intercepted their flight, and, with the aid of the

Indians, succeeded in killing or capturing their entire number. Among the fifteen taken prisoners was an old sergeant, who gave much important information respecting the position, height, and strength of Fort Mateo, towards which point De Gourgues was next to turn his attention. He prudently determined, however, first to fortify himself in one of the forts already captured, and thus guard against surprise from any attack the Spaniards might make upon him. He also busied himself with preparations for an assault upon Fort Mateo, making scaling-ladders, etc., and sending out reconnoitring parties to observe the operations of the Spaniards. One of these parties, headed by the young chief Olocatora, seized a Spaniard disguised as an Indian, and brought him in to De Gourgues. The Spaniard professed to have escaped from one of the captured forts, and said that he had disguised himself in order, as he hoped, to escape being killed by the Indians; but, being confronted with the old sergeant, he was found to be a spy from Fort Mateo, sent out to discover the strength of the enemy and obtain any other useful information he could. He said that the Spaniards supposed the French to be over two thousand strong, while their own garrison consisted of only two hundred and sixty men, and that they felt wholly unable to defend themselves against such vastly superior numbers. De Gourgues at once determined to hasten an attack upon the Spaniards, and so avail himself of an advantage which their overestimate of his strength would give him. Coming out under cover of night, he disposed his Indian forces in ambuscade around the fort to await the moment when their services would be required; and at day-dawn he approached with his own men, and was soon discovered and fired upon from a battery that had been so constructed as to cover the approach to the fort by water. De Gourgues fell back a little, and, turning aside, secured a position in which he was protected from the fort, while he could himself observe all the movements of the Spaniards. He soon discovered a party of some sixty armed men issue from the fort on a reconnoissance. As soon as they had advanced far enough from the fort to admit of it, De Gourgues threw some of his men in their rear, in order to intercept their return, and then, rushing out of his concealment, attacked the Spaniards in their front. They quickly fled before him, and, falling in with the French in their rear, were cut to pieces.

The garrison, becoming panic-stricken, attempted no resistance, and sought safety in flight; but, being surrounded on all sides by the French and their Indian allies, only a few, including the commander of the fort, escaped.

Most of them fell under the swords of the Frenchmen or the clubs of the Indians, while the few who were taken alive were reserved for a more awful doom.

There were found in the fort five double culverins, four mignons or moyennes, and other smaller pieces of iron and brass, besides corselets, arquebuses, pikes, etc., and eighteen large cakes of powder. The artillery De Gourgues had placed upon his vessels, but before he could secure anything more an accident occurred which destroyed everything. An Indian, broiling fish near the fort, set fire to a train leading to the magazine and storehouses, by which they were entirely destroyed.

The Spaniards who were taken prisoners were soon led out to the spot on which, in September, 1565, Menendez had caused the Huguenots of Fort Caroline to be hung. De Gourgues here arraigned them at the assizes of retributive justice. He told them of the wrongs they had done to the French king, how they had murdered his unprotected subjects, destroying the forts they had built, and taking possession of the country they had conquered. Such base treason and detestable cruelty could not go always unpunished, and he had taken upon himself, at his own risk and expense, to avenge the wrongs of his countrymen. He could not make them suffer as they justly ought, but must mete out to them such punishment as an enemy might fairly inflict, in order that their fate might be a warning unto others.

Having thus spoken, he caused the poor wretches to be suspended from the branches of the spreading oaks under whose shade the unfortunate Huguenots had suffered; and then, in place of the inscription which Menendez had written in Spanish over his bloody deed—"I do this, not as unto Frenchmen, but as to Lutherans"—De Gourgues caused to be engraved, on a tablet of pine, with a red-hot iron, "I do this, not as unto Spaniards, nor as to outcasts, but as to traitors, thieves, and murderers."

He now called together the Indian chiefs and their warriors, and told them that he had fulfilled his promises to them, and with their aid successfully carried out his purposes of retaliation upon the Spaniards, that their wrongs had been avenged, and that it only remained, to make their work complete, that the forts should be destroyed. This the Indians gladly undertook to accomplish, and so great was their zeal that by nightfall, it is said, not one stone remained upon another at Fort Mateo. They were anxious that De Gourgues should attack the fort at St. Augustine, but he felt that his means were altogether inadequate to such an enterprise. Moving down the river to the forts at its mouth, the thirty prisoners who had been captured and secured there were brought out and hung, and the forts totally destroyed. Among these last Spaniards who were put to death was one who confessed that he had taken part in the massacre at Fort Caroline, and had with his own hands hung five of the Huguenots. Acknowledging his guilt, he reproached himself greatly, and recognized the hand of God in the just punishment he was about to suffer.

De Gourgues now prepared to return to his vessels, which lay at the mouth of the river Tacatacouron; and as he marched along he found the paths everywhere filled with Indians, who had come to do him honor and offer him presents. Having reached his vessels and found them ready for sea, he assembled the Indians, and, addressing their chiefs, thanked them in his own behalf, and in the name of his countrymen, for their service, and exhorted them to continue the friendship which they had ever shown for the King of France and his subjects, who hoped ever to maintain peaceful relations with the Indians, and would protect them from the Spaniards and all other enemies. He warned them to be on their guard against surprise until his Majesty could send a sufficient force to protect them. The Indians parted from the French with tears and lamentations, and could be pacified only by a promise from De Gourgues to return to them within a twelvemonth with a larger force than he now had.

After weighing anchor, De Gourgues assembled his ship's company and called upon them to return thanks to God for the great success He had vouchsafed to their enterprise. "It was not," said he, "other than God who preserved us from shipwreck at the Cape Finisterre, and from our enemies at the Isle of Cuba, and at the river Halicamini, where He moulded the hearts of the savages to join with us. 'Twas God who blinded the understanding of the Spaniards, so that they were unable to discover the number of our forces or to know how to employ their own. They were four to our one in numbers,—had strong fortresses, well provided with artillery, ammunition, arms, and provisions. We had the just cause, and conquered those who contended without the right. Thus it was God alone, and not ourselves, who won the victory. Let us then always give thanks to Him, and pray Him ever to continue his favors to us, and now beg Him to guide and protect us on our homeward journey, and ask Him so to dispose the hearts of men that the dangers in which we have been placed and the labors we have undergone, shall find grace and favor before our sovereign,— and, before all, France,—for that we have sought nothing else than the service of our king and the honor of our country."

On Tuesday, the 3d day of May, 1568, they set sail for France with favorable winds, and on the 6th of June arrived at Rochelle, having lost on the passage the "tender" with eight men; a few had been killed at the assault on the forts.

De Gourgues was received with great honor and applause at Rochelle, but, the report of his exploits having reached Spain, a fleet was dispatched to capture him, which arrived at Rochelle the very day he had sailed for Bordeaux, and he was pursued as far as Blays. De Gourgues presented himself at court, gave an account of his doings in Florida, and tendered his services to the king to regain the possession of that country; but the anti-Huguenot party was then in power, and the temper of the court was not favorable to such an exploit, and, though there were doubtless many who rejoiced that the slaughter of Ribaut had been avenged, De Gourgues met with a cold reception, and was compelled to seek safety in concealment. Philip of Spain, the same king who had shortly before bestowed commendation and honor upon Menendez for his bloody acts in Florida, now had the unblushing assurance to demand of the French king the head of De Gourgues. The President of Parliament, De Marigny, and the Receiver, Vacquieux, shielded De Gourgues from the demands of Philip, and, after some years spent in obscurity, he was appointed by the king to the command of the French fleet, and died suddenly in the year 1582, greatly regretted.*

One can hardly fail to be struck with surprise at the success of this remarkable expedition. From the day of the destruction of Fort Caroline, Menendez had lived in hourly fear of the return of the French to avenge the slaughter of the Huguenots. Every passing sail, and every reverberation, had caused the Spaniards to grasp their arms and hasten to their ramparts to meet the expected foe. The fort, under its new name of San Mateo, had been rebuilt, and strengthened in such a manner that the Chaplain Mendoza records the boast, "that half of France could not take it." The Spaniards further strengthened their position, by erecting two forts near the mouth of the San Mateo River, and mounted guns of considerable calibre to command the passage of the river. Forts had been built at several points on the coast, every effort made to conciliate the Indians, and, in fact, Menendez had done all in his power to prepare his colony against any sudden surprise or attack.

Such was the condition of affairs when De Gourgues planned and executed his scheme of vengeance. Looking at the limited means and small force he had at his command, his enterprise seems the extreme of recklessness. With only two small vessels and a tender, a force of one

---

* We have followed the account given in Ternaux Compans, taken from a manuscript in the Royal Library of France,—"Reprise de la Floride."

hundred armed men and sixty sailors, without artillery, he was to attack a foe outnumbering his own four to one, occupying three forts which were mounted with heavy guns and provided with abundance of military stores, ammunition, etc.

On his arrival in Florida, De Gourgues had been met by a few Indian chiefs who were hostile to the Spaniards, and who were eager, with their followers, to join his expedition; but their only weapons were their bows and arrows, and no great dependence could be placed upon such allies. The success of his plan could be looked for only through one of those chances or accidents of war that sometimes reward confidence and audacity. The boldness of the assailants certainly deceived the Spaniards, who could not believe that any inferior force would assault them in their strongholds, and with a natural dread of the French they preferred to seek safety in flight, rather than stand their ground and risk the fate which would inevitably follow their defeat. Had the commander of Fort Mateo sustained the attack, De Gourgues must inevitably have been driven off, and compelled to abandon his purpose, or but imperfectly accomplish it in the capture of the smaller forts. Well might he be thankful for the success, and attribute it to the intervention of a higher power. We cannot, in this age of a more enlightened and refined Christianity, approve all the acts of De Gourgues. We feel that it would have been more noble to have spared his captives, and given an illustrious example of magnanimity to his enemies; but at that day such an instance of generosity would have been considered egregious folly. De Gourgues had himself, in reward for deeds of valor, been consigned by the Spaniards to the galleys, and was embittered alike by the remembrance of this personal grievance, and by the cruelty practiced upon his countrymen, the memorials of which perhaps still remained to animate his purpose of revenge. Thus incited, he believed that he was the minister of divine vengeance to execute justice upon "traitors, *thieves, and murderers.*"

The atrocities of Menendez, and the vengeance of De Gourgues, are alike sad records of the cruelty and vindictiveness of the human race.

CHAPTER XII.

Return of Menendez—Attack on St. Augustine by Sir Francis Drake—Missions to the Indians, and Massacre of the Mission Fathers—Attack on St. Augustine by Captain Davis—Establishment of a Spanish Settlement at Pensacola.

1568—1696.

WHILE De Gourgues was thus visiting with swift destruction the Spanish forts and garrisons on the St. John's River, Menendez still tarried in restless impatience at the Spanish court. He finally succeeded in obtaining a partial reimbursement of the funds he had expended, and procured from the Duke of Borja ten missionaries to accompany him on his return to Florida, who were to engage in the propagation of the faith among the Indians. Menendez had also been honored by being appointed Governor of Cuba, an appointment then considered of less importance than the command of Florida. He set sail on the 17th of March, 1568, and arrived in Florida shortly after the departure of De Gourgues, of whose attack he only learned upon his arrival there. His proud spirit must have chafed with unavailing rage at the severe blow which had been dealt upon his colony by so insignificant a force, but he had come too late to prevent or revenge it.

Menendez found his garrison demoralized, suffering from hunger and insufficiency of clothing. The Indians, aroused by the inroad of De Gourgues, were everywhere in open hostility, and he found ample occupation in restoring order, and re-establishing his posts along the coast. He gave particular attention to the missionary operations among the Indians, and, to his credit be it said, devoted himself with zeal and earnestness to this good work. The success of the missionaries was not equal to their labors, for it is said that although the Indians asked many questions, and gave apparent attention to the explanations and instructions of the worthy fathers while the corn which was daily given to them lasted, yet when that was gone they also disappeared; and notwithstanding four of the fathers labored in one locality most assiduously for a year, they succeeded in baptizing only seven persons within that period, of whom four were children and the others at the point of death.

These missions were soon extended through a large region; beginning at Cape Florida, they reached along the coast to St. Helena on the coast of Georgia, and an attempt was made, even at this early period, to plant a mission on the shores of the Chesapeake, then called the province of Axiocan.

Menendez had brought back with him an Indian who had been carried to Spain some time previously and educated in the Roman Catholic faith. This convert now proposed to guide a band of missionaries to his native province, of which his brother was the cacique or chief. An expedition having been fitted out, a party of missionaries, consisting of Father Segura, vice-provincial, with five other priests, and four junior brothers of the order of St. Francis, under the guidance of Don Luis, sailed to the Chesapeake, where they landed; and the treacherous convert, pretending to conduct them into the country, caused the massacre of the whole party, one of the junior brothers alone escaping, who was afterwards surrendered to Menendez.

Having learned of this bloody massacre of the missionaries, Menendez in the following year sailed to Axiocan, captured some of the Indians who had participated in it, and executed eight of them. Others of the mission were desirous to renew the attempt for the conversion of these Indians; but Menendez, in consideration of the distance from his settlements and the duplicity shown in the treatment of Segura and his companions, would not give his consent to their going. Had this company of missionaries succeeded in establishing themselves on the shores of the Chesapeake, it is not improbable that Virginia would have become one of the most important of the Spanish settlements in America.

The importance of Florida soon diminished in public estimation. None of the rich rewards which had been anticipated had followed its occupation, and it was only by the constant importation of provisions that the inhabitants could be sustained. The colony languished, and was supported only by the personal exertions of Menendez, to whom it was a profitless position, impoverishing him daily. Finally, leaving the government in the hands of his relative, the Marquis de Menendez, he returned to Spain, where his high reputation gave him position at court as one of the counselors of his Majesty, and it is said that no important enterprise was undertaken without his advice.

In the year 1574 he was appointed captain-general of the Spanish fleet, and at the mature age of fifty-five, at the summit of his honors, and surrounded with devoted followers, attracted by his brilliant reputation, when on the eve of assuming the command of a grand armada of over three hundred vessels, he was attacked by a violent fever, to which he succumbed after a short illness. It was said by some that he put an end to his own existence.

Menendez combined with many admirable and heroic

qualities others which have left a stain upon his name and memory. He was distinguished for the perseverance and energy of his movements, the fortitude with which he bore hardships and sufferings in the prosecution of his enterprise, and the possession of many of the virtues which constitute a great leader, and which, on a larger field, would have made him illustrious. Unfortunately, he was a cruel bigot, and was placed in a position calculated to develop the worst traits of his character. His portrait bears some resemblance to that of Henry VIII. of England—the forehead and upper portion of the face noble and full of intelligence, while the wide mouth and heavy chin bespeak the cruelty and selfishness of character which alike belonged to them. Under a leader of less resolution, the settlement of Florida would have been abandoned; and he is justly entitled to the credit of establishing the first permanent colony in the United States.

The settlement of the country progressed but slowly, consisting mainly of garrisons established at a few points. In 1586 Sir Francis Drake, returning from a freebooting expedition against the Spanish settlements in the West Indies, observed a lookout upon the shores of Anastasia Island, near the entrance to the harbor of St. Augustine. The English landed with a piece of ordnance, and, planting it at the nearest point, fired two shots, the first of which passed through the royal standard of Spain waving over the fort, and the second struck the ramparts. As it was nearly dark, the English suspended any further demonstrations until the following day. During the evening, several officers, making a reconnoissance in a boat, were fired at three or four times from the fort, which was at the same time being evacuated by the Spanish garrison to the number of one hundred and fifty, they supposing that the whole English force was about to attack them.

In the mean time the boat had returned to the English camp, when a French fifer, playing the Prince of Orange's March, approached in a canoe. He reported himself as one of the garrison, informed them of the flight of the Spaniards, and offered to act as a guide to the English forces.* The boats were immediately manned, and, upon approaching the fort, two shots were fired from it by some of the garrison who had remained; but, upon landing, the English found the place entirely deserted, the garrison having left in such haste that the treasure-chest, containing two thousand pounds sterling, destined for the pay of the troops, fell into the hands of Sir Francis. The fort then existing was constructed of the trunks of pine-trees, set upright as a palisade, but was without ditches; the platforms were of trees laid horizontally and filled in with earth; but the works were in an unfinished state, and not capable of defense against a superior force. Owing to heavy rains and some intervening creeks, it is said, the English were not able to approach the town by land. Upon their arriving at the town, after a slight show of resistance, the garrison and inhabitants fled, the former going to San Mateo. The English sergeant-major, pursuing the fugitives, was shot from an ambush, in retaliation for which the English pillaged and then burnt the town. Understanding that there was another Spanish settlement at St. Helena on the coast, and also that of San Mateo, Sir Francis determined to attack these points, but was unable, on account of the tempestuous weather, to make a landing.

St. Augustine, at the time of its destruction by Drake, boasted of a hall of justice, a parish church, and a monastery.

---

* This French fifer bore the name of Nicolas de Bourgoyne, and was one of the musicians said to have been spared at the time of Ribaut's massacre.

The combined garrisons of St. Augustine and San Mateo then numbered but four hundred men, and the only other post of any importance was St. Helena. With the departure of Menendez, the importance of the province had sensibly diminished, and, as no discoveries of the precious metals had been made, it was difficult to procure colonists to engage in mere agricultural pursuits.

After the departure of Drake, the Spanish governor returned to St. Augustine and commenced to rebuild the town. In the year 1593, twelve brothers of the order of St. Francis were sent to Florida to continue the missions among the natives, and were distributed at different points along the coast, the principal mission being on the island of Guale.

Five years afterwards the son of the chief of Guale, dissatisfied with the restrictions and reproaches of the priests, incited a general conspiracy for the destruction of the missionaries.

In the suburbs of St. Augustine were two Indian villages, called respectively Tolomato and Topiqui. At midnight, the young chief and his followers made an attack upon Father Corpa, who had charge of the mission of Tolomato, and dispatched him with their hatchets. Then, being urged by their chief to complete their cruel work, the band hastened to Topiqui, where they entered the habitation of Father Rodriguez, who begged the privilege of celebrating mass before he died. He had no sooner concluded than they fell upon him with the utmost fury, killing him at the very foot of the altar, and from thence dragging his lifeless body, they cast it into the fields. They then went to the Indian town of Assopo, on the island of Guale, where were two friars, Fathers Auñon and Badazoz, whom they quickly dispatched, their bodies being afterwards buried by their friends at the foot of a high cross, which Father Auñon had himself erected. From Guale, the infuriated savages went to the Indian town of Asao, where a friar resided by the name of Velascola, a man of great humility and piety, but endowed with remarkable strength, and of whom the natives stood in great awe. Becoming aware of their hostile intentions, he embarked for St. Augustine in a canoe. Enraged at his escape, the Indians hastened to intercept him, if possible, at the point of his landing near St. Augustine. Reaching this place in advance of him, they concealed themselves in the thickets, and, stealing upon him, seized him from behind and struck him repeated blows with their clubs and hatchets until they had deprived him of life.

Their thirst for blood still unslaked, they proceeded to Ospo, where Father Davila was stationed, who, hearing their yells and being made aware of his danger, sought safety by flight to the woods. But the night being clear, and the moon at the full, they soon discovered him and wounded him with their arrows. As he was seized and was about being sacrificed, he was saved by the intercession of an Indian woman, who claimed him as a captive and carried him to the interior, where he was forced to perform the lowest menial service, accompanied with much ill usage and severe treatment. Tired of their captive, they at last determined to complete their measure of vengeance against the missionaries by burning him alive. He was brought out for this purpose, and bound with thongs to an upright post in the *campus* of the town ; the fuel was heaped about him, and the torch about to be applied, when an Indian mother, whose son was held prisoner by the Spaniards at St. Augustine, begged that the priest might be delivered to her that she might procure the exchange of her son for him. With great difficulty she at last succeeded in having the father released from his great peril, and delivered to his friends in exchange for the Indian youth.

The savages had now visited all the missions except that of the island of San Pedro. With upwards of forty canoes they made a vigorous assault upon that mission, but were repulsed by the friendly cacique, whose tribe was at enmity with that of the assailants, and who followed up his success with such vigor that all who had already landed were destroyed, and the remainder forced to seek safety in flight.

In this massacre of the missionaries perished five priests, and another, Davila, was so maltreated that when he returned to his friends they were unable to recognize him.

The Spanish governor proceeded immediately to visit the murderers with exemplary punishment,—burning the dwellings and granaries of those whom he could not more directly reach.

In the course of the years 1612 and 1613, thirty-one missionaries of the order of St. Francis were sent to Florida, which was now erected into a religious province of that order, by the name of St. Helena; the principal house of which was established at Havana, and Juan Capelles chosen the first provincial.*

A catechism in the Indian language had already been prepared and printed, being probably the first work ever published in the Indian language.†

Three years later, twelve brothers of the order were added to the mission of St. Francis, and such progress was made in the ensuing two years that there were now twenty missions established in the principal Indian towns

---

* Ensayo Cronologico, p. 181.

† Mr. Buckingham Smith, former Secretary of Legation to Spain, to whose indefatigable labors Florida owes so much, in his researches abroad, discovered a copy of this Indian catechism, called " La Doctrina Cristiana," in the Timuqua language—a tribe occupying the larger part of the coast below St. Augustine, the name of which is still preserved in the Tomoka River.

through the country, and many of the friars preached to the natives with great success.

In the year 1638 a war broke out between the Spanish colonists and the Apalachee Indians, and although the garrison was very weak, not being able to furnish over one hundred effective men, the governor succeeded in repelling the assaults of the Indians and driving them back to their own province. A considerable number of Indians of this tribe, who had been captured, were set to work on the fortifications of St. Augustine, and they and their descendants were kept thus employed for sixty years.

St. Augustine remained the principal town of the Spaniards, and so slow was the progress of settlement that, although the recipient of government patronage and aid, in 1647 it is stated, with some degree of exultation, that the number of families or householders had reached three hundred, and that there were then domiciled in the city, at the convent of St. Francis, fifty members of that order.

The succession of the house of Menendez to the governorship of Florida had now terminated,—Hernando de Alas being the last of that family. Pedro Menendez, the nephew of the governor, had perished at the hands of the Indians, and De Alas had married his daughter Carolina. Diego de Rebellado was captain-general from 1655 to 1675, when Don Juan Hita de Salacar succeeded him, and held the government until 1680. He was succeeded by Don Juan Marquez Cabrera.

The settlement of Virginia had been commenced in 1607, and the other colonies to the north had been planted by the English and Dutch without opposition on the part of the Spanish crown. The wide separation of the Spanish and English settlements, for a time prevented difficulties between them, and the spirit of Menendez no longer animated his successors.

It was not until 1663, when the charter of Carolina was granted by Charles II., that the English settlements trenched on the ground which the Spaniards had at any time claimed by possession. With the settlement of Carolina there at once grew up a hostile state of feeling, which lasted for a century, between these neighboring colonies. At this period the buccaneers or free rovers filled the seas, to the destruction of the Spanish commerce, and to the great disturbance of the Spanish settlements.

In 1665, one of these piratical expeditions, under the command of Captain John Davis, made a descent upon St. Augustine, with some seven small vessels, and pillaged the town.* The garrison, consisting of two hundred men, do not appear to have resisted the attack, which, it is probable, was made from the south by boats. The fort is said to have been an octagon, with two round towers.†

The ill feeling existing between Florida and Carolina continued to increase; the Spaniards alleging that the pirates who preyed upon their commerce were received and sheltered in the harbors of Carolina, an accusation which was but too true. The Carolinians, on the other hand, complained that the Spanish authorities endeavored to incite the Indians to acts of hostility against them, and also seduced their servants from them and gave them protection at St. Augustine.

The Spaniards sent a force to attack some of the colonists on the Ashley River in the year 1676, but, the settlers having thrown up intrenchments for their protection, the Spaniards retreated. Two years later, an expedition, consisting of three galleys, from St. Augustine, made an attack

---

* Buccaniers of America, 53, London, 1684.

† This description of the fort is evidently erroneous; it was then unfinished, but was square, with bastions.

upon a Scotch settlement on Port Royal Island, which had been established by Lord Cardross. The settlers were too few in number to protect themselves, and their houses were pillaged. From thence the galleys ascended the North Edisto River to Bear's Bluff, where they made a landing, burnt the houses, and plundered the settlers. This expedition inflicted severe injury upon the colony, then in its infancy, and was characterized by all the atrocities of savage warfare. The property of the settlers was carried off, and their persons maltreated by the infliction of every indignity; one gentleman, of the name of Morton, a brother of the governor of the colony, was allowed to perish by the burning of the galley upon which he was confined. The utmost indignation was excited throughout the colony by these acts.

It was a part of the original contract with Menendez that he should carry into Florida five hundred negro slaves from the coast of Africa, but he does not appear to have complied with it, having introduced but a small number. One hundred years later, we find the privilege of introducing slaves accorded to one De Aila as a reward for meritorious services, and his arrival, in 1687, with negroes, seems to have occasioned much rejoicing in the colony.

Renewed efforts were made at this period to extend missions among the natives, and large numbers of priests and friars were sent across from Cuba to labor in Florida. The natives of South Florida had begun to have considerable commercial intercourse with Havana, carrying across skins, fish, and fruit in exchange for merchandise suited to their wants.

Don Juan Marquez Cabrera, the governor, about 1681 attempted to remove the various Indian tribes of Apalachees, Cowetas, and Casicas, as well as those of San Felipe, San Simon, San Catalina Sapala, and others, to the islands on the coast, and along the St. John's. This occasioned an insurrection of all these tribes, and several of them removed within the limits of Carolina, and subsequently made a sudden incursion into Florida, attacked the towns of the Timuquas, robbed the church and convent of St. Francis of the vestments and plate, burnt the town of Tomuqua, killed a large number of the Christian Indians, and carried many others away as prisoners to St. Helena, where they were made slaves of.*

At this comparatively late period in the history of America, by the energy and perseverance of Monsieur de la Salle, the course of the Mississippi was traced from the regions of the Illinois to the points of its discharge into the Gulf of Mexico. Although one hundred and seventeen years had passed since the actual settlement and occupation of Florida by the Spaniards, the spirit of enterprise and discovery had so far died out, that the information they had already derived from the expeditions of Narvaez, De Soto, and De Luna, apprising them of vast and fertile regions and magnificent rivers, had not stimulated them to undertake further explorations and occupation of the rich regions lying within the limits claimed by them as a part of Florida.

It was left to the insignificant expedition of La Salle—embarked in slight canoes and almost unarmed—to trace the mighty floods of the great rivers of the west to the sea, and thus to confer on France, by the claim of discovery, the right of appropriating the fairest portion of the American continent, the great valley of the Mississippi, to which they applied the name of Louisiana.

Spain, indifferent to other motives, was always accessible to the impulse of jealousy; and the successful voyage

---

* Ensayo Cronologico, p. 287.

of La Salle aroused her to the necessity of presenting her claims to the extensive regions about to pass under the sway of France. Hitherto she had been content to occupy the single fortified post at St. Augustine, and to make some feeble attempts at colonization. In 1692, however, an expedition was fitted out by the Viceroy of New Spain to explore the harbors on the western coast of Florida, and especially that of Santa Maria de Galva (which De Luna had occupied in 1561). In the year 1696, a Spanish colony was planted, called Pençacola,—a name derived from the locality having been formerly that of the town of a tribe of Indians called Pençacolas, which had been entirely exterminated in conflicts with neighboring tribes.

A fort of quadrilateral form, a church, and other public buildings were erected. To the fort the name of Charles was attached, in honor of Charles II. of Spain. Andres de Arriola was the first governor of the province; Don Lauseano de Torres was at that time governor of East Florida.

Two years later, D'Iberville arrived on the coast with three vessels sent out by Louis XIV. to establish a colony in Louisiana. He touched at Pensacola, then occupied by three hundred Spaniards. Sailing thence to the west, he entered Mobile Bay, and landed on an island, called by him Massacre Island, and subsequently known as Dauphin Island, where he established a colony.

The Spaniards, at this period, called the Mississippi the River of Palisades, from the number of tall trees standing singly along its shores. The English called it Mes-sa-che-be. While France and Spain were thus planting their colonies in the western portion of Florida, England was contemplating a similar enterprise, and three vessels were sent by King William to take possession of the country bordering on the Mississippi. But they were too late; D'Iberville had already occupied the country.

The interior of Florida was occupied by the Apalachians beyond the Suwanee. The tribes of Calos or Carlos were in the southern portion, and the Timuquans along the coast north and south of St. Augustine.* Many of these Indian names are still attached to various localities in Florida. There does not seem to have been much progress made in the civilization of the Indians during the Spanish rule; the natural ferocity of these savage tribes, their freedom from restraint, and their warlike propensities, made them impenetrable to the claims of a faith which inculcated love and forbearance towards one another.

Over one hundred years had now elapsed since Menendez had planted the standard of Spain on the coast of Florida, and a vast amount of labor and treasure had been expended in the almost fruitless effort to occupy and christianize the country. At the beginning of the seventeenth century no European colony existed on the Atlantic coast of North America, except St. Augustine. In 1607, and forty-two years after the founding of St. Augustine, the settlement of Virginia, by the English, began at Jamestown, and thirteen years later the Plymouth colony landed in New England. In the course of the next fifty years settlements were made on the whole coast by the French, English, Dutch, and Swedes; and from the Gulf of St. Lawrence to Port Royal harbor in Carolina, flourishing settlements had arisen and a very considerable commerce had grown up under the fostering care of their respective governments.

During the seventeenth century, Spain possessed, by

---

* These were apparently the dialects, the Timuquan being the language used at San Mateo, San Pedro, Asila, Machua, etc., as shown in the memorials in the Timuquan and Apalachian languages found by Buckingham Smith, Esq., in the Spanish archives at Madrid.

right of discovery and conquest, the claim to the most valuable portion of the American continent, but the history of this hundred years of Spanish domination is barren and fruitless. It is a record of feeble and spasmodic efforts at colonization, with a timid exploration of the regions adjoining the military posts.

Pensacola and St. Mark's had been established as isolated posts, and a few others. The history of Florida, during this period, presents but little more than a chronicle of the changes of governors, and petty details of local events. Having the fertile valley of the Mississippi, the rich plains of Texas, and the productive uplands of Alabama, Mississippi, and Tennessee within their reach, no exploration had been made, no colonies planted, no empire founded, and in this magnificent and then vacant domain the results of over one hundred years of Spanish domination were, three small fortified towns, and a few mission-houses. It is indeed quite probable that in the year 1700 they actually knew less of the country than did Menendez within ten years of his settlement. The mines of Mexico and the riches of the Spanish Main had drawn the attention of the Spanish monarchy from the more enduring wealth and power to be derived from a fertile and populous agricultural region, and the colony in Florida was allowed to languish, presenting but little more than a bare existence.

CHAPTER XIII.

Governor Moore's Attack on St. Augustine—Invasion of Moore, with the Creek Indians, of the Indian Missions and Spanish Posts in Middle Florida—Erection of a Fort at St. Mark's—Capture of Pensacola by the French—Recapture of Pensacola by the Spaniards—Recapture of Pensacola by the French—Transfer of Pensacola to Spain.

1696—1722.

From the time of the settlement of Carolina, constant sources of irritation and difficulty sprang up between the English and Spanish settlements, arising from their mutual jealousies. The aid of the Indian tribes was sought by both parties, and friendship towards one was regarded as necessarily involving hostility towards the other. The Spaniards, it will be recollected, had, in the year 1686, invaded the English settlements at Port Royal, inflicted great injury upon the settlers, and aroused great indignation throughout the colony. Prudential reasons had prevented the colonists from then resenting the attack by an invasion of Florida, but the purpose to do so was only deferred, not abandoned. More amicable relations had, however, sprung up subsequently between the colonies under the judicious administration of Governor Archdale. Unfortunately for the peace of the country, Governor Archdale was succeeded in the government of Carolina by Governor Moore, an ambitious man, who had secured his appointment by questionable means, and who was desirous of acquiring reputation by some signal enterprise.

By the influence of Governor Moore, the Assembly of South Carolina were induced to authorize an expedition against St. Augustine, which they had been informed was not in a very defensible condition, and might readily be reduced. Many of the settlers in the province of Carolina had lost servants, who had fled to Florida and been harbored and protected by the Spanish authorities, and many others of the inhabitants, doubtless, were quite willing to procure labor by making an inroad upon the Spanish Indians and reducing them to a state of servitude.*

A rupture had occurred between England and Spain, and Governor Moore, with the motive, as is charged by his enemies, of enriching himself, embraced the opportunity thus afforded of setting on foot an expedition against the Spaniards of Florida. Many of the inhabitants, with the recollection of former injuries sustained from the invasion of the Spaniards, seconded his plans, while others supported the proposal from mercenary motives.

The governor assured the people that the conquest of Florida would be an easy undertaking, and that the capture of considerable treasures of gold and silver would reward the enterprise. Some, however, opposed the project, and directed attention to the known strength of the castle at St. Augustine, the great expense certain to be incurred, and the fruitless nature of the enterprise. As is usual in such cases, the bold outnumbered the prudent, and the Provincial Assembly sanctioned the expedition, and voted two thousand pounds for the purpose, a sum which, although

---

* The failure of the expedition caused so much controversy between the friends and enemies of Governor Moore that it is not easy to find an impartial account of it by contemporaneous writers.

it seems insignificant compared with the cost of modern contests, was no inconsiderable amount to be raised by a poor colony of some five or six thousand people burdened with the expenses of a new government.

The force deemed sufficient to carry out this enterprise was placed at six hundred provincial militia, to be assisted by an equal number of friendly Indians. They were directed to rendezvous at Port Royal, in September, 1702. The plan of operations contemplated a march by land of one division, and an expedition by sea of the other, in order to effect a combined naval and land attack upon St. Augustine. The land forces were to proceed in boats by the inland passage to the St. John's River, and to ascend that river to the neighborhood of Picolata, whence they were to march across and invest the town in the rear. Colonel Daniel was assigned to the command of this portion of the expedition, the governor himself taking command of the naval force.

In the mean time the Spaniards, learning of the proposed attack, had availed themselves of all the means of defense in their power; provisions were stored in the castle, and preparations were made to sustain a long siege. The governor, Don Joseph Cuniga, had moreover succeeded in procuring some reinforcements.

The forces under command of Colonel Daniel, notwithstanding their circuitous route, reached St. Augustine in advance of the naval part of the expedition, and immediately attacked and gained possession of the town; the troops and inhabitants retiring to the protection of the castle. Governor Moore, with the vessels, soon after arrived, and invested the fortifications, but, on account of the want of siege-guns of larger calibre, no impression could be made upon the walls of the fort. Colonel Daniel was sent to Jamaica to procure heavier guns. While absent on this mission, two Spanish vessels appeared off the harbor. Alarmed by this circumstance, and fearing that his retreat might be cut off, Governor Moore hastily raised the siege, abandoning or destroying such of his stores and munitions as he was unable to remove. Before withdrawing, he committed the barbarity of burning the town. He was obliged to sacrifice his transports, fearing to encounter the Spanish vessels if he went to sea. Colonel Daniel returned shortly after, having succeeded in obtaining some mortars and heavy guns, and, being ignorant of the withdrawal of Governor Moore, narrowly escaped capture. Governor Moore carried the forces back to Carolina without the loss of a man.*

The expedition cost the colony of South Carolina some six thousand pounds, and led to the issue of the first paper money ever circulated in America.

In the same year the Spaniards had incited the Apalachian Indians to make an attack upon the English settlements in Carolina. The Apalachees had assembled a force of nine hundred warriors, and had commenced their march, when they were encountered by five hundred Creek Indians who were allies of the English and were organized by the Creek traders to repel the attack. The Creeks suspended their blankets in their camp, as though quietly reposing by their camp-fires, and placed themselves in ambush. The Apalachees, confident of an easy victory, rushed forward upon the supposed sleeping camp with great impetuosity, when they fell into the ambush prepared for them by the Creeks, and were routed with great loss.†

Although unsuccessful in this attack on St. Augustine,

---

* Carroll's Hist. Col. S. C., vol. ii.; Fairbanks's Hist. St Augustine, 131.
† MS. Report of Com. S. C. Assembly. St. Papers.

Moore appears to have been a man of much energy, and had influence enough to organize another expedition in the latter part of the following year, to attack the Indian towns under the Spanish protection, which were scattered mainly through the region between the Suwanee and Apalachicola Rivers, in what is now known as Middle Florida.

After being in the castle for three months, the inhabitants of St. Augustine were enabled, upon the retreat of Moore, to leave the close quarters in which they had been confined, but it was to find their homes destroyed and themselves without shelter until they could rebuild.

Aid to some extent was sent from Spain to help them to rebuild, but the prosperity of the unfortunate city must have received a great blow. Urgent representations were made by Governor Cuniga to the home government of the necessity for an increased force and larger means to strengthen the colony against its English neighbors. He pointed out the propriety of placing small garrisons at Apalachee,* eighty leagues distant from St. Augustine, at Timuqua,† thirty leagues south, and at Guale,‡ eighteen leagues north from St. Augustine. He also proposed to build a strong fort at the town of Ys,§ and on the coast below Cape Canaveral.||

The Indians of Apalachee, who for sixty years had been laboring upon the fortifications of St. Augustine, as a punishment for their revolt in 1640, were now, at the solicitation of their chiefs, released under a promise to renew their labors when it should become necessary.

Governor Moore, with a small force of militia, some fifty in number, and about one thousand Creek Indians, attacked the Spanish Indian towns with great impetuosity.

---

* St. Mark's. † New Smyrna. ‡ Amelia Island.
§ Indian River. || Ensayo Cronologico, p. 322.

Entering the province from the direction of the Flint River, he first attacked a town containing fifty warriors, which he reduced after a stout resistance. On the following day, the commander of the principal town, Fort San Luis, with a force of twenty-three Spaniards and four hundred Indians, encountered the English and Creek forces. Don Juan Mexia, the Spanish commander, was killed in the battle, with eight of the Spanish soldiers. The Apalachian Indians lost two hundred of their number. This battle decided the fate of all the Indian towns. The King of Atimiaca, who occupied a strong fort with a garrison of one hundred and thirty men, terrified by the defeat and death of Mexia, and by the terrible slaughter of the Indians on that occasion, offered his submission. Moore then visited all of the other Indian towns, without experiencing further resistance. Five of the towns were fortified, and it is probable that had Mexia met the English and Creeks behind his intrenchments he might have repelled their attack and rallied sufficient force to drive them from the province. Moore is said to have destroyed entirely two of the Indian towns, and to have carried away most of the people of seven others, to be held as slaves, leaving only one town undisturbed, which either by its strength or wealth was able to make terms with him.

The towns of San Luis* and Ayavalla† were burnt, with their churches and forts. All of the towns were plundered and robbed of everything of value, including the church plate and the sacred vestments; and desolation and ruin marked the track of the invaders.

There is much discrepancy in the accounts of the strength of the Spanish forces. A note attached to a manuscript map

---

* San Luis was two miles west of Tallahassee.
† Ayavalla was near the St. Mark's River.

found in the English State Paper Office says, "On the 15th of January, 1703, was a battle fought between the Carolinians, commanded by Colonel Moore, and the Spaniards, commanded by Don Juan Mexia, wherein eight hundred Spaniards were killed, whereupon the whole country submitted, being destroyed. Fourteen hundred Apalachee Indians removed to the savana towns, under English government."*

There seems to be also some discrepancy in the dates, some accounts giving the year 1703 and some 1704. Williams's account says that Mexia had a garrison of four hundred men; if it is meant that he had a Spanish garrison of four hundred men, it is certainly an error, as there were at that time not more than forty or fifty Spanish soldiers in that part of the country, and it is not likely Mexia had more than half of these.

The Indian missions in that part of the country were thoroughly broken up, and, it would seem, without excuse or provocation. The remains of these mission stations may be traced at several localities in Florida, and tradition has assigned to them far greater antiquity than they are really entitled to. A fort and chapel were erected together, and were surrounded with earthworks and ditches, with palisades sufficient to withstand an attack from Indians, the only enemies they were likely to require protection from. The outlines of these earthworks may be very distinctly traced at Lake City and elsewhere.

It is a sad reflection that the humble chapels, where the worthy fathers were accustomed to assemble congregations of the dusky sons of the forest to be instructed in

---

* I am indebted to Professor Rivers, of Columbia, S. C., for a copy of the manuscript map procured by him from the State Paper Office in England It appears to be one of the original manuscript maps from which the map of Florida in Molls' Atlas was compiled.—(*Author.*)

the knowledge of the true God, and the altars erected to his worship, should have been ruthlessly swept away by the arms of a nation professing itself to be Christian, and by a leader who claimed to be animated by peculiar zeal for the Christian faith, and that from the poor natives of Florida should be thus taken the light of eternal truth, glimmering feebly though it may have been, and that the altars thus thrown down were never more, so far as we know, restored.

We have a striking evidence of the manner in which interest sways the conviction of right and wrong, when we read that "the governor received the thanks of the proprietors for his patriotism and courage, who acknowledged that the success of his arms had gained their province a reputation;"* and the historian seems to utter a bitter sarcasm on the *patriotism* attributed by the proprietors to Governor Moore, when he adds, "but, what was of greater consequence to him, he wiped off the ignominy of the St. Augustine expedition, and procured a number of Indian slaves, whom he employed to cultivate his fields or sold for his own profit and advantage."†

The war between Great Britain, France, and Spain still continued to be carried on in Europe, and in the year 1706 an expedition was projected by the French and Spanish to make a descent upon Carolina. Monsieur Le Febvre commanded a French frigate and four sloops, with which he touched at St. Augustine to take on board a Spanish landforce to co-operate in an attack upon Charleston. The Spanish troops having been taken on board, the fleet pro-

---

* Hewitt, in Carroll's Hist. Col. S. C., p. 140.

† The Atimacian and Apalachian Indians, before Governor Moore's attack, had made some progress in civilization, and received instruction from the Roman Catholic missionaries, being very loyal to the Spanish government. Hewitt, in Carroll's Hist. Col., 203; Ibid., p. 140.

ceeded to the coast of Carolina, where, by mistake, the frigate entered Sewee Bay, the other four entering Charleston harbor. By the exercise of great prudence and some stratagem, the governor of Carolina was enabled to repel the attack with but slight loss, and eventually captured the frigate with a large number of the allies. The defeat of the French-Spanish expedition was complete, and the attempt at molestation of the colony was not repeated.

In 1708, Colonel Barnwell, of South Carolina, made an excursion to the Apalachian province of Florida, by way of the Flint River.* After visiting San Luis, and the region occupied by the mission towns, he passed on to the Alachua country and the St. John's River. It was perhaps at this period that Captain T. Nairn, of South Carolina, with a party of Yemassee Indians, penetrated to the headwaters of the St. John's, and the vicinity of Lake Okechobee, and and returned with a number of captives or slaves, as noted on a map of Molls' Atlas of 1719.

The year 1714 was signalized by a general outbreak of the Indian tribes in Carolina. This was charged to the instigation of the Spaniards, who, it is said, sent emissaries from Florida to stir up the Indian tribes bordering upon the English settlements to attempt their extermination; and, as evidence of the complicity of the Spaniards, it is said that the Indians, before commencing hostilities, removed their women and children to Florida, and placed them near to, and under the protection of, the Spanish garrisons. The Indians made a combined and powerful attack upon the English settlements, but were defeated and driven out of the province, retreating south to the Spanish

---

* On the MS. map before referred to, there is a note saying that the Apalachian region of Florida was destroyed by Carolinians in 1706.

possessions, and were welcomed at St. Augustine "with bells ringing and guns firing, as if they had returned victoriously from the field."* Above four hundred of the people of South Carolina lost their lives by this Indian outbreak before the Indians were overcome.

In the mean time, considerable progress had been made in establishing French settlements on the shores of the Gulf of Mexico. Injudicious locations had been made at the outset for these settlements, which had to be afterwards abandoned and better positions sought, and the usual difficulties and obstacles attending new settlements had retarded the rapid progress of French colonization; but, by the perseverance of those intrusted with the charge of the colonists, and the fostering care of the parent country, which supplied all their wants, even to the furnishing of their wives, the colonists succeeded in establishing themselves permanently, and were soon in a prosperous condition. The settlements at Mobile and Pensacola were in too close proximity to avoid jealousies and collisions, each charging the other with encroachments upon their territory.

For a long period all the Spanish plate fleets which were sent from Mexico to Spain pursued the route known as the Bahama channel, passing near the shores of Florida. In 1715, one of these fleets, consisting of fourteen vessels laden with a very large amount of gold and silver, was wrecked on Carysfort reef, and an immense amount of treasure was lost. Much of this was afterwards recovered by the wreckers employed for that purpose, but the knowledge of this recovery coming to the English at Jamaica they sent an expedition to the point where the wreckers were engaged, and robbed them of the amount saved, which was

---

* Hewitt, Hist. Col. S. C., vol. i. p. 199.

upwards of three hundred and fifty thousand dollars. The captors no doubt received great credit for this profitable exploit.

The Yemassees, who had been driven out of Carolina into Florida, maintained a constant and harassing warfare upon the settlements in Carolina, committing great havoc among the scattered families along the frontiers. The relation of the horrors of Indian warfare has ever drawn forth the sympathies of mankind. With a strange inconsistency, the most harrowing scenes of suffering occurring under our daily observation pass almost unnoticed, while the captivity and sufferings endured by some sturdy frontiersman or his family call forth all our sympathy and compassion. In every New England household the story of the sufferings of the Williams family, of the Dustans, and of Miss McCrea, excited the most tender emotions of pity. The history of the Southern colonies presents hundreds of such instances. It seems to be well established that the Spanish authorities in Florida instigated and protected these savage allies. A historian of Carolina relates that at this period a scalping-party of Yemassees from Florida penetrated as far as the Euhati lands, where, having surprised John Lent and two of his neighbors, they knocked out their brains with their tomahawks. They then seized Mrs. Barrows and one of her children, and carried them away with them. The child, frightened by the presence of the savages, began to cry, when it was immediately killed in its mother's presence, who was warned to cease her demonstrations of grief or she should share the fate of the child. She was then carried to St. Augustine, where she was delivered to the Spanish governor and thrown into prison, against the remonstrances of one of the Yemassee chiefs, who stated that he had known her a long time and that she was a good woman. The Spaniards, it is said, rejoiced with the Indians for the goodly number of scalps they had brought. Subsequently, Mr. Barrows went to St. Augustine to obtain his wife's release, but was thrown into prison, and died shortly afterwards. She, eventually, was permitted to return to Carolina, and gave an account of the barbarous treatment she had received. She reported that rewards were given to the Indians to incite them to these incursions, and that they were instructed to spare none but negroes, who were to be brought to St. Augustine.* Don Juan de Ayala was at this time governor of East Florida, and Don Gregorio de Salinas governor of Pensacola. Salinas was succeeded in 1717 by Don Juan Pedro Metamoras.

The increasing settlements of the French in Louisiana had already occasioned much uneasiness to the governor of Pensacola, and he had represented to the Viceroy in Mexico the importance of strengthening the fortifications of Pensacola. These representations were acted upon, and the requisite instructions given to Don Pedro, the new governor.

At the instance of the chief of the Apalachee Indians, the governor of St. Augustine sent Captain Don José Primo de Ribera to erect a fort at St. Mark's, in March, 1718, which was named *San Marcos de Apalache*. During the same year a small fortification was erected at St. Joseph's Bay by the French, and called *Fort Crèvecœur*, which seems to have been a favorite name with the French, although the heart of a Frenchman is not so easily broken as the name would seem to imply. The Spanish governor at Pensacola remonstrated against this occupation of the territory of Spain, and in a few months the fort was evac-

---

* Hewitt, Hist. Coll. S. C., vol. i. p. 213.

uated by the French. A Spanish fort was erected at the same place, but afterwards abandoned. Don Antonio de Benavides was appointed to succeed Juan de Ayala as governor at St. Augustine.

Monsieur de Bienville, the French commander at Mobile, upon being informed that hostilities existed between France and Spain, fitted out an expedition against Pensacola, and, having sent a large force of Indians by land, embarked with his troops, on board of three vessels, to make a sudden descent, in the hope of capturing the fort by surprise. He landed upon the island of Santa Rosa, where an outpost was situated, the garrison of which he soon overpowered, and some of the French, putting on the Spanish uniform of their captives, awaited the arrival of a detachment sent down to relieve the post, and captured and disarmed them. Taking the boat the Spaniards had brought, the French, still disguised, passed over to the fort, seized the sentinel on duty, and took possession of the guard-house and fort, making the commander a prisoner in his bed, and thus capturing the place without firing a shot. Such is the French account of the matter. The Spanish authorities confirm the statement of the surprise at the outpost at Point Siguenza, which was occupied by an officer and ten men only, but say that the fort was assaulted by four French frigates, which opened fire upon the Castle de San Carlos, and, after five hours of cannonading, the castle, being unable to reply effectively, and having only a garrison of one hundred and sixty effective men and provisions for fifteen days, and having sustained the loss of one man, agreed to capitulate, upon the following terms offered by Governor Metamoras:

That the garrison should march out with the honors of war, and retain all private property; that they should retain one cannon, with three charges of powder; that they should be transported in French vessels to Havana; and that the town should not be sacked, nor private property molested.*

The garrison was taken by two French vessels to Havana, where, by the perfidy of the Spanish commander at that place, the vessels were seized and their officers and crews cast into prison. An expedition for its recapture was immediately equipped, at the suggestion of Governor Metamoras.

The fort at Pensacola had been garrisoned by De Bienville with a force of some sixty men, under the command of Sieur de Chateaugué. The Spaniards had fitted up the French vessel called the Duc de Noailles, and a Spanish frigate, to retake the fort; and a ruse was adopted by sending in the French ship first, which, on being hailed, ran up the French flag and gave the name of the French captain who had commanded her, and was thereupon allowed to pass into the port. When abreast of the fort, she was joined by her consort, the flag of Spain was displayed, and the garrison summoned to surrender. A brisk cannonade ensued, with but trifling damage to the garrison. In order to gain time, Chateaugué asked for an armistice of four days. The Spanish admiral allowed him two days, and Chateaugué dispatched a messenger to Mobile asking for reinforcements, which De Bienville was unable to send. At the expiration of the armistice, the action was renewed until night, during which most of the garrison deserted,

---

* The Spanish account seems far more to be relied upon than that of the French. It is hardly credible that a force which could be transported in a single guard-boat could surprise a well-equipped fort and garrison and capture the governor in his bed, and, as the frigates were there, it is more probable that a bombardment effected the surrender.

and on the following day the French commander surrendered the fort.*

The Spanish account of the recapture of the fort places their own force at eight hundred and fifty men and that of the garrison at three hundred and fifty, and says the armistice was for but one day, when the fort surrendered, as well as the vessels lying in the harbor. So difficult is it ever to find an exact agreement in reference to the most simple transactions. The French who were captured were sent to Havana as prisoners of war.

The Spanish general proceeded immediately to strengthen the fortifications, and, having sufficiently secured his post from assault, he set out, with the forces under his command, to attack the French settlement on Dauphin Island. Owing to the skill and courage of Bienville, the Spaniards, although superior in point of numbers, were unable to effect a landing, and were forced, by the arrival of five French vessels, to retire to Pensacola.

The French, now strongly reinforced, determined to attempt the recapture of Pensacola, and returned there in September, 1719. A force was landed on the Perdido, to assail the town in the rear, and the fleet proceeded to the bar. A difficulty here presented itself in carrying in the flagship, the Hercules, which drew twenty-one feet of water; but, by the skill of a Canadian pilot, the ship was carried safely in.†

---

* The Spanish soldiers were much discontented at not being permitted to plunder the town, and, in order to gratify them, a detachment was sent by water to an Indian town not far distant, where a large number of slaves belonging to the French Company were, and one hundred and sixty of them were captured and given to the troops as plunder.—*Ensayo Cronologico*, p. 234.

† The pilot was afterwards rewarded for this service with a patent of nobility.

The French say that upon the appearance of their land-forces, accompanied by a large number of Indians, in rear of the fort, the garrison, after a very feeble resistance, retired to a new fort, which they had hastily erected at Point Siguenza, called *Principe de Asturias.* The Spanish accounts, however, contend that their troops fought with most heroic bravery until their guns were dismounted at Point Siguenza and their vessels forced to surrender, and that, the French vessels having then entered the port, the castle was forced to surrender, which took place on the 18th of September, 1719.

The French accounts of the capture award great credit to the commander at Fort Principe de Asturias for his gallant defense, which was continued until his ammunition failed, while it is said the commander at Fort San Carlos displayed great cowardice. On the following day a Spanish vessel entered the port with supplies and dispatches from the governor of Havana to the governor at Pensacola, the dispatches saying that he was confident the Spanish forces had succeeded in conquering all the places held by the French in that country, and directing him to send all the prisoners to work in the mines, in order to avoid the expense of feeding them.

The French, feeling unable to afford the amount of force necessary to hold the place, concluded to destroy the fortifications and public buildings and burn the town, leaving only a few small buildings to shelter a guard who were left in charge of one small battery.

Before leaving, the French commander caused the following inscription to be placed upon a tablet erected on the ruins of the fort:—

"In the year 1719, upon the 18th day of September, Monsieur Desnade de Champmeslin, commander of the squadron of his Most Christian Majesty, took this place by force of arms, as well also the island of Santa Rosa, by order of the King of France."

Returning first to Dauphin Island, the French fleet sailed for France, carrying with them the Spanish garrison of Pensacola as prisoners of war.

Thus, after having been thrice assaulted and thrice captured within a period of three months, Pensacola was laid in ashes, and the quiet of desolation allowed to rest over its remains; for there was no longer anything to capture or anything to defend.

The town first built by the Spaniards in 1696, and which was thus destroyed in 1719, was built where Fort Barrancas now stands, the fort being placed in the centre. On the opposite point, called Point Siguenza, Fort Principe de Asturias had stood, and was destroyed at the same time as Fort Carlos. When reoccupied in 1722 by the Spaniards, the town was rebuilt on Santa Rosa Island, near where Fort Pickens now stands. This location continued to be occupied until some time between 1743 and 1763, the inhabitants having begun to plant upon the northern side of the bay, and the location upon the island being peculiarly sterile and sandy, the settlement was gradually transferred, so that in 1763 it was laid out in the form of a city, the streets crossing at right angles, making squares four hundred by two hundred feet, with a large common fronting on the bay, about fifteen hundred feet in length by one thousand in breadth.* The present city of Pensacola may be considered to date back its existence to about the year 1750, being nearly two hundred years the junior in age of St. Augustine.

After the treaty of peace made in 1722 between France

---

* An engraved view of the town as it appeared in 1743 may be seen in Roberts's Florida, London, 1743.

and Spain, Pensacola was restored to the Spanish crown and a new town built on Santa Rosa Island, as has just been stated.

The difficulties between the neighboring provinces of Florida and Carolina had increased. The Spanish authorities at St. Augustine for many years harbored as well as encouraged the desertion of the negroes from the English settlements, against the continual and earnest remonstrances of the authorities of Carolina. The Spanish governors or officials had connived at, if not actually incited, the plundering incursions of the Yemassees upon the exposed frontiers of the English colony. To guard against these forays, a small fort had been erected on the banks of the Altamaha, called Fort King George. This was considered by the Spaniards an encroachment upon the Spanish territory, and representations were accordingly made to the British crown. A conference of the two governors was thereupon directed to be held, to endeavor to settle amicably the points in dispute between the two provinces. For this purpose Don Francisco Menendez and Don José Ribera came to Charleston, in 1725, to confer with Governor Middleton. In reply to their claim that the fort on the Altamaha was within the limits of Florida, Governor Middleton appealed to the chartered limits of Carolina in confirmation of the English claim to that region. This was, of course, no evidence of that claim; but as the Spanish governor could show no actual prior occupation since the days of Menendez, he could hardly gainsay the English claim. On the other hand, Governor Middleton demanded an explanation of the course pursued by the Spanish authorities at St. Augustine in enticing away slaves from the English colonists and offering refuge and protection to criminals and debtors, and refusing to surrender these fugitives.

The Spanish commissioners expressed their willingness to surrender the criminals and debtors, but said they were instructed by the Spanish crown not to surrender the fugitive slaves, on account of the great concern their king and master had for their *souls*, but that compensation would be made to their owners for their value. As might be inferred, no agreement was come to, and these irritating difficulties remained unsettled.

The incursions of the Yemassees became afterwards more frequent and injurious to the colonists. Murders were frequent, and every negro that could be reached was carried off. To put a stop to this state of things, Colonel Palmer, an energetic officer, in the year 1727 collected a militia force of some three hundred men, with a body of friendly Indians, made a rapid and unexpected descent upon the Indian and Spanish settlements in Florida, and carried desolation and destruction over the whole province, pushing forward to the very gates of St. Augustine, sparing nothing which was destructible, and driving off all the stock which fell in their way. The Yemassee towns were destroyed, many of the natives killed, and a great number carried off prisoners.* This chastisement seems to have repressed further incursions on the part of the Spanish Indians for a time, and a few years of comparative quiet ensued.

---

* One of these Yemassee towns, called Macariz, was about one mile north of St. Augustine.

CHAPTER XIV.

Attack on St. Augustine by Oglethorpe—Attack of Monteano on St. Simon's Island—Transfer of Florida to Great Britain.

1722—1762.

THE settlement of the new colony of Georgia, in 1732, increased the strength of the English settlements, and interposed another barrier between the Indians and Spaniards of Florida and the colonists of Carolina. The Altamaha was claimed as the southern boundary of the new colony, and a settlement of Scotch Highlanders was planted on the banks of that river. A fort was also built at Frederica, to command the approach to the settlements on St. Simon's Island. In the year 1736, the Spanish government, looking upon the settlement of Georgia as an encroachment upon their limits, sent a commissioner to Oglethorpe requiring him at once to surrender and evacuate all the territories south of St. Helena's Sound, as they belonged to the King of Spain, who was determined not to allow of their occupation by any other nation. Oglethorpe maintained the right of the English crown to all the territory occupied by him, and declined to comply with the requirements of the Spanish governor. From the imperious nature of the demand, Oglethorpe rightly conjectured that he might expect an armed invasion of his territory, and proceeded at once to England to direct the attention of the crown to the dangers that menaced the infant colony. English commerce had already suffered severely from the interference of Spain, and a feeling of hostility to the Spanish pretensions occupied the public mind. Supported by the king, and aided by popular sentiment, Oglethorpe was able to make strong preparations for the protection of Georgia against the anticipated attack. He returned in 1739, with the commission of major-general, a regiment of soldiers, and considerable pecuniary aid, and proceeded to erect forts on the coast and put the province in a state of defense. The Spanish force at St. Augustine was also strengthened, and both parties labored assiduously to prepare themselves for the impending conflict by securing the alliance of the Indian tribes of the adjacent regions. Of these tribes the Creeks were the most powerful, and they took the British side of the dispute.

Negotiations were meanwhile pending between the two governments. The English demanded redress for the injuries inflicted on their commerce, for which the Spaniards agreed to award compensation, provided the lands occupied by Oglethorpe were given up to them. This was refused, and the negotiations failed. The Spaniards at St. Augustine sent emissaries to the borders of Carolina to entice away the negroes, promising them freedom and protection. Many negroes had gone to them from time to time,—a sufficient number, it was said, to enable the Spaniards to form a regiment, with officers of their own, placed on the same footing, as to pay and uniform, as the Spanish regulars. In October, 1739, war was declared by Great Britain against Spain, and a squadron was sent to the West Indies to cooperate with General Oglethorpe in his intended operations against the Spanish provinces in Florida. Oglethorpe at once set on foot an expedition to operate against St. Augustine, and visited South Carolina to engage assistance from that colony, which was readily given, and a joint expedition, to operate by land and sea, was agreed upon.

A regiment of four hundred men was raised in Carolina, under Colonel Vanderdussen. The assistance of several Indian tribes was sought, and a naval force, to consist of four twenty-gun ships and two sloops, was to take part in the attack. Oglethorpe had ascertained that the garrison at St. Augustine was not very formidable in point of numbers, and was poorly provisioned, and therefore urged forward his preparations with great vigor, in order to make his attack before they could be reinforced. The expedition was not ready to march, however, before the latter part of April, 1740. In the mean time, the energetic governor of Florida, Don Manuel de Monteano, was making every preparation to strengthen his defenses against the menaced attack of Oglethorpe. The garrison was increased, the approaches to the fort were guarded, and the most urgent solicitations made for a supply of provisions from Cuba. There were at this time several outposts, where a few soldiers, under sub-officers, were stationed. One of these was on Cumberland Island, but was withdrawn on account of its distance and isolation. Another fort, called St. Nicolas, was on the St. John's River, a few miles above its mouth. At Picolata there were two forts: the larger, on the west bank of the river, and called Poppa,* was garrisoned by sixty men; the other, at Picolata, had only ten men. These forts were designed to keep in check the Indians, and to protect the passage of detachments marching from St. Augustine to Apalachee. An attack had been made upon Fort Poppa by a party from the English settlement, in December, which had proved unsuccessful. In January, however,

---

* The remains of Fort Poppa are still visible, near the ferry-house on the west bank of the St. John's River, opposite Picolata.

the fort at Picolata was taken, and Oglethorpe seemed to expect that the garrison at St. Augustine, being short of provisions, would become dissatisfied and desert in large numbers to him, while the rest, when driven into their castle and bombarded, would speedily surrender.* The vessels that composed the English squadron were the Flamborough, Captain Pearce, the Squirrel, Captain Warren, the Phœnix, Captain Fanshaw, and the Tartar, Captain Townshend, each of twenty guns. The force Oglethorpe had at his command in Georgia consisted of a regiment of regulars just arrived from England, a company of Scotch Highlanders from the Altamaha, under Captain McIntosh, and an inconsiderable body of Indians. The place of rendezvous appointed for the land-forces was the mouth of the St. John's River.

Oglethorpe felt the necessity of proceeding with the utmost energy; but, as is usual with such expeditions, made up of contingent forces and without regular military organization and discipline, there were delays, so that it was late in May—the 24th—before the land-forces reached the mouth of the river, about forty miles from St. Augustine.

About midway stood a fort, called San Diego, garrisoned by a few men, who fell back to St. Augustine and left the fort in the hands of Oglethorpe's party. On the 1st of June they reached a small fort, called Fort Moosa, about two miles north of St Augustine, and generally called The Negro Fort, it having been constructed for the fugitive slaves from South Carolina, and used by them as a place of security. This fort is described as being about twenty miles from Fort Diego, and within two miles' distance and in full sight of the castle of St. Augustine, and situated near the creek which runs between Point Cartel

---

* Report of Com. S. C., p. 430.

and the castle up to Fort Diego. Fort Moosa was built in the middle of a plantation, to protect the negroes from the Indians. It was square, with a flanker in each corner, banked around with earth, having a ditch without on all sides lined with prickly palmetto royal, and contained a house, a well, and a lookout. The English found this fort deserted, and, for some reason, concluding to destroy it, the gate and the house within the fort were burnt, and two breaches made in the ramparts, probably with the view of preventing its reoccupation by the enemy. Afterwards, concluding to garrison it, Colonel Palmer was sent there with one hundred and thirty-three men, consisting of McIntosh's Highlanders and some infantry, forty mounted men, and thirty-five Indians. Palmer protested against remaining with so small a force.*

Lieutenant Bryant was sent out to obtain information, and, returning, reported the town to be in great confusion, the inhabitants "screeching and crying," and recommended an immediate attack. Oglethorpe then made a reconnoissance in person, and, concluding that he would not be justified in exposing his men in so hazardous an attempt, determined to fall back to Fort Diego until joined by the remainder of his forces. It was not until the 6th of June that Colonel Vanderdussen arrived with his Carolina regiment, marching along the sea-beach to Point Cartel, and about the same time the fleet took position, and the siege was formally begun on the 20th of June.

On the 24th of June the English opened fire upon the town and castle from three batteries which they had erected on Anastasia Island. One of these batteries was on the point of the island opposite the fort, and consisted of five pieces,—four eighteen-pounders and one nine-

---

* MS. Report of Expedition to St. Augustine, S. C., p. 437.

pounder; another battery was on the margin of some high wooded ground on the same island, and consisted of two eighteen-pounders; the third battery was on the north beach, on North River Point, called San Mateo, and had seven pieces, six of which were of iron and one of bronze. The mortars and "mortarets" were thirty-four in number,—two of large size, two medium, and thirty of small calibre.*

On Sunday night, the 25th of June,† a force of three hundred men attacked Fort Moosa, then held by Colonel Palmer (who, it will be remembered, had remonstrated against being left there with so small a garrison). There had been much dissatisfaction from the first among the officers. Colonel Palmer believed the fort to be untenable, and desired his officers to go out and scout about the country, which they declined doing. There was some difficulty, too, about the command, between Colonel Palmer and Captains McIntosh and McKay, and this led to insubordination, and the garrison was not in condition to make as firm a resistance as would have been otherwise maintained and as might have proved effectual. As it was, they were taken by surprise and overcome.

As there was at that time much discussion and recrimination in reference to this matter, it may be as well to insert, verbatim, the account of one of the party engaged in the affair, as given before an investigating committee of the Carolina House of Assembly. The account is as follows:—

"On the 15th of June, about ten o'clock P.M., one of my rangers reported he had heard the Indian war-dance.

---

* Monteano MS. Dispatch, No. 205.
† The English account says 15th June. The discrepancy may arise from the difference in computation,—Old Style and New Style.

Thereupon Colonel Palmer said we might expect a brush before day, and ordered the men to lie down and take a nap, and he would awake them by three or four o'clock. Accordingly he did so, and all the rangers got up immediately and stood to their arms. Then the colonel went into the fort and aroused the garrison, and, telling them the danger they were in, urged them to stand to their arms. But, as usual, not regarding him, they all lay down again. This put him into a great passion, and, coming out, he said he did not know what they trusted to,—that the Spaniards would surely attack them after the Indian manner, and repeated that the general had sent them there to be sacrificed. He stood for some time after in the gateway, talking with one Jones. On a sudden one of the sentinels called out that there was a party of men coming. Colonel Palmer called out aloud, 'Stand to your arms; not a man of you fire; receive their first fire, then half of you fire and fall back, making room for the rest to come up, and we will kill them like dogs.' Some of the Highlanders, then upon guard in the bastions, fired notwithstanding. Directly the enemy poured in a large volley, upon which the colonel said, 'Are these the men I have to trust to? I thought so before,' and betook himself to the ditch. The rangers, who were about twelve yards without, followed the colonel as he had before directed them, because they would be in as much danger from the fire of the Highlanders within the fort as from the enemy without. Jones ran into the fort and got all the Indians together in one flanker, there being great hurry and confusion among the men, some being dressed and some undressed. Jones went into every flanker three times, yet could not find Captain McIntosh or see anything of the soldiers. He found Captain McKay in one of them, just got up, in his shirt, with a small-sword and a musket. Jones advised Captain McKay to support the gate with the Highlanders, but to no purpose. In the mean time the enemy, attacking in different parties, particularly endeavored to force their way into the fort through the gate. But it was so well defended during a constant fire on all sides for a quarter of an hour, from the two flankers that commanded that side, and by Colonel Palmer, who kept forming and encouraging his men, that they were repulsed twice. At length they came on again, sword in hand, and entered the gate, being led by an officer whom Jones shot at his entrance. At the same time another party entered at one of the breaches, and soon the fort was full of Spaniards, it being now about half an hour before day. McKay immediately jumped over into the ditch, sword in hand, and advised all to shift for themselves. Soon after McIntosh was carried out, a prisoner. They continued some time longer at club-work, cutting and slashing as fast as they could, until, the Spaniards being evidently masters, all that were able jumped into the ditch and made their way off through the enemy that surrounded the fort. Among these were Jones and six Indians, who on their way were joined by Colonel Palmer's two sons, the captain and his brother, and one of the rangers, who all together kept firing as they marched, and so, opening a way for themselves, escaped, Captain Palmer in particular killing a Spanish Indian. All this time Colonel Palmer maintained the ditch, with only two of his company by his side. At last he was shot from within the fort, and, bleeding very much inwardly from the mouth, he yet loaded his gun, and, when almost gone, reeling and panting, he cried out as he fell, 'Huzza, my boys! the day is ours! I have been in many a battle, and never lost one yet!'"

Others escaped to Point Cartel by the creek. Fifty whites and Indians were killed, and twenty prisoners were taken. Colonel Palmer was the only Carolinian killed.

The enemy's force consisted of three hundred forzadas (convicts) and negroes. They lost two officers, including their commander, and had as many killed as the English.*

Governor Monteano says that the attack on Fort Moosa was made with three hundred men, at eleven o'clock at night, with such impetuosity that sixty-eight of the English were left dead on the field and thirty-four were taken prisoners. The English force was stated by prisoners to be from one hundred and forty to one hundred and seventy, of whom thirty-five were Indians, Ychies and Uchies, commanded by a white chief. That an Indian reported he saw the body of Colonel Palmer, headless. Monteano acknowledges the loss of Lieutenant Don José de Aguilar and nine soldiers, and says his forces destroyed the fort and buried the dead.

It appears pretty clearly, from the accounts on both sides, that, although not actually surprised, the greater part of Palmer's forces were entirely unprepared and had made no preparations for a successful resistance. The number of killed would show that there was a somewhat desperate hand-to-hand conflict, and from Colonel Palmer's remark it would appear that many of the English suffered from the misdirected aim of their comrades in the fort.

Disorganization and want of discipline, and the lack of unity in the counsels at Fort Moosa, led to the natural result. The success of the Spaniards greatly encouraged them to make strenuous efforts for the defense of the castle, while the besiegers became depressed and anxious, and

---

* Captain McIntosh, in a letter written while he was a prisoner in Spain, says, " Seven hundred Spaniards sallied out to attack us. They did not surprise us, but put on with numbers. Twenty were taken prisoners, a few got off; the rest killed. The Spaniards lost three hundred killed on the spot, besides wounded."—*MS. in Ga. Hist. Soc. Library; Fairbanks's Hist. St. Augustine*, p. 147.

were daily suffering from the effects of the midsummer heat in this exposed position, where, too, they were annoyed by swarms of insects, from which they could invent no protection.

Oglethorpe, however, proceeded with his offensive operations, and, having completed his first battery, on the 19th of June formally summoned the Spanish garrison to surrender. On the following day, Governor Monteano returned his answer, in which he " swore by the Holy Cross that he would defend the castle to the last drop of his blood, and hoped soon to kiss his Excellencie's hand within its walls." It is said, however, on English authority, that the majority of the people of St. Augustine were in favor of a surrender, on condition that they should be permitted to go to Havana; but the governor and bishop, who, it is said, had come to a knowledge of the time our men-of-war intended to stay, would not consent.* This statement refers to a determination made by the commander of the fleet, and communicated to General Oglethorpe on the 6th of June, that he should deem it unsafe to remain on the coast later than the 5th of July, and which communication may have reached the ears of the Spanish government through deserters,† or through prisoners captured at Fort Moosa. A few days afterwards, some Chickasaw Indians brought into camp the head of a Spanish Indian, and presented it as a trophy to General Oglethorpe, who, wholly unaccustomed to the barbarities of savage warfare, spurned the offering and called the Indians barbarous dogs. This surprised and greatly exasperated them, and they soon after deserted. The batteries continued to play upon the town and fort, but with indifferent success, owing to the

---

* Report of Com. S. C. House of Assembly, pp. 453-4.
† Monteano says a deserter came over on the 14th of June.

short range of the guns and the want of precision in handling them, but still more to the peculiar nature of the material of which the castle was built; being constructed of a stone formed by the aggregation of small shells, thoroughly compacted, soft and yielding in appearance, but offering very much the same resistance to cannon-shot as that of moss or cotton on the face of a sand battery. The balls penetrated the stone to about their own depth, but made no fracture. Probably a continuous battering with modern rifled cannon might have cut through these walls and brought them down; but with such guns as were then used the castle was impregnable. The English claimed that all the shells fired except three broke either in the town or castle; but Monteano, in a report to the governor of Cuba, says that up to the 6th of July, although one hundred and fifty-three shells had fallen, his garrison and people had received no injury.

Oglethorpe knew that the Spaniards were short of provisions, and vigilantly guarded the entrances to St. Augustine by the main bar and Matanzas Inlet, but neglected to blockade a port some sixty miles south, at Mosquito. This port communicated by tide-water within a few miles of the head of the Matanzas River, so that vessels might unload their cargoes at Mosquito, to be transshipped by small boats to the intervening haul-over, and thence again to St. Augustine. It seems a little singular that in this fruitful country the people should have been so entirely dependent upon supplies furnished from abroad; but this was the case with all of the early settlers; and had Oglethorpe effectually blockaded Mosquito, or placed a vessel inside Matanzas River to cut off that communication, the Spanish garrison would soon have been reduced by starvation, for the tenor of Monteano's letters to his superior in Cuba was, "Provisions, or I starve." The communication with Cuba was kept up by way of Apalachee, and also by canoes sent to the Florida Keys, there to connect by fishing-smacks with Cuba.

The Spaniards had within the harbor some half-galleys, upon which they had mounted a few guns, and from time to time greatly annoyed the English by threatening a night-attack, so that they were kept in a continual state of anxiety. On the 1st of July there were fifty reported sick in the English camp, and Captain Wright, with the South Carolina volunteers, determined to return home. About this time, also, several deserters went over to the Spaniards, among them an Irishman,[*] and a man from New England, who reported to Monteano the condition of things in Oglethorpe's garrison. The latter had learned the inefficiency of his batteries, but still hoped to reduce the castle by starvation, until on the 27th of June he was informed by the captain of the vessel which lay off Matanzas Inlet that he had seen lying at Mosquito Bar a large sloop, two schooners, and some launches. Monteano says that on the 7th of July he received intelligence, through Luis Gomez, that vessels had arrived at Mosquito bringing him supplies; so it seems that, allowing for the difference in computation of time between the English and Spaniards, Monteano and Oglethorpe must have been informed about the same time of the arrival of the vessels which brought to the former confidence and relief and to the latter discouragement. On the same day the commander of the fleet informed Oglethorpe that, as the easterly winds were coming in, he felt obliged to ship his anchors and stand off.

Oglethorpe seems to have then concluded to make a night-assault upon St. Augustine, as a deserter informed

---

[*] Bayley, an Irishman, deserted, but was caught by a negro, tried by court-martial, and shot.— *S. C. Rep.*

Monteano of the intention of the English to attack him during one of the dark nights that were approaching. In the mean time, the supply-vessels were safely discharged at Mosquito, and the transshipment by the inland route was commenced and carried on securely, until rendered unnecessary by the removal of the English ships, which made it safe for small vessels to enter at Matanzas Inlet. On the 3d of July Colonel Vanderdussen's scouts on Anastasia Island discovered launches coming up Matanzas River, and he thereupon went with a detachment to the narrows, hoping to cut off the passage of the launches, but was driven off by the armed galleys that now guarded the river. The next day the question of abandoning the siege was discussed by the English commanders, and Colonel Vanderdussen, it is said, was opposed to withdrawing. But Oglethorpe felt that the force at his command was wholly inadequate for prosecuting the siege. Many of his men were sick, the fleet had withdrawn, and, the Spanish garrison having received supplies, there was no longer a hope of reducing them by starvation. It was therefore decided to raise the siege and abandon the enterprise for the present. On the 7th of July most of the guns from the batteries were placed on board the ships, which crossed the bar and went out on the 9th. Three six-pounders were buried in the sand at Point Cartel, and one eighteen-pounder at the battery nearest the fort.

The amount of stores destroyed did not probably exceed one hundred pounds in value. It is said that "the soldiers were loath to part with the liquor, and drank very freely of it." The troops marched on the 10th, with banners flying and drums beating, but were unable to provoke an attack from the Spaniards, Monteano doubtless thinking that "prudence was the better part of valor." The loss at Moosa was the only serious one sustained by the

English in battle. The Carolina regiment lost but eight men by sickness, four by accident, and two by desertion to the enemy. The small number of deaths speaks well for the healthiness of their encampment on Anastasia Island. But the siege was undertaken too late in the season, when there was much unavoidable suffering from the heat and insects, sand-flies and mosquitos, which must of course have interfered seriously with the efficiency of Oglethorpe's small command. Had he arrived sixty days earlier, he might have accomplished more than he did; but it is hardly to be supposed that, with his small numbers and insufficient siege-guns, he could at any season have reduced the castle at St. Augustine, fortified as it was with all the equipments known to the military engineers of that day. The shallowness of the water on the bar prevented the entrance of the English ships to participate in the attack, while the armed galleys of the Spaniards effectually protected the town from assault by small boats. St. Augustine is situated upon a narrow peninsula formed by the Sebastian and Matanzas Rivers, the waters of which are connected by a ditch at the north end of the town, where the fort stands. Palisades and batteries defended the only open side of the town, in front of which a space of fifteen hundred yards was kept clear of all obstructions, so that in order to attack the town from the land-approaches the enemy would have to pass over this open space under fire from the fort, batteries, and earthworks that protected it. If the town itself had been taken, the castle could have sustained a siege, unless forced to surrender for want of provisions. Had Oglethorpe effectually blockaded the ports, including Mosquito Inlet, or had he cut off inland communication with Matanzas River, it would have been almost impossible for Monteano to obtain supplies; but these avenues of communication with the Spanish garrison seem not to have been known or clearly understood by the English commander.

The failure of his expedition created great dissatisfaction in Carolina, and, as usual, recriminations were indulged in; disputes arose between the South Carolina and Georgia partisans, each endeavoring to throw the entire responsibility of the failure upon the other. The disputes were never settled satisfactorily, and criticisms have extended down even to our own time; but the conclusion arrived at by those who have thoroughly examined the matter seems to be, that no blame could be attached to either party, and that the want of success was owing to circumstances over which neither the commander nor his troops had any control. The season was certainly most unfavorable, and the force placed at the control of Oglethorpe was felt by him to be insufficient; but the urgency of the case seemed to admit of no delay, and doubtless, had the attempt not been made, greater dissatisfaction would have been felt than was created by the failure of the expedition. It has been supposed that a discrepancy existed in the English and Spanish reports as to the date at which supplies arrived from Cuba; but this is satisfactorily reconciled by observing that the computation in the Spanish accounts was made according to the New Style, and that in the English by the Old Style.

Monteano was informed by deserters that it was the purpose of Oglethorpe to return in the winter or spring with a larger force; and he accordingly labored with great diligence to strengthen his position, and urged upon the governor of Cuba the necessity of sending him strong reinforcements. The castle had sustained no material injury in the late bombardment, as its walls now, after a lapse of more than one hundred years, attest; but more men were needed, for, according to Monteano's statement, he had a nominal force of seven hundred and fifty men, and of these only three hundred and fifty-six could be relied on for active duty. He asked for three hundred and ninety-four to make up the complement of the garrison, and three hundred more to strengthen it against the return of Oglethorpe;* these three hundred to be "men of arms, mulattoes and free negroes," to be sent out immediately, the regulars and artillery not later than the ensuing December.† He urged constantly upon the governor of Cuba the necessity of sending him reinforcements to meet the apprehended attack of the English; and it undoubtedly was the intention of Oglethorpe to return to St. Augustine whenever he had such force as experience had proved to be necessary.

Eight companies of infantry were sent to Monteano; and in the following spring, finding the attention of the English apparently withdrawn from further offensive operations, he advised the invasion of South Carolina and Georgia. A destructive fire had occurred in Charleston, consuming three hundred of the best buildings in the place; and, the province being greatly depressed by the heavy indebtedness in which the expedition to Florida had involved her, Monteano thought that the misfortunes of his neighbors invited an invasion of their province with the greater promise of success. He hoped to strike them with terror by an attack which would threaten them with an insurrection of their slaves, and which, by the destruction of their city and some of their plantations, would create consternation, and perhaps cause the flight of many.

The proposition of Monteano does not appear to have been acted on immediately, and the year 1741 passed

---

* Monteano MS., Carta de 7 Agosto, 1740.
† Monteano MS.

away without active operations on either side. Preparations were, however, made by the Spaniards with the view of invading the English colonies with a large force in the following spring. Early in the spring of 1742, the governor of Cuba dispatched an expedition designed to operate against the settlements in Georgia. It consisted of some two thousand men, and went first to St. Augustine, where great delay occurred, from the difficulty of organizing that portion of the expedition that was to be formed from the garrison at that place. In the mean time, Oglethorpe was apprised of the proximity of the Spanish fleet. He at once called to his aid the friendly Indians attached to his service, and sent a message to Carolina, urging prompt assistance. No effort was spared to strengthen his position and to use to the best advantage his very limited means, and, without professional engineers, he went to work to construct batteries to command the approach to St. Simon's Island.

The Spanish fleet, consisting of thirty-six sail, received at St. Augustine an additional force of one thousand men, and was placed under the command of Governor Monteano. On the 5th of July, 1742, he entered the harbor of St. Simon's, where he met with strong resistance from Oglethorpe, who had mounted guns on two vessels in the harbor, and kept up a steady fire from these and his batteries on the shore. After four hours' engagement, Monteano succeeded in passing these and getting beyond the range of the guns; whereupon Oglethorpe determined to abandon the works and retire to Frederica. Having destroyed the fort and batteries at St. Simon's, he succeeded in safely retreating to Frederica with several vessels, and there awaited the attack of Monteano. Two days later the Spanish general landed his troops and commenced his march. In order to reach Frederica he was obliged to pass over a narrow causeway through the marshes, and, while crossing this place, he was attacked, and sustained such heavy losses that he fell back to the cover of his camp, leaving many prisoners in the hands of the English. A few days afterwards the Spaniards attempted to ascend the river and attack Frederica by water, but they encountered such a warm reception that they again fell back. Oglethorpe learned that in the action at the causeway Monteano lost four captains and over two hundred men, and that a number had also been killed at the action with the batteries. The English general determined to avail himself of the evident discouragement prevailing in the Spanish camp, and by a night-attack add to their apprehension and dissatisfaction, and accordingly marched his forces to the neighborhood of the Spanish camp. But the desertion of a Frenchman, who betrayed his plans to the enemy, compelled him to abandon the attack. This apparently unfortunate incident was, however, used to good effect by the ready genius of Oglethorpe. Calling in one of his Spanish prisoners, he gave him a sum of money and promised him his liberty if he would carry a letter from him to the French deserter. This letter was in French, and purported to be written by a friend of the Frenchman, desiring him to persuade the Spaniards that the English forces were weak and could be easily overcome; and he was then to induce them (the Spaniards), if possible, to allow him to pilot them up a safe passage to the English fort, but he was to bring them directly upon concealed batteries; and, if the plan was carried out faithfully, the Frenchman was to receive a liberal reward. When the Spaniard arrived in camp, he was carried immediately before the governor and questioned as to his escape and whether he had letters. He said he had none, but, upon being searched, the letter was found. The Frenchman denied knowing the writer of it or anything of its contents; but, on trial, he was condemned as a double spy, and so the object of Oglethorpe's intrigue was effected, in having awakened the distrust of the Spaniards towards the French deserter. Monteano was, however, greatly perplexed by the letter, and re-embarked his troops. Just at this critical time, three vessels, that had been sent from Charleston to aid Oglethorpe, appeared in sight, and Monteano, believing that the English would be heavily reinforced, determined to retire. An attack was made upon Fort William by a portion of the fleet, but was unsuccessful; whereupon the entire Spanish force retired to Cuba and St. Augustine, deeply chagrined at the failure of their enterprise.* There appears to have been a want of cordiality and co-operation between Oglethorpe and the Carolinians on this occasion, caused, it is said, by their distrust of the general's abilities as a military leader,—the unfortunate expedition to St. Augustine being still fresh in their memories; but Oglethorpe's repulse of Monteano restored their confidence and established his reputation as one of the most distinguished colonial governors on this continent. In March of the next year, 1743, Oglethorpe made a sudden descent upon Florida, and marched to the gates of St. Augustine, offering battle, and the Indians attached to his force advanced with so much celerity that they captured and slew forty of the Spanish troops under the very walls of the fort where they were seeking shelter.† The Spaniards refusing to fight, Oglethorpe retired; and, though it was reported that troops were to be sent from Havana to destroy the English colonies, no further hostilities occurred, and comparative peace pre-

---

* General Oglethorpe's letter to the Duke of Newcastle, July 30, 1741.

† General Oglethorpe's letter, 21st March, 1743.

vailed for many years, although the Indians in the Spanish interest continued to molest and ravage the English border settlements. The garrison at St. Augustine was greatly reduced after the necessity for defensive operations had ceased, and in 1759 Governor Palazir reports his command as only five hundred men in all on duty there.

A treaty was concluded between Great Britain and Spain in the year 1748, which caused a suspension of hostilities between the colonies. The progress of French settlements in the West began to create uneasiness, as a conflict of interest threatened between the trading-houses of the three rival nations. Upon the renewal of hostilities between Spain and Great Britain, in 1762, Havana fell into the hands of the English, which at once isolated St. Augustine from its home government and sources of supply. England had long desired to complete her colonial boundaries by the acquisition of Florida, and the capture of Havana seemed to offer a favorable opportunity, by arranging for its transfer to Spain in exchange for Florida. This was effected in concluding the treaty between England, France, and Spain, November 3, 1762, and ratified on the 10th of February, 1763. By this treaty, the provinces of East and West Florida were ceded to Great Britain, and Cuba was restored to Spain.

CHAPTER XV.

Policy of the English Government for the Settlement of Florida—Land-Grants—Dr. Turnbull's Colony of Greeks and Minorcans at Smyrna—Governor Grant's Administration—Governor Tonyn's Administration—First Colonial Assembly—Revolutionary War—Burning of Effigies of Hancock and Adams.

1763—1779.

THE change of flags was excessively distasteful to the Spanish population of Florida. Apart from the feelings engendered by the long continuance of hostilities between themselves and the neighboring English colonies, there was the utter repugnance arising from religious prejudices and traditional animosities, extending back to the days of Henry VIII.

The nineteenth article of the treaty between Spain and England provided that Great Britain should grant to the inhabitants of the countries ceded "the liberty of the Catholic religion, and that his Britannic Majesty will, in consequence, give the most exact and the most effectual orders that his new Roman Catholic subjects may profess the worship of their religion according to the rites of the Roman Church, so far as the laws of Great Britain permit." His majesty further agreed that the Spanish inhabitants or others who have been subjects to the Catholic king in the said countries, may retire in all safety and freedom, etc. These guarantees, though in liberality and toleration far in advance of the principles and practice of the Catholic King of Spain, were insufficient to overcome the repugnance of the inhabitants to passing under the domination of England.

On the 7th of October, 1763, the King of Great Britain, taking into consideration the extensive and valuable acquisitions in America secured to his crown by the treaty of the preceding year, issued a royal proclamation, in which he declared that, with the advice of his privy council, he had granted letters-patent, under the great seal, "to erect, within the countries and islands ceded and confirmed to us by the said treaty, four distinct and separate governments, styled and called by the names of Quebec, East Florida, West Florida, and Granada."

The government of East Florida was declared to be bounded to the westward by the Gulf of Mexico and the Apalachicola River; to the northward, by a line drawn from that part of the said river where the Chattahoochee and Flint Rivers meet, to the source of the St. Mary's River, and by the course of the said river to the Atlantic Ocean; and to the eastward and southward, by the Gulf of Florida, including all islands within six leagues of the sea-coast.

The government of West Florida was declared to be bounded to the southward by the Gulf of Mexico, including all islands within six leagues of the sea-coast, from the river Apalachicola to Lake Pontchartrain; to the westward, by said lake, the Lake Maurepas, and the river Mississippi; to the northward, by a line drawn due east from that part of the river Mississippi which lies in thirty-one degrees (31°) of north latitude, to the river Apalachicola or Chattahoochee; and to the eastward, by said river.

It will thus be seen that Florida in 1763 embraced all of the coast of Alabama, Mississippi, and a part of that of Louisiana.

The letters-patent constituting the new governments gave express power and directions to the governors of the respective provinces, that, so soon as the state of the colonies would admit, they should, with the advice and consent of the members of their several councils, summon General Assemblies within their respective governments, in such manner and form as were used and directed in those colonies and provinces in America which were under the king's immediate government. Power was also given to the said governors, with the consent of the councils and the representatives of the people, to make laws for the public peace, welfare, and good government as nearly as might be agreeable to the laws of England, and under such regulations and restrictions as were used in other colonies; and until such assemblies could be called, the governors, with the assent of their respective councils, were authorized to establish courts of judicature in their respective colonies.

This was the first admission of representative government within the bounds of Florida, and indicates the source of the unexampled prosperity which attended the efforts of Great Britain in the work of colonization. The narrow and autocratic regulations with which other powers had endeavored to regulate their colonial dependencies, and which were aggravated by the distance from the seat of power, gave no voice in the government to the colonists, and had a tendency to repress all enterprise and chill all public spirit. Colonies are usually increased by the favorble representations of their first settlers; and their opinions will be influenced, favorably or otherwise, quite as much by the institutions of a country as by its physical advantages.

The Spanish system of colonial administration advanced none of the material interests of the country, and the government never treated the inhabitants as capable of self-government, but collected around its garrisoned posts a crowd of parasites and dependents, who were contented to live in safety under its protection, satisfied with salaries and petty employments.

With the view of encouraging the speedy settlement of the newly-acquired territories, the English governors were empowered and directed to grant lands, without fee or reward, to such reduced officers as had served during the late war, and to such private soldiers as had been or should be disbanded in America, and were actually residing there, and should personally apply for such grants, subject, at the expiration of ten years, to the same quit-rents as other lands in the provinces in which they were granted, as also to the same conditions of cultivation and improvement. These grants were to be proportioned to the rank of the applicants. A field-officer was to receive five thousand acres; a captain, three thousand; a subaltern or staff-officer, two thousand; every non-commissioned officer, two hundred acres; and every private soldier, fifty acres.

At the period of the cession of Florida, the Spanish flag had floated over the city of St. Augustine for one hundred and ninety years. Within that period, the French had made settlements in Louisiana, and on the Mississippi from its mouth to the Falls of St. Anthony, and thence eastward along the great lakes to the Gulf of St. Lawrence, as well as on the Ohio and other principal rivers. The English had occupied the whole Atlantic seaboard with her colonies, which now comprised a population of nearly three millions. At the close of nearly two hundred years from her occupation of Florida, Spain occupied but little more territory than at the beginning; and the entire population of Florida at the time of the cession hardly exceeded six or seven thousand, and the interior of the country was almost as much of a wilderness as ever. The Spanish population was gathered within the towns of St. Augustine and Pensacola and Mobile, and hardly any agricultural population existed. The people were mostly dependents upon the military and civic employment of the government, and seem to have been greatly deficient in industry and enterprise.

The change of government of course involved the loss of official employment, and this portion of the inhabitants withdrew at once to the West Indies and Mexico. The oppressive conduct of Major Ogilvie, who held the temporary command of the province immediately after its cession, is said to have had much influence upon the removal of the Spanish inhabitants, which was so complete that not more than five persons remained; and had it not been for the efforts of the commanding officer the retiring inhabitants would have destroyed every house and building in St. Augustine. The governor destroyed his fine garden, and the inhabitants before they left not only assumed to sell their houses in town, but the whole country, to a few gentlemen who remained there for that purpose.*

General James Grant was appointed the first English governor of East Florida in 1763, and proceeded to adopt the most salutary measures to promote the settlement of the province and to develop its resources. In a proclamation, issued in October, 1767, he especially refers to the great salubrity of the country and the extreme age which its inhabitants had attained. He refers also to the advantages which the climate offers for the production of indigo and the fruits and tropical productions of the West Indies.

Under the impetus of the patronage of the government,

---

* Forbes's Florida, p. 18.

attention was drawn to Florida, and emigration from the British Islands to its shores encouraged. Public roads were laid out, and so well constructed that they remain to this day the best roads in the State, and are still known as the "king's roads." Bounties were offered upon indigo, naval stores, etc., in order to stimulate their production. Pamphlets descriptive of the country were issued in England, and letters recounting its many advantages appeared in the newspaper publications of the day, and two or more works with engraved illustrations were issued from the press.*

In the year 1765, a general council of the western tribes of Indians was held at Mobile, attended by the head-men and warriors of the Chickasaws and Choctaws, and by the British governor of West Florida. At this council a tariff of trade was settled to the satisfaction of the Indians.

The road from Fort Barrington, on the St. Mary's, to St. Augustine, now called the King's Road, was constructed in 1765 by the subscription of several public-spirited gentlemen, among whom were Governors Grant and Moultrie, and Messrs. Forbes, Fish, Izard, Pinckney, Gerard, Walton, Manigault, Oswald, Huger, Henry, Laurens, Elliot, Murray, and others, names which indicate that the distinguished families of South Carolina bearing those names once belonged to Florida.†

A considerable emigration, consisting of some forty families, went from Bermuda, in 1766, to Mosquito, with the purpose of applying themselves to ship-building. The fine groves of live-oak in that neighborhood had attracted the attention of the British government, and the abundant supply of ship-timber was considered among the most valuable fruits of the acquisition of Florida.

---

* Roberts's Florida, London.
† Forbes's Florida, 73; Stark's Florida, London.

An association was formed in London, at the head of which was Dr. Andrew Turnbull, a Scotch gentleman, having in view the settlement of the large and very valuable body of land lying near Mosquito Inlet. They proposed to accomplish this purpose by procuring settlers from the south of Europe and the Mediterranean islands of Minorca, etc., who, living in a similar climate, might successfully transplant to and cultivate the productions of their country on the rich lands of Florida.

Sir William Duncan and Dr. Turnbull, at an expense of one hundred and sixty-six thousand dollars, brought from Smyrna, under indentures, fifteen hundred Greeks, Italians, and Minorcans, who formed a settlement at Mosquito and called it New Smyrna. Their indentures required them, in consideration of the sums paid for their passage and support, to labor for the proprietors a certain number of years, at the end of which they were to be entitled to receive grants of land in proportion to the number of persons in their families. The location of the settlement was well chosen, on the line below the region of frost, situated upon a river abounding in fish, turtle, and oysters, with a rich and productive soil, in the hammocks bordered by pine ridges favorable to health. Much labor was expended in opening canals and ditches, and in making various permanent improvements, among which was the stone wharf which still remains. The operations of the colony were carried on with much system, and, it is said, with success. Indigo and sugar were the principal articles cultivated, but the vine and fig were planted.

The settlement of the new town of Pensacola, upon the mainland, where it now stands, had been commenced by the Spanish inhabitants before the cession, and the old settlement on Santa Rosa Island almost entirely abandoned. The arrival of the English gave an impulse to the growth of the new city, and its being now made the capital of the colonial government of the province of West Florida, and the presence of a large garrison, for whose accommodation extensive barracks were constructed, made it a place of considerable importance. The expenditures of the British government in carrying on the government of West Florida during the last three years of the English occupation amounted to the large sum of four hundred and five thousand pounds. Those for East Florida, during the same period, were about one hundred and thirty-five thousand pounds. The expenditures of the Spanish government were for both provinces about one hundred and fifty thousand dollars per annum. The population of West Florida did not increase so rapidly as that of the eastern province, being more distant and less accessible from the Atlantic coast. There seems to have been the usual amount of provincial intrigue and local politics in West Florida, as in other small communities.*

Published letters, written by officers of the garrison at

---

* One of the officers, writing from Pensacola in 1770, says, "Affairs in our unlucky province have as yet been upon a very unstable footing. Whether this ill fate is still doomed to be our lot, or whether we are about to emerge from such unhappy circumstances, a little time will discover."

"Pensacola has been justly famed for vexatious lawsuits. It is contrived, indeed, that if a poor man owes but five pounds, and has not got so much ready money, or if he disputes some dollars of imposition that may be in the account, or if he is guilty of shaking his fist at any rascal that has abused him, he is sure to be prosecuted; and the costs of every suit are about seven pounds sterling . . . I have known this province for a little more than four years, yet I could name to you a set of men who may brag of one governor resigned, one horse-whipped, and one whom they led by the nose and supported while it suited their purpose and then betrayed him. What the next turn of affairs will be, God knows."—*Forbes*, p. 180.

Pensacola, abound with unfavorable criticisms upon the place and its society. One is often forced to observe how apt persons composing such limited circles are to be engrossed with the petty details of their narrow limits, to exaggerate their inconveniences, magnify their own troubles, and gossip freely of their neighbors; imputing sometimes the grossest derelictions in morals upon mere conjecture, and illustrating in a thousand ways the weaknesses and infirmities of poor human nature. The history of every colony is replete with discussions, backbitings, jealousies, conspiracies, harsh oppression, unjustifiable revenge, and often bloody retribution. Exiled far from their homes, and requiring every alleviation of sympathy and mutual aid, the colonists oftentimes appeared to exhibit the spirit of the Evil One, increasing and embittering the unavoidable hardships and privations of their position.

Many writers have labored to frame a theoretical form of government which should be adapted to human society, wherein all the acknowledged evils and misfortunes of existing social organization should be remedied, the evil tendencies of human nature corrected, its good impulses excited, all that is venerable, good, and pure respected, virtue occupying high places, and the law of justice universally acknowledged. While these theorists might well say to their objectors that no sufficient test could be applied in the midst of old and organized societies, they would find it impossible to deny that in the settlements of the New World, where the fairest field existed for the successful reformation of the abuses of old societies, these evils became intensified, selfishness exhibiting itself as the main principle of action, and these new settlements were, for the most part, the most wretchedly disagreeable, unsatisfying, and miserable assemblages of people which could anywhere be found. Those who will carefully peruse the annals of our early colonial settlements will find abundant proof of these observations.

Many grants of land were made in the province of West Florida in 1776, under the regulations established by the crown, and were mostly located along the banks of the rivers.

An eminent naturalist, who visited Pensacola in the year 1778, says there were at that time some hundreds of houses. The palace of Governor Chester was a large stone edifice, surmounted with a tower, which had been built by the Spaniards. The city was defended by a large fortress, the plan of which was a tetragon, having at each corner a salient angle, and a small round tower was elevated one story above the curtains, upon which were placed the smaller cannon. The fort was constructed of timber: there were contained within the walls the council-chamber, office of records, an arsenal, and magazine, with lodgings for the garrison.* There were in the city many merchants and professional gentlemen, who occupied well-built houses. A fort also existed on the point of Santa Rosa Island, which defended the entrance to the harbor.

General Grant continued to fill the office of governor of East Florida from 1763 to 1771, and, by his wise and judicious administration of public affairs, acquired the respect and affection of his people, as well as the confidence of the home government. During this period the colony received a large accession of inhabitants of the best class from Carolina, among whom was Major Moultrie, afterwards lieutenant-governor of the province, and William Drayton, Esq., who became chief-justice. Several English noblemen, among whom were Lords Granville, Hillsborough, Egmont, and Hawke, received large grants of land

---

* Bartram's Rep. Florida, vol. ii. p. 252.

upon the condition of settlement and cultivation. Several gentlemen of fortune also procured land, upon the same conditions, among the most prominent of whom were Richard Oswald and Dennis Rolle. Mr. Oswald established a plantation on the Halifax River, at a place still known as Mount Oswald. Dennis Rolle, Esq., father of Lord Rolle, obtained from the British government a grant of forty thousand acres, and embarked in 1765 from England with one hundred families, intending to settle in Middle Florida near St. Mark's; but, being driven by stress of weather to enter the St. John's River, and wearied with having been a long time on shipboard, he decided to remain, and selected a location on the east side of the St. John's River, two or three miles above Pilatka, which he named Charlottia,* and made his settlement between this point and Dunn's Lake. After incurring very great expense, the settlement, owing to the bad management of his agents, was abandoned, and most of the settlers removed to Carolina.† Traces of the old settlement are still to be seen.

There was a large plantation opened about the same time on the upper St. John's, known as Beresford, and still bearing that name, and another at Spring Garden. A colony of Scotch Highlanders made a settlement on the St. John's River, and afterwards removed to Georgia. The cultivation of sugar-cane was begun on the Halifax River, and, under the fostering care of the British government, would, in the course of a few years, have become a very important staple of Florida.

The colony established by Dr. Turnbull at New Smyrna in 1767 remained until 1776. Having put the land in a proper condition for cultivation, they turned their atten-

---

* This place is still known as Rollstown.
† Bartram, vol. i 177.

tion to the production of indigo, which then bore a high price in the London market. The net value of their first crop reached the sum of three thousand dollars; but difficulties soon arose between the proprietors and the colonists, the latter alleging that the former had not complied with their agreements, and that they were restricted in the quantity of provisions allowed them, and otherwise treated with great tyranny and injustice.

In 1769 an insurrection had taken place among them, in consequence of the infliction of severe punishments upon some of their number. The insurrection was put down, and the leaders brought to St. Augustine for trial: five of the number were convicted and sentenced to death, two of whom were pardoned by the governor, and a third was released upon the condition of his becoming the executioner of the remaining two.

The Smyrna colony upon its establishment consisted of fourteen hundred persons, but in nine years their numbers had become reduced, by sickness, to about six hundred. In the year 1776, two of their number came to St. Augustine, and placed before the attorney-general, Mr. Yonge, a statement of their wrongs and grievances, with the view of finding some means by which they might be relieved from their indentures, and from the thraldom in which they were held by the proprietors.

The statement of the cruelties practiced upon these colonists, it is presumable, is greatly exaggerated, as it does not seem probable that a course so opposed to the dictates of humanity, and not less so to those of self-interest, should have been pursued.

Proceedings were instituted in the civil tribunals at St. Augustine, which resulted in a decree requiring the indentures to be cancelled and the colonists released from their engagements to the proprietors. Liberal offers were now made to retain them as freeholders, and to continue the cultivation of their lands; but the colonists had suffered so greatly from sickness and trouble that they were unwilling to remain. The entire number removed to St. Augustine, where they received allotments of land in the northern part of the city, which are occupied by their descendants at the present day.

Of the character of Dr. Turnbull we have little knowledge, except the prejudicial inferences to be derived from this transaction. He was a Scotchman, and undoubtedly strict and exacting in business matters. His position in the province appears to have been highly respectable, as he was one of the privy council, and possessed great weight in the management of the affairs of the province, and it was expected that he would be appointed governor to succeed Governor Grant in 1771. The colony which he established at New Smyrna must have proved almost a total loss to him, as it was abandoned before it could have reached the point of success when it would have proved remunerative. The location, although a highly favorable one, has never been reoccupied to the same extent; but it is not unlikely that at some future day the lands first settled by the Greek colonists will be the centre of a highly cultivated and wealthy community.

Governor Grant retired from office in 1771, and was succeeded by Lieutenant-Governor Moultrie, who had acquired some reputation in the Cherokee war under Colonel Montgomery. Governor Moultrie was a brother of General Moultrie, a conspicuous officer of the American army in the Revolutionary War. The chief-justice of the province, William Drayton, a gentleman of high social position and much political influence, was unwilling to yield to Major Moultrie the deference which he claimed in his new position, and these gentlemen were soon at variance in respect to all public measures, and the chief-justice, having taken means to thwart the lieutenant-governor in his official acts, was suspended from his office by Governor Moultrie. Mr. Drayton was charged with being friendly to the revolutionary party in the American colonies, and his appeal to the English ministry for reinstatement to his office was unsuccessful. He retired from East Florida, and, after remaining some time in England, went to South Carolina, where he bore a conspicuous part in the struggle for American independence.* One of the assistant judges was appointed by Governor Moultrie to the place of chief-justice, but, being suspected of republican principles, his appointment was not confirmed, and a new appointee was sent to fill the place.

In 1774, Governor Tonyn came out from England to assume the government of East Florida. Upon his arrival, he issued a proclamation to the loyalists of the colonies of Georgia, South Carolina, etc., inviting them to remove to Florida, and promising them the protection and patronage of the government. A considerable number availed themselves of his invitation, and settled upon plantations in the neighborhood of St. Augustine.

The transfer of Florida from Spain to Great Britain was too recent, and was too great and favorable a change from its former condition, to allow of the growth of the feeling of disaffection which pervaded the other North American colonies. There were, however, some who sympathized very strongly with the movements of the republicans, and shared their opinions. Upon the news of the adoption by Congress of the Declaration of Independence being received at St. Augustine, the effigies of John Adams and John Hancock were burnt upon the public square at St. Augustine, on the spot where the monument now stands.

---

* Forbes's Sketches of Florida, p. 22.

A British vessel, called the Betsey, commanded by Captain Lofthouse, sent from London, and having on board one hundred and eleven barrels of powder, was captured off St. Augustine bar, in August, 1775, by a privateer from Carolina, which ran alongside and discharged her in sight of the ships of war in the harbor and in plain view of the garrison. This capture was very mortifying to the governor, and, in order to avenge the insult, he immediately ordered a predatory expedition to advance upon the frontier settlements of Georgia. The expedition was placed under the command of Colonel Brown, who afterwards became very prominent as a partisan leader, and was one of the most successful and enterprising officers in the British service. His force was made up of Indians and irregular troops. Privateers were also fitted out, and a fort erected at the mouth of the St. Mary's for their protection and that of their prizes.

East Florida, with the inauguration of active hostilities between Great Britain and her colonies, began to assume more importance as a rendezvous and base of operations. The governor called out the militia, in the summer of 1776, to join the royal troops in resisting what he called "the perfidious insinuations" of the neighboring colonists, and repelling their future incursions into the province, and to prevent any more infatuated men from joining their "traitorous neighbors." It would appear from this that some persons from Florida had joined the Americans.

President Gwinnett, of Georgia, issued a counter-proclamation, offering protection to the persons and property of those "who would join the American standard in opposition to tyranny."*

In addition to the rangers, who were considered as reg-

---

* Forbes's Sketches, p. 26.

ularly enrolled, there was a volunteer militia, organized and officered under their own choice when called out. Many loyalists now began to arrive from Georgia and Carolina, who increased the effective strength of the province, as well as introduced an element of additional bitterness towards the rebel colonies.

An invasion of Florida was now contemplated by the patriots in Georgia, and forces for that purpose directed to assemble in Burke County, to march from thence, under command of the governor, against Florida; but the purpose was not carried into effect. The province was at the same time threatened by the Indian tribes friendly to the American cause.

Captain Elphinstone, of the navy, and Captain Moncrief, a distinguished officer of the engineer corps, having arrived at St. Augustine with a promise of reinforcements, the fears of an invasion were allayed, and an expedition against Georgia was fitted out and placed under the command of Colonel Fuser, of the 60th Regiment, who, with a force of five hundred infantry and the aid of several pieces of artillery, made an attack on Sunbury. He failed in the object of his expedition, and fell back into Florida to await promised reinforcements.

During the year 1778 nearly seven thousand loyalists from Carolina and Georgia moved into Florida. Among those who came in 1777 was one Captain Roderick McIntosh, better known as Rory McIntosh, who had been with the company of Highlanders who were surprised at Fort Moosa in 1740, in the Oglethorpe expedition. At the time he went to Florida he was sixty-five years of age, about six feet in stature, strongly built, with white frizzled bushy hair, fresh complexion, and large muscular limbs. In 1763 he carried a drove of cattle to St. Augustine, and received his pay in Spanish dollars, which, putting in a canvas bag, he carried on his horse. Some miles from home the bag gave way, and part of the money fell out. Paying no attention to what had fallen, he fastened the sack and went on, and some years afterwards, being in want of money, he returned to the spot and picked up the amount he required. He had a favorite dog, which he had taught to track his back scent. On one occasion he laid a wager that he would hide a doubloon and send his dog back three miles to fetch it. The dog returned without it. "Treason!" cried Rory, and returned to the log under which he had hidden the gold, but found it had been removed. Seeing a man in a field some distance off, he galloped up to him, and, drawing a dirk, threatened to kill him unless he produced the piece of gold, which the man surrendered. Rory threw it back to him. "Take it, vile caitiff!" said he; "it was not the pelf, but the honor of my dog, I cared for!"*

Governor Houston of Georgia, in conjunction with General Howe, projected an attack upon St. Augustine in the spring of 1778; but, owing to sickness among the troops, disagreements among the commanders, and deficiency of supplies, the expedition was not carried out. To meet this attack, a force was organized in Florida, to proceed from St. Augustine, under command of Captain Mowbray, of the navy, and Major Graham, of the 16th Regiment, with one hundred and forty men, and Major Prevost, of the 60th, the whole force being under the command of Colonel Fuser, of the 60th Regiment. From the same causes which paralyzed the movements of the American expedition,—the disagreement and jealousies of the commanders of different arms of the service,—the English forces did not cross the St. John's, but contented themselves with erecting

---

* White's Georgia.

a fortification at St. John's Bluff. Colonel Fuser also ordered out all the militia of the province to resist the anticipated invasion.

Further alarm was created in the province, at this juncture, by the sudden death of Captain Skinner, Deputy Superintendent of Indian Affairs, an active and energetic officer. The expedition of the Americans against St. Augustine, if it had been carried out, would probably have met with entire success, as the English forces were then weak in numbers and divided in counsels.

CHAPTER XVI.

English Occupation, continued—Capture of Pensacola by De Galvez—Capture of New Providence by the English—Retransfer of Florida to Spain.

1779—1784.

REINFORCEMENTS having been received at St. Augustine, Major Prevost, who had been promoted to the rank of general, leaving the militia to guard the province, advanced, in December, 1778, to join the forces on their way from New York to attack Savannah. Rory McIntosh had attached himself to the 60th Regiment, which was engaged in this expedition. On their way the English forces laid siege to the fort at Sunbury, commanded by Captain, afterwards General, McIntosh, the same officer who had been taken prisoner by the Spaniards in 1740 at Fort Moosa. Rory McIntosh was in the British lines, in front of the fort at Sunbury. Early one morning, when he had imbibed rather too freely of mountain-dew, he insisted on sallying out to demand the surrender of the fort. His friends could not restrain him, and out he marched, claymore in hand, followed by his slave Tom, and, approaching the fort, roared out, "Surrender, you miscreants! how dare you presume to resist his Majesty's arms?" Captain McIntosh, the commander of the fort, knew him, and, seeing his condition, forbade any one firing on him, and, throwing open the gate, said, "Walk in, Mr. McIntosh, and take possession." "No," said Rory, "I will not trust myself among such vermin; but I order you to surrender." Some one fired a rifle at him, the ball from which passed through his face immediately below his eyes. Stumbling, he fell, but recovered, and retreated backwards, flourishing his sword. Several shots followed, and Tom called out, "Run, massa! dey kill you." "Run, poor slave," says Rory; "thou mayest run, but I am of a race that never runs,"* and succeeded in getting back safely into the lines.†

The attack upon the fort at Sunbury and Savannah, under General Prevost, proved successful, and that officer's gallant defence of Savannah against the combined attack of the forces of D'Estaing and Lincoln, in 1779, added very greatly to his reputation.

Don Bernardo de Galvez, a young and enterprising Spanish general, had been placed in command of the Spanish possessions west of the Mississippi, and of New Orleans and its dependencies. Upon the breaking out of hostilities between England and Spain, in September, 1779, he invested the English fort at Baton Rouge, which was within the then limits of West Florida. Lieutenant-Colonel Dickson, who was in command, found himself unable to resist the forces brought against him, and surrendered to De Galvez.

After Charleston had fallen into the hands of the British forces, the general in command at that place, in order to remove from Carolina those whom he supposed to have been the principal promoters of the Revolutionary cause, caused some forty gentlemen, of high standing, to be

---

* White's Ga. Hist. Coll., p. 471.

† When at St. Augustine, upon one occasion, Rory was introduced to a Scotch gentleman of the name of Morrison. Rory addressed him in Gaelic. Mr. Morrison regretted his ignorance of that language. "I pity you," said Rory; "but you may be an honest man, for all that." —*White's Ga. Hist. Coll.*, p. 470.

transferred, in August, 1780, to St. Augustine, and at a later period twenty-one others were forwarded to the same point.

The following list comprises the names of these distinguished prisoners of state: John Budd, Edward Blake, Joseph Bee, Richard Beresford, John Berwick, D. Bordeaux, Robert Cochrane, Benjamin Cudworth, H. V. Crouch, J. S. Cripps, Edward Darrell, Daniel Dessaussure, John Edwards, George Flagg, Thomas Ferguson, General A. C. Gadsden, Wm. Hazel Gibbs, Thomas Grinball, William Hall, Thomas Hall, George A. Hall, Isaac Holmes, Thomas Heyward, Jr., Richard Hutson, Noble Wimberley Jones, William Johnstone, William Lee, Richard Lushington, William Logan, Rev. John Lewis, William Massey, Alexander Moultrie, Arthur Middleton, Edward McCready, John Mouatt, Edward North, John Neufville, Joseph Parker, Christopher Peters, Benjamin Postell, Samuel Prioleau, John Ernest Poyas, Edward Rutledge, Hugh Rutledge, John Sansom, Thomas Savage, Josiah Smith, Thomas Singleton, James Hampden Thompson, John Todd, Peter Timothy, Anthony Toomer, Edward Weyman, Benjamin Waller, Morton Wilkinson, and James Wakefield. Subsequently, General Rutherford and Colonel Isaacs, of North Carolina, were added to their number. These gentlemen were taken early in the morning from their beds, and placed on the vessels, in violation of the paroles which had been granted to them.[*] Upon their arrival at St. Augustine, upon giving new paroles, they were allowed the freedom of the city. General Gadsden refused to accept a parole, and, with a sturdy independence, bore a close confinement in the castle for forty-two weeks, rather than give a second parole to a power which had violated the

---

[*] Ramsay's Hist. of S. C., vol. i. pp. 370–373.

engagements contained in the first. These prisoners of state were officially treated with great indignities at St. Augustine, and were annoyed by being informed of several decisive battles, which were represented as having destroyed all chance of success by the rebels, and told to expect the fate of vanquished rebels; they were also told, from high authority, that the blood of the brave but unfortunate André would be required at their hands, and were cut off from all intelligence of their friends. The English governor, Patrick Tonyn, in an official letter to Lord St. Germain, says that "to prevent" these rebel prisoners "from poisoning the minds of the people, and for their former conduct, they are treated with great contempt, and to have any friendly intercourse with them is considered as a mark of disrespect to his Majesty and displeasing to me." This conduct, it is said, tended to increase the number of the disaffected rather than to excite the inhabitants to acts of aggression against them. These prisoners remained at St. Augustine nearly a year, when they were sent to Philadelphia, to be exchanged at the general exchange of prisoners in the year 1781.

An order was issued in 1780, by Sir Guy Carleton, directing the entire evacuation of the province of East Florida, but, remonstrances having been forwarded, the order was countermanded.*

The letters-patent of the king, in 1763, upon the occupation of Florida, had provided that the governors of the colonies, so soon as the state of the country would admit, should summon General Assemblies. This, however, had never been carried into effect in Florida during the seventeen years of British occupation, the governors having availed themselves of the discretionary power placed in

---

* Forbes's Florida, p. 50.

their hands as to the period of calling such Assemblies, and being quite willing to withhold as long as possible a partition of power. In 1780, the state of public opinion in the province forced Governor Tonyn, apparently a weak-minded and conceited individual, to call a General Assembly, which assembled in December, 1780.

This step was taken very reluctantly by the governor. In a dispatch to the British Secretary of State, he says, "I have, my lord, maturely weighed the expediency, necessity, advantages and disadvantages, benefits and danger, of convoking a House of Representatives, and nothing but the necessity of it (to remove deep-rooted prejudices) for the benefit of this province could have induced me to request instructions from your lordship relative thereto, how to proceed further on this point; but these great objects must actuate my conduct, and determine me to take this arduous and dangerous step. I perceive the cry for a provincial legislature to remedy local inconveniences is as loud as ever, and suggestions are thrown out, that without it people's property is not secure, and that they must live in a country where they can enjoy to their utmost extent the advantages of the British Constitution and laws formed with their consent. But mention the expediency, propriety, reasonableness, justice, and gratitude of imposing taxes for the expenses of government, they are all silent, or so exceedingly poor as not to be able to pay the least farthing."*

In a dispatch of January, 1781, the governor informs the Secretary of State that the first General Assembly of the province had met, and that the freeholders had elected the most substantial, sensible, and best-affected persons in the province as their representatives. The business was

---

* Forbes's Sketches, p. 35.

transacted with moderation and zeal, and the governor seems to have been relieved of the fear of revolutionary tendencies, very naturally suggested by the example of the neighboring American colonial assemblies. If there were any in the Provincial Legislature of Florida who had sympathies with the American cause, they must have been too few in number to make any demonstration. The Assembly appears to have confined itself to the enactment of a few laws of local importance, and the organization of a militia force.

The governor made an address to the two Houses at the opening of the session, in which he congratulates them that during his administration of the government the province had arrived at such a state of affluence and importance as to enable him with propriety to fulfill his Majesty's most gracious engagements in his Royal Proclamation of the 7th of October, 1763, by establishing a Provincial Legislature, for the purpose of making constitutions, ordaining laws, statutes, and ordinances, as near as may be agreeable to the laws of England, under such regulations and restrictions as are used in other colonies, for the public welfare and good government of the province and its inhabitants. "Of late," he says, "the increase of property from your success in commerce and planting has been considerable, and the industry and the judgment of a few may evince to Great Britain that ample returns in produce may be made for money laid out in raising a produce equally beneficial to the planter and mother-country, in one of the most healthy and fertile climates upon earth."[*]

The condition of the province at this period appears to have been prosperous, and, by the influx of a hardy race of planters from Georgia and Carolina, experienced in

---

[*] Forbes's Sketches, p. 47.

farming and inured to the difficulties and obstacles attending new settlements, a new impetus had been given, and the province had attained a position which promised to make it, aided by the fostering power of the home government, quite as prosperous as the other colonies. The commerce of the colony had steadily increased, the agricultural productions, stimulated by the liberal bounties offered upon indigo, rice, and naval stores, had been constantly growing larger, and nothing seemed now to forbid the hope that Florida would become one of the most productive and valuable of the English transatlantic possessions. The climate, especially upon the coast, had proved eminently favorable to health, and the variety and value of its natural productions gave promise of a bountiful reward to industry and labor. All who had explored Florida gave animated accounts of the beauty of its forests, lakes, and rivers, the wonderful growth of vegetation along its streams, and its adaptation to all the productions of the tropics. Among the most valuable articles which could be profitably cultivated were enumerated sugar-cane, cotton, rice, indigo, oranges, lemons, figs, grapes, bananas, pineapples, etc., while the forests abounded in timber of the best description, and the waters teemed with fish, oysters, and turtles. It is hardly to be doubted that had Florida remained a British colony it would at this time have equaled any of the seaboard States of the South in population. One can even now hardly penetrate a swamp or hammock along the Atlantic coast of Florida without finding distinct traces of the English cultivation and remains of improvements made by them.

As an evidence of the healthiness of the country, the important fact may be referred to that the 9th British Regiment remained in St. Augustine eighteen months without losing a single man by sickness; and it was also observed that a detachment of artillery which arrived from the West Indies with a great deal of sickness soon recruited, and left no traces of the contagious disease from which it had suffered. During the whole period of the British occupation there were but ten medical men in East Florida. Mr. Rolle, under date of September 1, 1766, indicates the favorable impression made upon him by saying, "Everything in nature seems to correspond towards the cultivation of the productions of the whole world, in some part or other of this happy province,—the most precious jewel of his Majesty's American dominions."

The exports of the province of East Florida amounted in 1768 to the sum of £14,078; in 1778 they had increased to £48,236; in 1781 they were £30,715.

During the year 1770 there were fifty schooners entered the port of St. Augustine coastwise, besides several square-rigged vessels in the trade to London and Liverpool. In 1771, five vessels arrived at St. Augustine from London, seven from New York, and eleven from Charleston; and there were imported into the province about one thousand negroes, of whom one hundred and nineteen were directly from Africa.

The Florida indigo brought the highest price of any sold in the London market. Forty thousand pounds were exported in 1772. During the year 1779, forty thousand barrels of naval stores were shipped, and an increase in the quantity was anticipated the following year. The British government allowed the very liberal bounty of ten shillings per barrel upon turpentine shipped from Florida; its value at St. Augustine was thirty-six shillings per barrel.

A large trade was also carried on in peltries by several Indian trading-houses, among the more important of whom were Panton & Leslie, Spaulding, Kelsull, McLatchie, Swanson, and McGillivray & Strother; and in West

Florida by Panton, Leslie & Forbes, and Matthew & Morgan.

The Spanish governor of Louisiana, Don Bernardo de Galvez, who had captured in 1779 the English post at Baton Rouge, made an investment of Pensacola with a vastly superior force, in March, 1781, assisted by a naval force under Admiral Solana. The place was strongly fortified, and held by a garrison of one thousand men, under the command of General Campbell. The English occupied two strong forts, called St. Michel and St. Bernard, which were bravely defended for a long time against the heavy bombardment of the troops of Galvez and the ships of Solana. The Spaniards were able to make no impression on the works until an unlucky accident occurred, by a chance shell entering the magazine of Fort St. Michel at the moment it was opened to take out ammunition. This explosion carried away the principal redoubt, and enabled the Spanish troops to possess themselves of Fort St. Michel. Preparations were then made to avail themselves of the position, in order to carry Fort St. Bernard by assault. Being satisfied that St. Bernard was now untenable, General Campbell capitulated on honorable terms, being allowed to withdraw with his whole force, under an engagement not to serve against Spain until exchanged.

In consequence of the necessity of employing all their disposable forces in the military operations with the American colonists, the English commanders in America were unable to send reinforcements to General Campbell, and much mortification was experienced at the capture of so important and well-fortified a post. The same causes which prevented the sending of reinforcements made any attempts to recapture it out of the question at that time, and from Pensacola westward to the Mississippi the country and all the military posts remained in the possession of

Spain until the treaty of 1781, when they were formally re-ceded to her by Great Britain.

The mortification which the British government experienced in the loss of West Florida, Pensacola, Mobile, and Baton Rouge was in part compensated by the capture of the Bahama Islands. An expedition fitted out by Colonel Devereux, who had come to Florida from Carolina, and had a high reputation for spirit and gallantry, sailed from St. Augustine, in 1783, in two private armed brigs, for the purpose of attacking New Providence. The brigs carried twelve guns each, and the forces on board consisted of some fifty adventurers, who were desperate and reckless enough to engage in an expedition to capture strong fortifications well garrisoned. The vessels stopped at Eleuthera, where they took on board a number of negro recruits. The vessels arrived off the point on which Nassau is built, at night, and the men were landed without discovery on the east side of Fort Montague, which stands at the entrance of the harbor. The garrison, resting in fancied security, exhibited so little vigilance that the English troops reached the ramparts without alarming the Spaniards. Colonel Devereux rushed upon and surprised the sentinel before he could challenge or give an alarm, and without difficulty disarmed the sleeping garrison and obtained possession of the fort.

The colonel then proceeded to the summit of a ridge opposite the governor's house. In order to deceive the inhabitants in reference to their numbers, he arranged a show of boats passing to the fort, crowded with men, and returning apparently empty to the vessels, with their occupants concealed by lying down. Men of straw were posted as sentinels on the heights, and some of the party were dressed up and painted as Indians to strike the inhabitants with terror. One or two galleys in the harbor were taken possession of with an appearance of being sustained by a considerable force. Colonel Devereux, with a pompous description of his force, summoned the governor to surrender. The governor hesitating in complying with his demand, he directed a shot to be fired over the governor's house, which produced an immediate capitulation. The Spanish troops, as may well be imagined, were astonished and chagrined when they discovered the number and character of the troops to whom they had surrendered, and by what a miserable force they had been deceived.* The consequences of the expedition were very important, as these valuable islands have ever since remained a part of the British Empire.

At a period when the inhabitants of Florida were flattering themselves with the prospect of a long career of peaceful prosperity, and when they had attained the fullest measure of constitutional liberty, they found themselves suddenly made the victims of one of those political set-offs, or *equivalents*, by which diplomats endeavor to make amends for the ill success of cherished plans, and by a new arrangement of political divisions, the acquisition of new territory, and the transfer of equivalents, shield themselves from the acknowledgment of failure. At the close of the American Revolution, the ministry of Great Britain found themselves compelled to acknowledge the independence of the colonies. They were also desirous of closing a fruitless war with Spain. In order to effect this, they assumed that the provinces of East and West Florida, extending from the Atlantic to the Mississippi, and the island of Minorca, were of little value to the crown, as all the colonies north of Florida had passed from under the British flag, and it was proposed to make a re-

---

* Forbes's Sketches, p. 53.

cession of these provinces, and also of Minorca, for the comparatively insignificant Bahama Islands, important only as a naval station.

Almost the first intelligence the unfortunate people of Florida received of the coming disaster was the promulgation of a treaty, entered into on the 3d September, 1783, ceding East and West Florida. In this treaty the religious toleration which was exacted by the King of Spain for his Roman Catholic subjects from his Britannic Majesty in 1763 was not reciprocated, but it was simply provided that the English inhabitants might have eighteen months within which to remove with their property, or to dispose of their effects. The evacuation was to take place within three months after the ratification of the treaty.

The unfortunate inhabitants of Florida, who were thus summarily disposed of, were placed in a most miserable predicament. For years the British government had been offering to its subjects every inducement to establish themselves in the province; they had come there relying implicitly upon the good faith of the government, and had undergone all the hardships incident to the settlement of a new country. Many of them had left the adjoining colonies in consequence of their adherence to the royal cause, and could not return. Their property consisted largely in slaves and lands, and they had no point of refuge except the unwelcome rocks and barren islets of New Providence and the Bahamas.

In June, 1784, Governor Zespedez, the new Spanish governor, arrived at St. Augustine with a few troops, to take possession of Florida in the name of the King of Spain. The British government had sent to the harbor of Amelia, at the mouth of the St. Mary's River, a fleet of transports to remove the inhabitants of East Florida. Some returned to England, some went to Nova Scotia, some to the Bahamas. A large number of others carried their negroes to Jamaica, where they were received with much jealousy, and a system of government and regulations adopted in reference to them, so injurious that they made application to the home government for relief, which was tardily granted, but not until many had sunk under the pressure of difficulties and annoyancès. Afterwards, some of the inhabitants of Florida preferred returning to the American States and trusting to the generosity of their former fellow-citizens to obliterate past differences. Many of those who thus returned to Carolina had emigrated to Florida before the war, and had not therefore to encounter the odium attaching to the tories and refugee loyalists who had taken up arms on the British side. These parties carried back with them to South Carolina one thousand three hundred and seventy-two negroes. Of the number carried to Jamaica and the Bahamas we have no account, but it must have been very considerable.

The time for removal was extended four months by the Spanish crown, and in April, 1786, a further order was passed in consequence of representations made by the governor of Louisiana, allowing the former inhabitants to remain on condition that they should take a solemn oath of fidelity and obedience to his Catholic Majesty; that they should not change their residence or go away without leave of the government; that "at Natchez, and other places of both Floridas, where it is convenient, parishes of Irish clergy be established, in order to bring said colonists and their children and families to our religion with the sweetness and mildness which it advises."*

St. Augustine was the only town of any importance in East Florida at the period of the evacuation by the Spaniards,

---

* Vignoles, Observations on Florida, p. 196.

in 1763. It contained three thousand inhabitants at that time. All the gardens in the town were well stocked with fruit-trees, such as figs, guavas, plantains, pomegranates, lemons, limes, citrons, shaddocks, bergamot, China and Seville oranges. The city was three-quarters of a mile in length, and about a quarter of a mile in width. It had four churches, ornamentally built of stone in the Spanish style. One was pulled down during the English occupation, the steeple of which was preserved as an ornament to the town. One of the churches was attached to the Convent of St. Francis. The houses were all built of stone, their entrances shaded by piazzas supported by Tuscan pillars or pilasters. Upon the east the windows projected eighteen inches into the street, and were very wide and proportionably high. On the west side the windows were commonly very small, and there was no opening of any kind to the north, upon which side they had double walls, six or eight feet asunder, forming a kind of hall for cellars and pantries. Before most of the entrances, which were from an inner court, were arbors of vines, producing fine and luscious grapes. None of the houses were supplied with chimneys or fireplaces. For the purposes of warmth, stone urns were filled with coals, and placed in the rooms in the afternoon to moderate the temperature in weather sufficiently cool to require it.

The governor's residence had piazzas on both sides, also a belvidere and grand portico, decorated with Doric pillars and entablatures. At the north end of the town was the castle, a casemated fort, with four bastions, a ravelin counterscarp, and a glacis, built with quarried stone, and constructed according to the system of Vauban. Half a mile to the north was a line, with a broad ditch and bastions, running from the Sebastian Creek to St. Mark's River; a mile from that was another fortified line, with some redoubts, forming a second line of communication between a staccata fort upon St. Sebastian River, and Fort Moosa, upon the St. Mark's River.* Within the first line, near the town, was a small settlement of Germans, who had a church of their own. Upon the St. Mark's River, within the second line, was also an Indian town, with a stone church built by the Indians themselves, and in very good taste.

During the English occupation, large buildings were erected for barracks, of sufficient extent to quarter five regiments of troops. The brick of which they were built was brought from New York, although the island opposite the city afforded a much better building-material, in the coquina stone. The lower story only of the British barracks was built of brick, the upper story being of wood, These barracks stood at the southern extremity of the town, to the south of the present barracks, and the length and great extent of the buildings fronting on the bay added greatly to the appearance of the city as viewed from the harbor.

The city, in English times, contained many gentlemen of distinction, among whom were Sir Charles Burdett, Chief-Justice Drayton, Rev. John Forbes, the Admiralty Judge, General James Grant, Lieut.-Governor Moultrie, William Stark, Esq., the historian, Rev. N. Frazer, Dr. Andrew Turnbull, Bernard Romans, Esq., civil engineer, James Moultrie, Esq., and William Bartram, the naturalist.

Some few English families remained after the evacuation by the British in 1784, and the entire settlement of Greeks

---

* These lines may be still distinctly traced. The churches spoken of, outside the city, as well as Forts Moosa and Staccata, have long since disappeared, but their sites are known. The outer line passed through the grounds formerly occupied by the writer.

and Minorcans, who had come up from Mosquito from Dr. Turnbull's colony. As they were all Roman Catholics, and were accustomed to a language resembling the Spanish, they were not affected to any great degree by the change of rulers.

It is a sad thing for an entire people to be forced to give up their homes and seek an asylum in some foreign land; and melancholy was the spectacle presented on all the routes leading to the harbor designated for the embarkation of the English inhabitants of Florida. Families separating perhaps forever, long adieus between neighbors and friends who had together shared the privations and pleasures of the past, leaving behind them places endeared by the most sacred associations, and containing, perchance, the precious dust of the departed. Homes embowered among the orange-groves, and made pleasant by the fragrant blossoms of the honeysuckle, the rose, and the acacia; a land where Nature had lavished her choicest beauties, and created a perpetual summer,—such was the land upon which the unfortunate residents of Florida were obliged to turn their backs forever.

CHAPTER XVII.

Condition of the Province after its Recession to Spain—Notice of McGillivray—Operations of Bowles—Patriot Rebellion—Operations of United States Troops in Florida—Indian Hostilities, between the Americans and King Payne the Seminole.

1784—1813.

UPON the reoccupation of Florida by the Spaniards, in 1784, but few of its former inhabitants returned. Twenty years had scattered them through other lands, where they had made new homes, and new occupations and associations had weakened or wholly destroyed their attachment to Florida. The few inhabitants left in St. Augustine felt their weakness and insecurity, and hardly ventured to go beyond the range of the guns of the castle.

The fine estates upon the coast, and upon the St. John's River, left by the retiring English proprietors, remained unoccupied, a prey to that rapid decay which so soon reclaims to its native wildness the improvements and cultivation which it had been the labor of years to effect. The boldness of the Indians, in their intrusions upon the whites, created a feeling of insecurity, which was greatly increased when, a short time after the departure of the English, they destroyed Bella Vista, the beautiful country-seat of Governor Moultrie, seven miles from St. Augustine. Some attempt was made to induce settlement, by offers of lands; but they were accompanied with such conditions that very few cared to avail themselves of them. Some of those who had left with the English, and gone to the Bahama Islands, became disgusted with the poverty of the soil, from which they found it impossible to reap a subsistence, and, returning to Florida, made a settlement at New Smyrna. But the policy of the Spanish government, which seemed always averse to individual prosperity, soon forced them to abandon their settlement and seek homes in the States, where more liberal institutions encouraged industry, protected property, and honored integrity. The Spanish authorities soon endeavored to enter into negotiations with the neighboring Indian tribes, upon whose friendship so much depended for the Spaniard.

At this time the principal chief among the Creeks was Alexander McGillivray. This remarkable person was the son of a half-breed Creek woman and Lachlan McGillivray, a Scotchman who was engaged in the Indian trade. The son was carefully educated, and on his return to the nation acquired great influence from his superior intelligence, gained the confidence of the tribes, and was made their chief. During the Revolutionary War he attached himself to the royalists, and received the rank of colonel from the British government, and was an active and useful ally to them in their operations against the frontiers of Georgia. In 1784 he formed a treaty with the Spanish governor in behalf of the Creeks and Seminoles, and engaged to adhere to the government of Spain and prevent all white men from entering their country without a Spanish permit. The Spanish authorities gave him the rank and pay of a colonel in their service, and he was very useful to them in the control he exercised over the neighboring Indian tribes, whom he succeeded in preventing from attaching themselves to the American interest.

About the year 1789, a bold attempt was made by a

General William Augustus Bowles to dispossess Spain of Florida by a concerted and general attack of the Indian tribes upon the borders. This individual was a native of Maryland, and held a commission in the British army in the latter part of the Revolutionary War. He sailed with his regiment to Jamaica, and afterwards to Pensacola, where he was dismissed from the service. While he was at Pensacola, a party of Creeks visited the post for the purpose of receiving their annuities. Animated by a love of adventure, Bowles returned with them to their nation, where he learned the Indian language and married the daughter of an Indian chief. Gaining the confidence of the Indians, he was able to obtain the command of the party who went as allies to the English at the siege of Pensacola, and by his good conduct on that occasion he was restored to his former position by the English commander. After West Florida was ceded to Spain, in 1784, he went to New York, where he joined a company of play-actors, and subsequently went to the Bahamas. While there he followed the profession of comedian, and added to this the business of portrait-painting. The versatility of his talents, and his acquaintance with the Creek Indians and familiarity with their language, induced Lord Dunmore, the governor of the Bahamas, to appoint Bowles as an agent to establish a trading-house among the Creeks. His own ambition seems to have led him to hope that he might attain a much higher position, and perhaps be able to establish an extensive empire in the southwest, under English protection, in which he might fill a conspicuous and honorable place.

He left New Providence with about sixty followers, and landed at Mosquito. From thence he crossed over to the St. John's River for the purpose of attacking an Indian trading-house, called Hamblys, near Lake George. The traders had been advised by friendly Indians of Bowles's intention, and the delay occasioned by his attempts to bring from his vessel several small iron cannon gave the traders time to prepare for him, and they had received fifty Spanish soldiers from St. Augustine. Bowles found them so well fortified that he was discouraged from making the proposed attack, and directed his steps towards Cuscowilla, an Indian town in Alachua, which stood near the present site of Micanopy, and was the chief town of the Seminoles under King Payne.

Finding the Indians here unwilling to join him, his followers deserted him, and he fled to the Creeks. Here he married a daughter of Pennyman, an Indian chief, and was joined by a Spanish subject, one Daniel McGirth, who had been conspicuous in the border war waged by McGillivray against the Georgians during the Revolutionary War.* They induced the Creeks to believe that the goods contained in the various trading-houses were intended as presents for them, and were improperly withheld from them

---

* Daniel McGirth was a native of South Carolina, and in the beginning of the American Revolution was a valuable partisan scout. While stationed at the Satilla River with the American troops, he was court-martialed for using disrespectful language to an officer who desired to dispossess him of a favorite mare, and he was sentenced to be whipped. This indignity was borne by him in silence, but he soon managed to escape, and became from that day one of the most vindictive, untiring, and revengeful enemies of the Georgians, upon whom he inflicted a vast amount of injury. After the war he remained in Florida, and was concerned with Bowles, and probably on this account was arrested by the Spanish government and thrown into the dungeon of the castle at St. Augustine, where he was confined for five years a close prisoner. Subsequently, with his health totally destroyed by his long and cruel confinement, he returned to his wife in Sumter District, S. C. A small tributary that empties into the St. John's River, near Jacksonville, bears his name.—*White's Hist. Col.*, page 281.

by the Indian traders. The Indians credited this story, and several of the chiefs agreed to assist attacking the houses and taking possession of the stores. They established their head-quarters at Miccosukie, a town in Middle Florida, and, fortunately for their purpose, a vessel arrived at Apalachee, with goods for Bowles, from New Providence. These he distributed among his followers, telling them that they were a part of the same goods the traders had in their possession. Having taught navigation to an Indian crew, he kept a vessel running from New Providence to Apalachee, until the traders, having determined to break up his party, prevailed upon the Seminoles to take Bowles prisoner. McGirth, hearing of the approach of the Seminoles, informed Bowles in time for him to escape to the Oclockony River and hide himself. Nothing is said of the escape of McGirth, who, it is probable, on this occasion fell into the hands of the Spaniards, who had instigated the Seminoles to make the attack.

The Creeks who were with Bowles and McGirth professed a willingness to return home, and entered into a treaty of peace; but after the Seminoles had dispersed they again joined Bowles, and aided him in the capture of a vessel laden with goods for the traders. Bowles was emboldened by his success to make an attack upon St. Mark's, and, finding the garrison off their guard, he captured the fort, and for several weeks kept possession of it, until Governor O'Neil, coming down from Pensacola, drove him out, without making any effort to capture him or his Indian allies. Orders were afterwards sent out for his arrest, and, a large reward being offered for him, the Indians gave him up. He was sent in chains to Cuba and confined in Moro Castle, where he is said to have died.

At one time his influence with the Creeks was so great that he destroyed their confidence in their great chief

McGillivray, whom he represented to them as a traitor who had sold them to Spain and afterwards to the United States. This accusation was not without foundation, as McGillivray had entered into a treaty with Washington, by which he promised that after a certain date all of the commerce of the Creek nation should pass through the ports of the United States. This gave great dissatisfaction to the Indians as well as to the Spaniards, who now began to distrust McGillivray. It was proved that while receiving thirty-five hundred dollars a year as agent of Spain, he was filling the same office under the United States government with a salary of twelve hundred, sometimes wearing the Spanish uniform, and at other times that of a brigadier-general in the American army. But there is no doubt that he was mainly inclined to the Spanish interest, as it does not appear that he ever carried out the provisions of the treaty with Washington. Carondelet, the Spanish Governor, endeavored to unite the four Indian nations under McGillivray, and secure their services in his effort to prevent the advance of American settlements on the coast, and also on the Mississippi. But the race of McGillivray was run. In 1793 he died, and was buried at Pensacola, with Masonic honors.

By the treaty of 1790, in which McGillivray had represented the Creek Nation, the United States had set aside a previous treaty between General Twiggs and the Creeks, and agreed to a new boundary-line, less advantageous to Georgia. This gave great dissatisfaction to General Elijah Clarke, who had been a party to the treaty of General Twiggs, and one of the most active and useful officers in the Georgia service. He was greatly incensed, and determined to take possession of the territory so improperly surrendered.* He had no difficulty in finding adherents,

---

* Stevens, Ga., p. 401.

and, having established himself in the disputed territory, made several incursions into Florida, and drove in the Spanish outposts. It was supposed that he was acting in the interest of France; but the French consul at Savannah denied the charge. Having set at defiance the authorities of Georgia, Clarke crossed the river Oconee, and erected a fort, whereupon an expedition was sent out against him, and he was forced to abandon the enterprise.

Some ten years after the change of flags, General John McIntosh removed to Florida with his accomplished and devoted wife, and settled upon the St. John's River, at a plantation which he called Bellevue. He had been a distinguished officer in the War of the American Revolution, and carried with him to Florida several families devoted to his interests. The Spanish governor, Quesada, jealous and suspicious of the consideration with which General McIntosh was treated, affected to believe that he was engaged in projects inimical to the interests of Spain. He pretended to be on friendly terms with the general, but upon one occasion, when he was on a visit to St. Augustine, Quesada had him arrested and thrown into the castle. A detachment of soldiers was then sent out to the general's plantation, who searched the house, and carried off all the private papers they could find. All communication with his family was prevented, and soon after General McIntosh was sent to Havana and immured in the dungeons of Moro Castle. His resolute wife made every effort in her power to procure his release. Though deprived of her sight, she wrote to the Governor-General of Cuba several able letters, declaring the innocence of her husband, and urged that he should be brought to trial and confronted with his accusers. She also appealed to the sympathies of her husband's old comrades in arms, and enlisted the services of Washington himself to procure the release of the general. Finally, after having been kept a year in close confinement, the Governor of Cuba released him, and allowed him to return, without trial, to his family. Incensed and disgusted with the treachery of Quesada, General McIntosh determined to abandon Florida forever, and, gathering his adherents, some of whom had been fellow-sufferers, he descended the river, and returned to Georgia, not without having first destroyed a Spanish fort at the Cowfords, opposite Jacksonville, and several Spanish galleys that lay in the river. General McIntosh was engaged in the War of 1812, and died in 1826.

In 1795 Spain receded to France all that portion of West Florida lying west of the Perdido River, thus cutting off from West Florida the most valuable and important portion of her territory. The progress of the great campaigns in Europe, in which the interest of Spain was so deeply involved, left the Floridas with but little care from the home government. White, who was for many years Governor of East Florida, had strong prejudices against the Americans, and opposed their settlement within his province. In the mean time, France, becoming satisfied that in the progress of events Louisiana and her West India colonies would be taken from her, entered into negotiations with the United States, and, in the year 1803, agreed, for the pecuniary consideration of fifteen millions of dollars, to cede the territory of Louisiana to the United States.

Thus, at the end of two hundred and thirty years, France withdrew from the last of her possessions in North America. If we examine a map of the country as it was held by various European powers in the early part of the eighteenth century, we shall see on the north, the great territory of New France, extending along the Gulf of St. Lawrence, including part of Newfoundland, Nova Scotia, Cape Breton, and Canada, lying on both sides of the river St. Lawrence and the lakes, along the Ohio River to its junction with the Mississippi, and the whole valley of the Mississippi, extending on the east to the Alleghany Mountains, on the west to the Rocky Mountains, and south to the Gulf of Mexico. Her forts and trading-houses were scattered along the borders of all the great lakes, and upon the Mississippi, from the Falls of St. Anthony to the Gulf of Mexico, and along all the tributaries of this great river. From these vast possessions France had retired step by step, receding from the frost-bound regions of Canada and the Northwest to the mild and sunny borders of the Gulf of Mexico. One by one she had parted with her possessions by the fortunes of war and treaty stipulations, and at last transferred, for a few millions of dollars, an empire in extent, reaching from the Gulf of Mexico to the far distant sources of the mighty river Mississippi. The towns upon its banks, the tributaries that swell its flood, the bold bluffs that overhang its currents, all bear to this day the names given them during the French possession. All the saints in the calendar are honored, and many an historic name perpetuated, along with the designation of the various tribes who once inhabited the land.

The English colonies occupied a narrow strip along the coast, from the St. Croix on the north to the Altamaha on the south, with an average breadth of not over three hundred miles, not one-half of which was occupied. Upon the cession of Louisiana, the United States possessed themselves of the territory lying west of the Perdido, and thus inclosed the Spanish province of Florida within narrow boundaries. In the year 1811 the difficulties between the United States and Great Britain began to assume a threatening aspect. On the north the provinces of Upper and Lower

Canada extended along the entire border, and offered every advantage for assailing the people of the border States. It was suspected that a design was on foot to seize Florida, and thus secure to the British a frontier along the whole southern border. The matter was thought of sufficient importance by the President to bring it to the attention of Congress, and, in secret session, a resolution was passed, authorizing the President, in the event of an attempt being made by Great Britain to get possession of Florida, that territory should be occupied by the American forces. The President appointed General Matthews, of Georgia, and Colonel John McKee, commissioners to confer with the Spanish authorities of Florida and endeavor to procure a temporary cession of the province to the United States. They were, if successful, to establish a provisional government over the colonies; if the governor so required, they were to stipulate for the redelivery of the country at some future time to Spain. But, in case of refusal, "should there be room to entertain a suspicion that a design existed on the part of any other power to occupy Florida," they were authorized to take possession of the province with the force of the United States. As might have been anticipated, the Spanish governor declined a surrender of the province, and protested against any trespass upon his rights or domain. The plans of the government of the United States had, however, become generally known, and a number of frontiersmen along the borders of Georgia eagerly awaited an opportunity of making a descent upon Florida. In the spring of 1812 a number of these persons, and some of the settlers from the northern borders of Florida, assembled near St. Mary's, and organized themselves as patriots seeking to establish republican institutions in Florida. A provisional government was formed, and officers were elected.* General John H. McIntosh was chosen governor or director of the republic of Florida, and Colonel Ashley was appointed military chief.

Fernandina had been occupied as a Spanish port for some three or four years, and was becoming a place of some importance. During the existence of the embargo imposed by the United States in the war of 1812 with Great Britain, Fernandina had become a depot of neutral trade, and as many as one hundred and fifty square-rigged vessels, it is said, could have been counted at one time within her harbor, and the town then contained a population of about six hundred persons. In 1812 a small Spanish garrison held possession of the place, commanded by Captain José Lopez. It was deemed important to secure possession of Fernandina, and nine American gunboats, under the command of Commodore Campbell, had come into the harbor, under the pretense of seeking to protect American interests. General Matthews, having determined upon the occupation of Amelia Island, used the patriot organization as a cover to effect his purpose. The gunboats were drawn up in line in front of Fernandina, with their guns bearing upon the fort. Colonel Ashley then embarked his patriots in boats, and approached the town with a summons to surrender. The commandant, Don José Lopez, seeing a line of gunboats, with their guns bearing upon the town, flying the flag of a neutral power, but prepared to enforce the demand of the soi-disant patriots, had no alternative but to haul down the Spanish flag. Articles of capitulation were entered into at four o'clock on the 17th of March, 1812, between Don José Lopez, Commandant, etc., on the part of the Spanish government, and John H. McIntosh, Esq., commissioner named and duly authorized by the patriots of the district

---

* A copy of this constitution is in the possession of the writer.

of the province lying between the rivers St. John's and St. Mary's. The fifth article of capitulation provided "that the island shall, twenty-four hours after the surrender, be ceded to the United States of America, under the express condition that the port of Fernandina shall not be subject to any of the restrictions on commerce that exist at present in the United States, but shall be open, as heretofore, to British and other vessels and produce, on paying the lawful tonnage and import duties; and, in case of actual war between the United States and Great Britain, the port of Fernandina shall be open to British merchant vessels and produce, and considered a free port until the 1st of May, 1813."

The articles were witnessed by George Atkinson, George I. F. Clarke, Charles W. Clarke, and Archibald Clark.

The succeeding day, Lieutenant Ridgley, of the United States Army, assumed command, and Colonel Ashley, with his patriot army, numbering some three hundred men, were marched towards St. Augustine. On their way they arrested Zephaniah Kingsley, a well-known planter, and afterwards induced him to join in the enterprise. They marched to within two miles of St. Augustine, and camped at the place known as Fort Moosa. Colonel Smith, with a detachment of one hundred regulars, here joined the patriots. Soon after they became dissatisfied with Colonel Ashley, and suspended him from the command, and William Craig, one of the Spanish judges, was put in his place. Colonel Estrada, the acting governor of Florida, was unwilling to meet these insignificant forces in the field, but, managing to get some small guns on a schooner, he shelled Fort Moosa from the water approaches, and compelled the patriots and their supporters to fall back to Pass Navarro and intrench themselves; but soon, finding that their force was wholly insufficient to take St. Augustine, the patriots fell back to the

St. John's, leaving Colonel Smith and his regulars at the pass.

The occupation of Fernandina, and subsequent movement upon St. Augustine, coming to the knowledge of the Spanish Minister at Washington, he remonstrated with the American government against this violation of treaty stipulations, and the British Minister also protested against this invasion of neutral territory.

The President was in an embarrassing position. General Matthews was his accredited commissioner, and had his written instructions to occupy the country should there be room to entertain a suspicion that a design existed on the part of any other power to take possession of the province. The alternative existed of boldly justifying his own acts, assuming the responsibility, and accepting the consequences, or of sacrificing his agent and disowning his acts. The President pursued the usual course of those in power: he politely ignored the measures that had been taken by his commissioner, and declared that he had transcended his authority; regretted the mistake, and promised to have it corrected. General Matthews was relieved from his position, and Governor Mitchell, of Georgia, appointed in his place, with instructions to restore the condition of affairs which existed before the invasion, and to act in harmony with Governor Estrada. While these diplomatic movements were in progress, and just after the appointment of Governor Mitchell, an affair took place which was very disgraceful to the Spanish governor and tended greatly to exasperate the United States military authorities. On the evening of the 12th of May, a detachment of United States troops, mostly made up of invalids, under the command of Lieutenant Williams, of the United States Marine Corps, with a number of wagons, were on their way from Colonel Smith's camp, at Pass Navarro, to Colonel Briggs's camp on the St. John's, when they were attacked by a company of negroes, under the command of a fellow by the name of Prince, sent out by the governor of St. Augustine. These negroes, concealing themselves in Twelve-Mile Swamp at a point where the road is lined on both sides by a dense thicket, poured in upon the unsuspecting party a deadly volley. Lieutenant Williams fell, mortally wounded, pierced with six bullets. Captain Fort, of the Milledgeville Volunteers, was wounded, and a non-commissioned officer and six privates were killed. The soldiers immediately charged upon the negroes, who instantly broke and fled.

Governor Mitchell promptly called for reinforcements, to enable him to attack St. Augustine. In the mean time, Governor Kindelan had been sent out as Governor of Florida, and in June he made a formal demand for the withdrawal of Colonel Smith from the province, and the President, finding that Congress was opposed to entering into any further hostilities with Spain while serious difficulties were threatening with England, felt obliged to make arrangements for withdrawing all the United States troops from Florida. The camp at Pass Navarro was broken up, and Colonel Smith withdrew with his command, now greatly reduced by sickness, to Davis's Creek, on the King's Road. In the mean time, the Indians, under their chiefs Payne and Bowlegs, had begun a predatory warfare upon the settlements, carrying off all the live stock they could find, burning houses, and stealing negroes, and were preparing to extend their incursions into Georgia. It was determined to make an effort to disperse the Indians, if possible, before they collected in sufficient numbers to be formidable. Colonel Newnan, of Georgia, the Inspector-General of that State, who was a volunteer, offered to lead a party against Payne's town in Alachua. Organizing a command of one hundred and ten men only, from the patriots in Florida, he undertook to penetrate the enemy's country over one hundred miles, and attack two formidable chiefs surrounded by their warriors and with every advantage of position and thorough knowledge of the country.

Crossing at Picolata, Colonel Newnan and his men arrived the third day at the foot of Lake Pithlachocco, a few miles from Payne's town. They here unexpectedly encountered an Indian force of about one hundred and fifty, under their leaders Bowlegs and Payne, who had just set out on the war-path. Both sides prepared for the conflict, which began about mid-day. Captain Fort, of the infantry, was posted on the left, Lieutenants Broadnax and Reed in the centre, and Captain Humphreys, with a detachment of marines, held the right. King Payne, mounted on a white horse, displayed great gallantry in leading his men into action. At first they fired from the shelter of a swamp, so well protected on both sides that but little effect was produced by the return fire of Newnan's men. A feigned retreat on their part, however, drew the Indians out in pursuit, when, suddenly turning upon them, Newnan killed a great number, and mortally wounded Payne. Dismayed by the loss of their leader, the Indians fled from the field; but, knowing the Indian character so well, Newnan felt confident they would soon renew the attack, and lost no time in throwing up temporary breastworks to protect his small force. About sundown Bowlegs returned, heavily reinforced, and began the attack with great vigor. They came forward yelling, and charged nearly up to the intrenchments.

Newnan's forces received them with great coolness, and returned a galling fire, which drove them back with great loss. The Indians returned to the attack several times, but the steady valor of the whites forced them finally to retreat, carrying off their dead and wounded. Confident that Bowlegs would again return, Newnan still further strengthened his position, and prepared for a siege. Fortunately, they killed an ox, and subsisted on that and the one horse they had left, the Indians having carried off all the others. The night of the eighth day they effected a silent retreat, and, carrying their wounded on litters, marched slowly back towards the St. John's. The Indians were not long in discovering that their enemy were on the retreat, and quickly followed in pursuit. Newnan's party was overtaken when on their way to Picolata, and attacked by a band of fifty Seminoles, under their young governor. Three of the whites were killed at the first fire, but, notwithstanding their exhausted condition, they roused themselves, and made a charge on the Indians which put them to flight, leaving their chief dead on the field. A few miles farther on, Newnan halted and threw up breastworks, and sent a messenger in for the relief they so much needed. Their provisions were exhausted, and their wounded men suffering for want of care and rest. A party was sent out foraging, but could find nothing but two alligators, and on these they subsisted until the arrival of sixteen horsemen with provisions. The wounded men were mounted, and in two days they all reached Picolata. The death of Payne greatly discomfited the Indians, and for the time put a stop to their preparations for war, but they still continued, in small bands, to annoy the border settlers. Among these was Mr. Kingsley, whose plantation the Indians kept in a state of siege, and carried off his cattle and negroes. The patriots retaliated upon the loyalists, and lawless bands were scattered over the country, plundering and destroying property, until scarcely a house or plantation remained uninjured in the province.

CHAPTER XVIII.

Occupation of Pensacola by the English—English driven from Pensacola by General Jackson—Destruction of Negro Fort on Apalachicola by Colonel Clinch—Defeat of Florida Indians by General Jackson—Occupation of Pensacola by General Jackson—Treaty with Spain, ceding Florida to United States.

1813—1821.

ABOUT the year 1812 a party of Georgians visited the Alachua district of country, carrying with them a surveyor to run out the lands which they expected to conquer and occupy. The surveyor was killed by the Indians, and it is said that his field-notes and plots were carried in by the Indians to Geo. I. F. Clarke, Esq., the Spanish Surveyor-General, and formed the basis of all the Spanish land-grants in the Alachua district of country, now covered by Alachua and Marion counties. The promoter of this expedition was a General Harris, of Georgia. The Indians attacked the party and forced them to retire.

The American troops were not finally withdrawn from Florida until the early part of the year 1813. Governor Mitchell had been superseded by General Pinkney, but no active operations were carried on against the Spanish inhabitants. This incursion of the United States troops into Florida ruined the agricultural interests of the country, which had begun to revive, and were attended with very encouraging success. The civil war and unbridled license which prevailed for a year and a half broke up and disheartened the planters, who saw the fruits of their well-applied industry made the prey of lawless invaders, their homes rendered insecure, their stock carried off, their slaves scattered, their crops and fences destroyed, and all they possessed plundered and pillaged under the immunity and protection afforded to the perpetrators of these wrongs by the flag of the United States. The planters retired in despair to St. Augustine, and sought shelter and protection under the guns of the fort. The Spanish forces were too weak to contest with the invaders the possession of the country, and during the years 1812 and 1813 Florida was virtually in the condition of a conquered province.

The war of 1812, between the United States and Great Britain, to some extent involved Florida. In August, 1814, a British fleet entered the harbor of Pensacola, and landed troops, which were placed in garrison in Forts Michel and Barrancas, with the assent of Governor Manrequez; the British flag was raised over the forts, and the Indians of that region taken under British protection and pledged to carry on hostilities against the Americans, being furnished with arms and ammunition and promised liberal bounties.

General Jackson was directed by the government of the United States to counteract these movements, and, having raised a body of troops, marched against Pensacola in November of the same year. His forces consisted of five thousand Tennessee volunteers and a large force of friendly Indians. A flag which General Jackson had sent forward to open communication with the Spanish governor was fired upon, and he immediately determined to storm the town. Marching his troops to the eastward of the city, he pushed forward his columns for a direct assault. The town was protected by a fort, several batteries, and seven vessels of war lying in front of the city. The advance of General Jackson's column was rapid, and they soon entered the streets of the city. A battery of two guns, which had been planted so as to sweep with grape and canister the street upon which they entered, was stormed and captured by Major Laval. The town soon yielded, and with Fort Michel was taken possession of by the American troops. Fort Barrancas was blown up by Colonel Nichols, the English commander, who, with the British troops and their Indian allies, escaped on board the vessels and went to sea. The Indians were landed on the Apalachicola River.

After holding the town two days, and having destroyed the fortifications, General Jackson withdrew his troops and proceeded with his command to New Orleans, then threatened by the British forces. The Spanish governor, after General Jackson's forces had withdrawn, commenced rebuilding the fortifications, declining the assistance proffered by the English for that purpose.

Colonel Nichols, having been expelled from Pensacola, devoted his attention to organizing an Indian and negro territory on the river Apalachicola, for the purpose of establishing a place of refuge for runaway negroes from the Southern States, who, in connection with the Indians, might operate with effect upon the frontier settlements. Selecting a place admirably suited for the purpose on that river, he superintended the erection of a strong fortification upon a high bluff, making out into the river, well protected by a deep morass in the rear. A garrison of three hundred British troops was placed in it, and it was made a point of rendezvous for the Creek Indians called Bluesticks. During the following year a large number of runaway negroes congregated in this region of country, and settled along the banks of the Apalachicola River for some fifty miles, bidding defiance to both the Spanish and American governments. After the close of the war with Great Britain, the British garrison was withdrawn, and the fort was left in the hands of the runaway negroes, who were closely allied with the Indians, and were under the leadership of a negro by the name of Garcia. The fort was situated on the east side of the river, at the point where Fort Gadsden was afterwards built. The parapet was fifteen feet high and eighteen feet thick, and it was defended by nine pieces of artillery, several of which were of large calibre. Besides the swamp in the rear, it was protected by a large creek above it and a small creek below it. Two large magazines were well supplied with ammunition, and three thousand stand of arms had been furnished by their British allies. Thus situated, the fort commanded the navigation of the Apalachicola River, and of the Flint River also, and menaced the settlements along the borders, while affording a refuge for all runaway slaves.

In August, 1816, Colonel Duncan L. Clinch, of the United States Army, was stationed at Camp Crawford, on the Chattahoochee River, about one hundred and fifty miles above the Bay of Apalachicola. General Gaines had directed a supply of provisions, with a quantity of ordnance-stores, two eighteen-pounders, and one howitzer, to ascend the river to Camp Crawford; and, as the hostile attitude of the Indians and negroes at the negro fort made it probable that some opposition would be made to the passage of the expedition up the river, General Gaines instructed Colonel Clinch, in case of such opposition, to take measures to reduce the fort.

An Indian chief by the name of Lafarka was sent down the river from Fort Crawford, to obtain some information of the convoy and vessels guarding it, and soon returned with dispatches from Sailing-Master Loomis, advising Colonel Clinch of his arrival in the bay with two gunboats and two transports, with provisions, etc. Colonel Clinch immediately set out with one hundred and sixteen men in boats to descend the river. These forces were divided into two companies, under command of Major Muhlenberg and Captain Taylor. On their way a junction was accidentally effected with a large body of Creek Indians, who, without any knowledge of the movements of the United States troops, were also on their way to attack the negro fort, and capture the runaways for the benefit of their owners.

These Indians were under the command of Major McIntosh, and the next day were joined by another party, under Captain Isaacs and Kateha-haigo—*mad-tiger*. A council was held, and the Indians agreed to act in concert with the whites. Scouts were kept in the advance, who captured an Indian with a scalp, which he was carrying into the fort. The prisoner informed Colonel Clinch that the black leader, Garcia, and a Choctaw chief, had been down the bay the day before, saying they had killed several Americans and taken a boat from them. It appears that Lieutenant Loomis, the commander of the gunboats, had sent out Midshipman Luffborough, with four seamen, into the river to get a supply of fresh water, where they were attacked by a party of negroes and Choctaws, who fired upon them, killing the midshipman and two of the seamen; one was taken prisoner, and the fourth escaped.

The command of Colonel Clinch landed within a short distance of the negro fort. The Indians were posted around it, so as to cut off all communication, and an irregular fire kept up to harass the besieged. They replied by a constant discharge of artillery, which inflicted no damage upon the besiegers, but greatly reduced their supply of ammunition. Some days before, a party of Indian chiefs had entered the fort and demanded its surrender, but they were received with abuse, and the negro commander told them that he had been placed in command by the British government, and he intended to sink any American vessels which should attempt to pass his fort, and that when he found that he could not hold the fort he would blow it up. After this declaration, he hoisted the red flag with the English Jack over it.

The vessels from below were brought up to within four miles of the fort, and, after a careful examination of the ground, a position was selected for a battery on the west side of the river, opposite to the fort. The troops under Major Muhlenberg and Captain Taylor occupied the west side of the river, and Major McIntosh and his Indians, and a detachment of American troops, invested the fort in the rear. On the morning of the 24th of August, the two gunboats came up and took position in front of the battery. The negroes immediately opened fire upon them from a thirty-two-pounder, which was replied to with such effect that, at the fifth discharge, a hot-shot from Gunboat 154, commanded by Sailing-Master Basset, entered one of the magazines of the fort and blew it up, thus rendering any further defense of the fort impossible. The garrison consisted of about one hundred effective men, including twenty-five Choctaws, and there were over two hundred women and children, of whom not over fifty escaped the effects of the explosion.

The Americans sustained no loss whatever. A large amount of property was taken, estimated at two hundred thousand dollars in value. One hundred and sixty barrels of powder were saved from an uninjured magazine. The negro commander, Garcia, and the outlawed Choctaw chief, were condemned to death by a council of the friendly Indians, for the murder of the midshipman and seamen. The sentence was carried into effect immediately. The runaway Spanish negroes were turned over to the Spanish Agent, and the American negroes delivered to Colonel

Clinch to be restored to their owners. A body of Seminoles had come down the river to aid the besieged, but, the news of the capture of the fort having reached them, they scattered to their homes.

The destruction of this fort broke up for the time the Indian and negro settlements. The English government appear, in this instance, to have encouraged their agents to violate all the rules of civilized and honorable warfare, by permitting them to instigate an atrocious Indian war, in connection with a hostile negro organization, to prey upon the defenseless frontiers of the Southern States. Bounties were offered and paid for the scalps of Americans, a strong fortress was built for the protection of outlaws, murderers, and runaway slaves, and large sums of money were spent in supplying them with arms, ammunition, and provisions, and the British flag allowed to float over this mongrel crew. The evil influences of the course pursued by these English agents were felt for a long time, and finally forced the American government, in self-defense, to adopt measures for putting to an end forever the atrocities of the savage allies of Great Britain.

Instigated by the English emissaries Nichols and Woodbine, the Seminoles, with scattering bands from other tribes, continued to annoy the border settlements in Georgia, and several times attacked transports on the Apalachicola River, in one instance mustering twelve hundred men and continuing the fight for several days. In January, 1818, General Jackson made a treaty with the Creeks, and engaged them to join him in an attack upon the Seminoles of Florida. In the spring of the same year, with a force of one thousand militia, five hundred regulars, and nearly two thousand Indians, he started on an expedition against the Seminoles, with the purpose of destroying their power and putting an end to their depredations.

Marching rapidly upon the Miccosukee towns of East Florida, he destroyed them, and soon afterwards attacked and destroyed the Fowl towns, the Indians making but a feeble resistance. General Jackson then marched upon St. Mark's, which was strongly fortified and had twenty guns mounted. The fort surrendered without resistance, and Prophet Francis and another Indian chief fell into the hands of the Americans, and were immediately hanged.

At Miccosukee, General Jackson found three hundred scalps of men, women, and children, most of them fresh, and which had evidently been recently exhibited with triumph. From St. Mark's General Jackson marched to Suwanee, where he dispersed a large number of Indians, and took many prisoners, among them two Englishmen, Arbuthnot and Ambrister, who were accused of being the chief agents in supplying the Indians with arms and ammunition and directing their operations against the whites. A court-martial was held to try them, and both being found guilty were sentenced to suffer death, one by hanging, the other to be shot, and the sentence was promptly executed. This action of General Jackson was severely criticised, both at the time, and subsequently in the political contests in which he became engaged. General Jackson afterwards marched against Pensacola, having been informed that the Spanish government, while furnishing arms to the Indians who were hostile to the United States, refused to allow provisions to pass up the Escambia for the American troops. Upon the approach of General Jackson, the Spanish governor retired to Fort Barrancas, which, being menaced by the United States troops, was surrendered after a slight show of resistance.

A treaty of peace, consisting of sixteen articles, was concluded between Spain and the United States on the 22d of February, 1819, ceding the Floridas to the United States. The sixth article of this treaty provided that "the inhabitants of the territories ceded to the United States should be incorporated into the Union of the United States, as soon as might be consistent with the principles of the Federal Constitution, and admitted to the enjoyment of all the privileges, rights, and immunities of the citizens of the United States."

The eighth article provided "that all the grants of land made before the 24th of January, 1818, by Spain, should be ratified and confirmed to the same extent that the same grants would be valid if the territories had remained under the dominion of Spain."

The ninth article provided that "the United States would cause satisfaction to be made for the injuries, if any, which by process of law should be established to have been suffered by the Spanish officers and individual Spanish inhabitants by the late operations of the American army in Florida."

These articles of the treaty have given validity to what are now known as Spanish grants and claims for losses, in which so many of the people of Florida were interested.

The treaty was finally ratified on the 19th of February, 1821. The change of flags in East Florida took place at St. Augustine, 10th of July, 1821, under Governor Coppinger on the part of Spain, and Colonel Robert Butler on the part of the United States; in West Florida, at Pensacola, on the 21st of July, 1821, Governor Callava representing the Spanish government and General Jackson that of the United States.

CHAPTER XIX.

Organization of the Territory of Florida—Condition of the Indians—Treaty of Fort Moultrie—Indian Agency—Treaty of Payne's Landing—Collisions between the Races.

1821—1833.

UPON the change of flags the civil administration of affairs devolved upon the military authorities until the passage of an act of Congress, on the 3d of March, 1822, for the establishment of a territorial government in Florida, which provided that the territory ceded by Spain to the United States, known by the name of East and West Florida, should constitute a Territory of the United States, known by the name of the Territory of Florida. The government was to be administered by a governor appointed by the President, who was to be ex-officio Superintendent of Indian Affairs, and authorized to appoint all local officers. The legislative power was vested in the governor and in "thirteen of the most fit and discreet persons of the Territory," to be called the "Legislative Council," to be appointed annually by the President. The judicial power was vested in two superior courts, one for each division of the Territory. The governor was allowed a salary of two thousand five hundred dollars, the secretary fifteen hundred dollars, and the judges of the superior courts fifteen hundred dollars each; members of the Council three dollars per day. The first governor appointed was William P. Duval, of Kentucky. The first Legislative Council met at Pensacola, in June, 1822. An amended act of Congress, relative to the civil government of Florida, was passed 3d March, 1823, and the second session of the Legislative Council was held at St. Augustine. At the session of 1822 West Florida was divided into two counties, Escambia and Jackson, and East Florida into the counties of St. John's and Duval.

Dr. William H. Simmons and John Lee Williams, Esq., were appointed commissioners to select a site for the seat of government. They chose the old Indian fields of Tallahassee, then covered in part by a noble growth of live-oaks and magnolias, and in the vicinity of a beautiful cascade, which has long since disappeared. Their choice was approved by the Council in October, 1823, and the seat of government permanently established, retaining, with great good taste, the euphonious Indian name of Tallahassee. The first house was erected in the new capital in the spring of 1824, and the construction of the State-house began in 1826, but was not completed for many years. Gadsden and Monroe Counties were established in 1824, and subsequently Walton, Leon, Alachua, and Nassau. In 1825, Washington and Mosquito Counties were established. In 1827, Jefferson County, and, in 1828, Hamilton and Madison Counties were set off from Jefferson.

The settlement of the country would have progressed much more rapidly but for the difficulty of disposing of the Indians, who occupied so large a portion of the country.

The acquisition of Florida was regarded as a matter of great national importance, occupying, as it did, so large a portion of the Southern coast-line, and rendering its possession by an unfriendly power hazardous to the commerce of all the States bordering on the Mississippi and the Gulf of Mexico. It was also regarded with much interest as adding to the United States a tropical region, beyond the limits of frost, where the sugar-cane and tropical fruits could be cultivated.

The change of flags in Florida transferred the Indian tribes from the mild and timid control, almost nominal in its character, of the Spanish governors, to the exacting and ever-encroaching domination of the Americans. The previous difficulties, caused by the irruptions of the Georgians under Harris and Matthews, had created a strong feeling of repugnance between the Indians and the border white men. The Indians had so long remained in undisputed control of the country that they had never realized that any authority could be exercised superior to their own, and understood nothing of the idea of a sovereignty over their domain by any government or power. The chastisement inflicted upon them by General Jackson had considerably broken their power and diminished their numbers, but they still occupied the whole interior of Florida. The Spanish settlement had never extended far from the coast in the neighborhood of St. Augustine and Amelia Island on the east, and Pensacola on the west, while all the extensive range of country lying between the Cape of Florida on the south, the St. Mary's River on the north, and the Perdido on the west, some eight hundred miles in extent, was occupied by the tribes of Seminoles or Miccosukies.

The Miccosukies were considered to be the original occupants of the country, and the Seminoles were, as their name indicates, runaways from the Creek tribes living along the Chattahoochee River. A considerable number came into Florida in the year 1750, under Secoffee, a noted Creek chief, and settled in Alachua, the central part of the peninsula, a country possessing many very attractive features to an Indian. Secoffee left two sons, who became head chiefs, Payne and Bowlegs. In 1808 another band of Creeks settled in the vicinity of Tallahassee.*

The parent nation, originally called Muscogees or Creeks, was one of the most powerful tribes of natives on the continent; their villages, sometimes numbering two thousand souls, extending along the whole course of the Apalachicola and Chattahoochee Rivers.

The Seminoles were never very numerous, but occupied a vast extent of country. William Bartram, the celebrated botanist, visited a considerable part of the Indian country nearly a century since, in 1773, and gives this flattering account of the Seminoles in that day:

"They possess all of East Florida and a large part of West Florida, countries which, divided as they are by nature into innumerable islands, hills, and marshes, marked with many rivers, lakes, streams, and vast prairies, offer such a number of desirable localities convenient for settlement and inaccessible to enemies. This country, so irregular in its form, and so well watered, furnishes, besides, so great a quantity of the means of subsistence for wild animals, that I do not hesitate to say that no part of the world contains so much game, and so many animals suitable for the support of man.

"Surrounded with this great abundance, guaranteed from all extraneous attacks, the inhabitants of this region possess the two great requirements for men in their union as a society,—security for person and for property. With the skins of the deer, the bear, the tiger, and the wolf, they purchase from the traders clothing and other necessary articles. They have no wishes to gratify, or wants for which they are required to provide; no enemies to fear, no disquietudes, unless such as they may entertain from the

---

* Sprague's Florida War, 19.

continual progress of the white settlements. Content and tranquil, they seem as free from care as the birds of the air; like them they are light and volatile, like them they sing and coo. The Seminole presents the picture of perfect happiness. The joy, the internal content, the tender love, and the generous friendship, are imprinted on his very countenance, they show themselves in his demeanor and in his gestures, they seem to form his habitual state of existence, and to be a part of his nature, for their impress only departs from him with life."*

A pressure of interest was brought to bear upon Congress and the President, immediately after the cession of Florida to the United States, in order to have the country thrown open to settlement.

According to the usual practice, the governor was made Superintendent of Indian Affairs, and an Indian Agent appointed. Both were gentlemen of high character and unblemished reputation, and were, moreover, imbued with a very warm degree of sympathy for the Indians and a determination to protect them from aggression. The Indian Agent was Colonel Gad Humphreys, who had served with credit in the war with Great Britain.

The number of Indians in Florida, in the year 1822, was ascertained to be about four thousand, with perhaps one thousand negroes associated with them as slaves or otherwise. They had scattered villages throughout the territory, with an inconsiderable amount of land in cultivation, their main dependence being hunting and fishing.

The first demand made by citizens of the States adjoining Florida, was that the Indians of Florida should be removed from the northern and western part of the Territory and restricted within narrower limits. Efforts were at

---

* Bartram's Voyages, Paris edition, vol. i. p. 363.

once made by Colonel Humphreys, under the direction of the government, to obtain the meeting of a council of the principal chiefs, for the purpose of making a treaty on this subject.

A considerable number were induced to assemble at Fort Moultrie, six miles below St. Augustine, on the 18th September, 1823, where they were met by Governor W. P. Duval, James Gadsden, and Bernardo Segui, as commissioners on the part of the United States, and a treaty, called the Treaty of Fort Moultrie, was negotiated, by which the Indians agreed to remove within certain limits, the northern line of which was about twenty miles south of Micanopy, the United States agreeing to compensate them for all improvements they might abandon. A bonus of six thousand dollars was to be paid them, and an annuity of five thousand dollars per year for twenty years. The treaty was signed by a majority of the chiefs, but six of the most influential had to be conciliated by further concessions and liberty to retain their improvements.

Colonel Humphreys established his agency at Fort King, in the midst of the Indian settlements, and remained in charge of the agency until March, 1830, maintaining, during the whole period, a sincere and earnest championship for the rights of the people committed to his charge.

The usual difficulties attended the progress of the settlement of the country: the Indians stood in the way of the white settlers, who regarded them with an unfriendly eye. They, moreover, did not confine themselves to their limits, and thus gave ground for complaint. As the population of the country increased, a desire grew up to have the Indians entirely removed from the Territory.

The Legislature memorialized Congress, asking their speedy removal from the Territory, and "that commissioners should be appointed to hold a new treaty with them, stipulating for their immediate removal to the new country west of the Mississippi."

A considerable number of negroes were living with the Indians, mostly runaways. The parties from whom they had escaped were desirous of reclaiming them. The demand was resisted by the Indians, and hence difficulties continually arose.

On the 29th October, 1828, a *talk* was held at McKenzie's Pond, by Colonel G. Humphreys, Indian Agent, with Hicks, head chief, and a number of other chiefs, sub-chiefs, and warriors, for the purpose of prevailing on the chiefs of the Seminoles to send a delegation to examine the country west of the Mississippi, which it was proposed by the government to give to the Indians of Florida. At this talk it was determined by the chiefs that "they would organize a deputation for that purpose, to start early the ensuing spring, provided the agent himself would accompany the deputation on its tour of exploration; that their expenses should be paid; and provided, further, that nothing should be inferred from the journey of said deputation in the character of an obligation on the nation (or any part of it) to remove to the country visited by said deputation; and that such removal was not to be expected from them unless of their own free will and accord, after making the proposed examination."

This proposition of the Indians was transmitted to the Indian Bureau, but no action was had upon it. Procrastination discouraged the Indians, who soon after declared their determination to remain upon the land.*

The relations with the Indians became more and more troublesome. The interior of Florida was a fine grazing country, and stock-raising was exceedingly profitable, and

---

* Sprague's Florida War, 65.

was the readiest employment, as well as the most lucrative, to which the white settlers could give their attention. The Indians remained in the best grazing region, and they also owned considerable stock. This stock, both hogs and cattle, was only to be recognized by marks and brands; and, for the purpose of marking and branding, the cattle were gathered every spring by the cattle-drivers. Of course they did not always get up all the stock they had a claim to, and left in the woods a considerable number of wild cattle, unmarked, and called in the Florida vernacular *heretics* and wild hogs. Collisions and difficulties grew out of the disputed ownership of cattle, and invasions of each other's limits in pursuit of stock were frequent. All losses were naturally charged upon the Indians, and complaints were unceasingly made, and demands of indemnity. Another source of trouble was the harboring of fugitive slaves in the Indian towns. From a long period anterior to the change of flags, runaway negroes from Georgia and South Carolina had joined the Indians, and, by intermarriage, had become connected with and intermingled with them. They naturally received, and were disposed to protect, the runaways who might escape from the neighboring white settlements. The negroes were so numerous among the Seminoles in 1816 that at the destruction of the negro fort on the Apalachicola, by the United States troops, there were three hundred in the fort who were killed or captured; and some five hundred negroes were engaged in the battle at Suwanee Old Town, in 1818. Their number in 1836 was estimated at fourteen hundred.* It is said by many familiar with the subject that they exercised a very powerful influence over the Indians; and they certainly added a very important difficulty to the many others involved in negotiations with the Indians.

---

* Gidding. Exiles of Florida, p. 97.

A restlessness and distrust began to pervade both the Indians and white settlers, and a constant pressure began towards an enforced emigration of the Indians to the West. The Indian tribes remaining in Georgia were also a subject of annoyance to the people of that State, and a feeling had grown up and was then generally entertained in the South and Southwest, that all these Indian tribes should be removed to the west of the Mississippi.

The prevalence of intoxication, induced by the fondness of the Indians for strong liquors, and promoted by the unprincipled venders of this poison, from the sale of which they not only derived large profits, but still larger advantages from the trades consummated with drunken Indians for their property while in a state of inebriation, occasioned numberless petty difficulties and brawls, which laid up in the Indian mind revengeful memories.

The agent, Colonel Humphreys, was accused of being too partial to the Indians,—certainly not a common charge, —and influences were brought to bear, at Washington, by which his removal was effected in 1830.

He was succeeded by Mr. John Phagan. The secretary and acting governor of the Territory, in an official letter dated 5th November, 1833, said that he found, on his visit to the agency, evidences of fraud and improper conduct on the part of Major Phagan; that he had sub-contracts with employees of the agency for much less than the amount they receipted for to the government, and that even then he was a defaulter to them.* It may therefore be presumed that his character and conduct would have been unsatisfactory to the Indians.

The proposals made by Colonel Humphreys, to send a delegation West, were revived, and after many delays

---

* Sprague's History of the Florida War, p. 72.

Major Phagan succeeded in getting together a respectable portion of the chiefs of the Seminoles at Payne's Landing, a point on the Ocklawaha near Orange Springs, on the 9th of May, 1832, where they were met by Colonel James Gadsden, as a commissioner on the part of the United States, and the treaty of Payne's Landing was formed.

The preamble to this treaty recites that the Seminole Indians, regarding with just respect the solicitude manifested by the President of the United States for the improvement of their condition, by recommending a removal to a country more suitable to their habits and wants than Florida, are willing that their confidential chiefs, Jumper, Fuch-lus-to-had-jo, Charley Emathla, Coi-had-jo, Holati Emathla, Ya-ha-had-jo, and Sam Jones, accompanied by their agent, Major John Phagan, and their faithful interpreter, Abraham, should be sent, at the expense of the United States, to examine the country assigned to the Creeks west of the Mississippi River, *and should they be satisfied with the character of the country,* and of the favorable disposition of the Creeks to reunite with the Seminoles as one people, the articles of the compact and agreement herein stipulated at Payne's Landing, on the Ocklawaha River, the ninth day of May, 1832, between James Gadsden for and on behalf of the United States, and the undersigned chiefs and head-men for and in behalf of the Seminole Indians, *shall be binding on the respective parties.*

The first article surrendered their lands in Florida for an equal extent of country west of the Mississippi.

The second article stipulated for the payment of the sum of fifteen thousand four hundred dollars, to be divided among them.

The third article provided for giving a blanket, etc. to each, on their arrival at their destination.

The fourth article gave an annuity of three thousand dollars for ten years.

The fifth article provided for the payment by the United States for their cattle.

The sixth was as follows:—

"The Seminoles being anxious to be relieved from the repeated vexatious demands for slaves and other property alleged to have been stolen and destroyed by them, so that they may remove unembarrassed to their new homes, the United States stipulate to have the same (properly) investigated, and to liquidate such as may be satisfactorily established, provided the amount does not exceed seven thousand ($7000) dollars."

The seventh article provided that the Indians would remove within three years after the ratification of this agreement, the emigration to commence as early as practicable in the year 1833, and the remainder of the Indians in equal proportions in the years 1834 and 1835.*

The language of the preamble, it will be observed, is that the Indians are willing that their *confidential* chiefs, Jumper, etc., shall be sent out to examine the country west of the Mississippi River, and if *they* were satisfied with it, then the articles of the treaty relative to their removal should be binding on the respective parties. Whatever may have been the understanding and intention of the Indians, the language used is susceptible of but one construction : the pronoun *they* must necessarily relate to the confidential chiefs just before named, and does not sustain Captain (now General) Sprague's remark that "the fulfillment of the treaty was clearly conditional. If the Indians, that is, the nation, were satisfied with the country,

---

* For the complete text of the treaty, see Sprague's History of the Florida War, 75.

as represented by those sent to explore it, a voluntary emigration would take place." (Page 76.) Even Mr. Giddings, with his strong desire to censure the whole transaction, does not attempt to raise any question as to the plain language of the treaty, merely referring to it as *vague language.**

The confidential chiefs, or Indian Commissioners, as they may properly be called, commenced their journey in September, 1832, accompanied by Major Phagan, their agent, and were engaged in examining the country west of Arkansas until the last of March, 1833,—a period, one would suppose, permitting of a very careful examination.

The executive, acting upon the plain language of the treaty, appointed Messrs. Montfort Stokes, H. L. Ellsworth, and J. F. Schermerhorn commissioners on the part of the United States to meet the confidential chiefs, who had been appointed by the Seminoles, at Fort Gibson, to ascertain the result of their examination, and, if satisfactory, to make such other arrangements as might be deemed requisite to carry the treaty into effect. What is called an "additional treaty" was made at Fort Gibson on the 28th day of March, 1833, by the aforenamed commissioners on the part of the United States, and by Jumper and all the other delegates of the Seminole nation of Indians on the part of said nation. The preamble recites the principal provisions of the treaty of Payne's Landing, and says that "Whereas, the special delegation appointed by the Seminoles on the 9th of May, 1832, have since examined the land designated for them by the undersigned commissioners on behalf of the United States, and have expressed themselves *satisfied* with the same, in and by their letter dated March, 1833, addressed to the under-

---

* Exiles of Florida, p. 84.

signed commissioners: Now, therefore, the commissioners aforesaid, by virtue of the treaty made with the Creek Indians on the 14th February, 1833, hereby designate and assign to the Seminole tribe of Indians, for their separate future residence *forever*, a tract of land lying between the Canadian River and the North Fork thereof, and extending west to where a line, running north and south between the main Canadian and north branch thereof, will strike the forks of Little River; and the undersigned Seminole chiefs, delegated as aforesaid on behalf of their nation, hereby declare themselves well satisfied with the location provided for them by the commissioners, and agree that their nation shall commence the removal to their new home as soon as the government will make arrangements for their emigration satisfactory to the Seminole nation."*

This treaty was ratified by the Senate of the United States, as was also that of Payne's Landing.

Looking at the transaction as it appears upon its face, there seems no ground to assume anything but good faith and fair dealing on the part of the government. The country designated for the Seminoles was as fertile and as well situated for their support as the one they surrendered. The climate was colder, and their favorite light-wood was wanting; they were, however, relieved of the vexatious and increasing hostility of their white neighbors; they had a boundless region lying west of them, and game, including the buffalo, in the greatest abundance.

It is said that, when they returned, the nation was dissatisfied with what they had done, and that they disowned their own acts; that the Seminoles charged them with having been circumvented by the United States. Some of those who had signed the treaty, in deference to the pop-

---

* Sprague's Florida War, p. 77.

ular clamor, became the warmest opponents of removal, and in the war which succeeded took arms against the government. All this may be true, without there being any cause for reflection upon the government or its agents. The removal of the Indian tribes from the States fast settling up with the white race was a necessity, unless the richest and most productive portions of the United States were to be surrendered to them as hunting-grounds. Five thousand Indians were scattered over a country equaling in extent the State of New York. In Georgia and Alabama the Indian tribes still lingered, and there were continually influences at work to induce the Indians to hold possession of the country and to resist all attempts at removal. It is easy, in every community, for the young, the thoughtless, the restless, and the foolish to create resistance to a wise policy or a necessity, and to raise a clamor which passes for the voice of the people, when, in fact, it is but the noise of the few prevailing over the silence of the many. Thus it was in Florida; young warriors, who had no experience in warfare, restless men, who desired excitement, and the runaway negroes, who believed their security imperiled by emigration, excited a resistance which the older men and chiefs had little part in organizing, but had no power to withstand.

The treaty and additional treaty were ratified by the Senate on the 9th of April, 1834, and a proclamation to that effect was issued by President Jackson on the 12th of April, 1834.

Measures were at once taken to effect the removal of the Indians. Major Phagan, the Agent, was superseded by General Wiley Thompson, and Colonel Duncan L. Clinch, an experienced army officer, was placed in command of the United States forces.

General Thompson was informed, in October, 1834, by

the United States officers in command at Fort King, of the determination of the influential chiefs not to emigrate, and of the hostility felt towards Charley Emathla, who had declared himself in favor of emigration.

Violent language was used by some of the chiefs in a council called by General Thompson, and Osceola drew his knife in anger, and, driving it into the table, said, "The only treaty I will execute is with this." As he was only a sub-chief of the Red Sticks, and a half-breed of inferior standing, this something like stage-trick attracted but little attention.

The negroes exercised, it is asserted, a wonderful control,* and they undoubtedly added very much to the barbarity and savage manner with which the war was prosecuted.

The subject of emigration was, of course, a constant topic of conversation, and, when at the Agency, the Indians were impudent, and treated the matter of their removal with ridicule. Charley Emathla alone, of the old chiefs, took decided ground in favor of emigration, and pointed out to the Indians the destruction and eventual defeat which awaited them.

General Thompson, in a report to the Secretary of War, of October, 1834, says that he had observed that the Indians were buying powder in considerable quantities, and he understood that they had a deposit of forty or fifty kegs. In November, he writes that he is satisfied that they have been tampered with by designing and unprincipled whites.

---

* Sprague's Florida War, 81.

CHAPTER XX.

Hostile Disposition of the Indians—Murder of General Thompson, Indian Agent—Massacre of Major Dade's Command—Battle of the Withlacoochee—General Scott's Campaign.

1834—1836.

As time elapsed, it became evident to the Indian Agent and the military and civil officers in Florida that the Indians had determined not to emigrate, and would altogether repudiate the treaty of Payne's Landing and the supplementary treaty of Fort Gibson. Ten companies of troops were placed at General Clinch's disposal, to enforce the provisions of the treaty. In February, 1835, the Secretary of War directed General Clinch to fully explain to the Indians the determination of the government to insist upon their removal, and that they should be made fully aware of the consequences of resistance, and then, "if necessary, let actual force be employed and their removal effected."

General Jackson, then President of the United States, sent a "talk" to be read to the chiefs, urging their compliance with the treaty. Preparations for supplies, transportation, etc. were made by the War Department, upon a scale supposed to be fully equal to any probable requirement.

On the 24th of April, 1835, another council was held at the Indian Agency, which was attended by Colonel Clinch and General Thompson, the Agent, and by a large number of the influential chiefs. The chiefs had agreed, beforehand, to interpose an unqualified negative to the proposal for their removal. On their assembling, Jumper acted as their mouthpiece, and declared their determination to remain in Florida. General Thompson responded with some warmth, which led to recriminations, and a scene of confusion ensued. General Clinch interposed, and urged their fulfillment of the treaty, telling them of his orders to use his troops to enforce it. Eight of the chiefs came forward and agreed to emigrate, and five refused to abide by it; these were Sam Jones, Jumper, Micanopy, Alligator, and Black Dirt. General Thompson at once struck the names of these five from the roll of chiefs, which created great ill feeling and was a most injudicious step, afterwards disapproved of by the Secretary of War and the President. At the solicitation of the eight chiefs, the time for preparation for removal was extended until the 1st of January following, when they promised that they would assemble at the points designated for their embarkation. The Indians seemed quieted, for a time at least, but how far they acted in good faith in making this promise is more than questionable, and it seems quite probable that they sought nothing more than the delay necessary to secure their crops and ammunition and mature their plans. They continued to purchase ammunition and arms, until an order was issued by the Agent forbidding the sale of these articles to the Indians. This the Indians regarded as an act of hostility and an insult. Osceola was refused the privilege of purchasing powder, and in a burst of savage indignation exclaimed, "Am I a negro—a slave? My skin is dark, but not black! I am an Indian—a Seminole! The white man shall not make me black! I will make the white man red with blood, and then blacken him in the sun and rain, where the wolf shall smell of his bones and the buzzard live upon his flesh!"

This daring and impetuous leader was frequently at the Agency, comporting himself with reserve and sullenness, and using violent and intemperate language, and, on one occasion, carried his disrespect to General Thompson to such an extent that it was deemed necessary to arrest him and confine him in irons several days, until he professed to be penitent: on the solicitation of other chiefs he was released. He then expressed an entire willingness to emigrate, and subsequently brought in seventy of his followers, who made the same pledge.

In October, Major Llewellyn Williams and six of his neighbors discovered a party of Indians near the Cannapa-ha Pond, butchering a beef. As the Indians were a long distance outside of their boundaries, the white party disarmed them and flogged some of them, but one escaped, and two Indian hunters coming up fired on the party of Major Williams. A skirmish ensued, in which two of the Indians were killed, and three of the white men wounded, one mortally.

About the same time, the express-rider from Tampa Bay to Fort King was murdered by the Indians.

Charley Emathla had commenced his preparations for removal, and gathered his cattle for appraisement and sale. Osceola, at the head of a party of Miccosukies, met the old chief on the trail to his village, in the latter part of November, and shot him down. A friendly chief, with a large number of women and children, now sought protection at Tampa Bay.

General Clinch asked for additional troops, and fourteen companies were directed to report to him from various military posts. The estimated number of Indians was three thousand, including women, children, and negroes, and, in all, from four to five hundred fighting-men. The number of Indians was very greatly underestimated, as the government soon ascertained; but upon their estimate the force placed under command of General Clinch seemed ample to compel submission. The ignorance of the government agents as to the real number of the Indians in Florida seems strange, considering the intercourse maintained through the Indian Agency and the traders. The error was a very fatal one, and the remissness of the War Department, in not sending troops in sufficient numbers as soon as the hostile intentions of the Indians were known, was very censurable. The authorities at Washington seem hardly to have comprehended the warlike character of the Seminoles, or their powers of resistance. It is not surprising that this supineness of the government should have emboldened the Indians, the majority of whom were too young to recall the campaign of Jackson in 1818. They had never seen more than a few companies of troops, and had learned to despise the supposed feebleness of the government of the United States, while the many councils and "talks" held with them, to persuade them into acquiescence, undoubtedly seemed to betoken conscious weakness.

Osceola had dissembled his real feelings and intentions to such a degree as to deceive the agent and people into the belief of his sincerity; but, brooding over his arrest and imprisonment, he thirsted for revenge. Gathering a band of some twenty of his followers, he approached the Indian Agency, seeking an opportunity to glut his vengeance. For two or three days no opportunity presented itself; but, on the afternoon of the 28th of December, General Thompson walked out after dinner in company with Lieutenant Constantine Smith, enjoying a cigar. The day being pleasant, they extended their walk towards the military sutler's, some distance from the fort. Unsuspicious of danger, they were already covered by the watchful eyes and unerring rifles of Osceola and his companions. At a given signal, the whole number of Indians fired upon them. General Thompson and the lieutenant fell, pierced by many balls. The Indians rushed out with a yell, and scalped and mutilated their victims within sight of the fort. Proceeding to the sutler's store, they fired upon the party within, and, after scalping them and cutting in pieces their bodies, set fire to the building.

The force in the fort consisted of only forty-six men, and it was supposed that the number of attacking Indians was much larger. It was consequently deemed imprudent to weaken the garrison by sending out any portion of the troops. Osceola and his band, however, contemplated nothing further than the destruction of the agent, General Thompson, and the sutler, Mr. Rogers, who had probably also incurred their enmity. The Indians left immediately after they had fired the sutler's store.

Major Francis L. Dade, of the 4th Infantry, had been ordered from Key West to Fort Brooke, and on the 21st of December arrived at Tampa Bay, with Company A of his regiment, thirty-nine men, and a small supply of ammunition. To this force was joined Captain Gardiner's company, C, of 2d Artillery, and Frazer's company, B, 3d Artillery, fifty men each. This force was directed to proceed to Fort King to strengthen that post. The distance was about one hundred and thirty miles, and the route lay through an entirely unsettled country. No one connected with the expedition being acquainted with the country, Major Dade secured the services of a negro slave named Lewis, belonging to a sutler of the name of Antonio Pacheco.*

---

* Giddings's Exiles of Florida, p. 101. Mr. Giddings makes a very pretty romance out of this negro Lewis, who must have been, by his

This guide, it is said, informed the Indians of the date of departure and the intended route, with the view of affording them a favorable opportunity of making an attack. The point of rendezvous agreed upon by the Seminole leaders was the Big Wahoo Swamp. Osceola, however, had determined to first wreak his vengeance upon General Thompson, which he so successfully accomplished.

The troops under Major Dade commenced their march on the 24th of December. The officers attached to the command were Major F. L. Dade, 4th Infantry, Captain S. Gardiner, Second Lieutenant W. E. Basinger, Second Lieutenant R. Henderson, 2d Artillery, Captain U. S. Frazer, Second Lieutenant R. R. Mudge, Second Lieutenant J. L. Reais, 3d Artillery, Assistant Surgeon J. S. Gatlin, and about one hundred men belonging to the 4th Infantry and 2d and 3d Artillery. One six-pounder fieldpiece and one light wagon, with ten days' provisions, accompanied them. On reaching the Hillsborough River they were delayed some time on account of the bridge having been burned by the Indians.

On the 27th they reached the Withlacoochee, and camped. The next morning they continued their march through an open pine country, and in apparent security, utterly unapprehensive of danger. Their road was skirted, however, by the low palmetto, which afforded a covert for the Indians, who were stationed on the west side of the road, where it passed near a pond. The troops were marching along in open order, and extending a considerable distance. The Indians, posted near trees, and well concealed,

---

account, an Admirable Crichton. "He had been well bred, was polite, accomplished, and learned. He read, wrote, and spoke with facility the Spanish, French, and English languages, and spoke the Indian." This accomplished negro, it is said, had formerly belonged to Genera Clinch. He was the subject of the celebrated Pacheco Claim in 1848.

were to await the signal of attack, to be given by Micanopy, when each should select his object. They were mostly within a distance of thirty or forty yards, and, of course, their fire could hardly fail to be destructive. Nearly half the command fell at the first fire, which, proceeding from an unseen foe, gave no opportunity of seeking shelter from, or returning it. The number of Indians engaged was, according to the report of Alligator, one hundred and eighty warriors, and, having secured the advantage of the loss inflicted by the first fire, they were enabled to reload.

Those who escaped the first discharge took shelter behind trees, and Lieutenant Basinger poured in five or six rounds of canister upon the Indians, which checked them for some time. They retreated over a small ridge and disappeared. Captain Frazer was killed at the first fire; Lieutenant Mudge was mortally wounded, and Lieutenant Reais had both arms broken; they were bound up, and he reclined against some logs until he was killed late in the action. Lieutenant Henderson had his left arm broken, but continued to load and fire his piece until late in the second attack, when he too was killed. Captain Gardiner, Lieutenant Basinger, and Dr. Gatlin were the only officers who escaped unhurt by the first volley.

On the retreat of the Indians, Captain Gardiner commenced the erection of the breastwork of pine-trees. In about three-quarters of an hour the Indians returned to the attack and commenced a cross-fire on the breastwork with deadly execution. Lieutenant Basinger continued to fire the six-pounder until all the men who served the piece were shot. Captain Gardiner at length fell. Dr. Gatlin, with two double-barreled guns, continued to fire on the Indians until he fell, late in the action; and Lieutenant Basinger was wounded. About two o'clock the last man fell, and the Indians then rushed into the breastwork, headed by a heavy painted savage, who, believing that all were dead, made a speech to the Indians. They then stripped off the accoutrements of the soldiers and took their arms, without offering any indignity, and retired in a body.

Soon after the Indians had left, about fifty negroes galloped up on horseback and alighted, and at once commenced a horrible butchery. If any poor fellow on the ground showed signs of life, the negroes stabbed and tomahawked him. Lieutenant Basinger, being still alive, started up and begged the wretches to spare his life; they mocked at his prayers, while they mangled him with their hatchets until he was relieved by death.

After stripping the dead, the negroes shot the oxen and burned the gun-carriages. Shortly after the negroes retired, a soldier named Wilson, of Captain Gardiner's company, crawled out, and, discovering that Rawson Clark was still alive, asked him to go back to Tampa with him. As he jumped over the breastwork, an Indian shot him. Clark lay down, and at night, with De Coney, another wounded man, made the best of his way to Tampa. The next day, De Coney was killed by an Indian; Clark concealed himself in a scrub, and the following day reached Tampa. Another soldier, named Thomas, bribed an Indian and was allowed to escape.

Captain Hitchcock, with a detachment of troops, passed over the ground on the 20th of February following, and thus describes the appearance of the battle-ground, which had not before been visited by the United States forces:

"Our advanced guard had passed the ground without halting, when General Gaines and his staff came upon one of the most appalling scenes that can be imagined. We first saw some broken and scattered boxes, then a cart, the two oxen of which were lying dead, as if they had fallen asleep, their yokes still on them; a little to the right, one or two horses were seen. We then came to a small inclosure, made by felling trees in such a manner as to form a triangular breastwork for defense. Within the triangle, along the north and west faces of it, were about thirty bodies, mostly mere skeletons, but much of the clothing was left upon them. These were lying, almost every one of them, in precisely the same position they must have occupied during the fight,—their heads next to the logs over which they had delivered their fire, and their bodies stretched, with striking regularity, parallel to each other. They had evidently been shot dead at their posts, and the Indians had not disturbed them, except by taking the scalps of most of them. Passing this little breastwork, we found other bodies along the road, and by the side of the road, generally behind the trees which had been resorted to for covers from the enemy's fire.

"Advancing about two hundred yards farther, we found a cluster of bodies in the middle of the road. These were evidently the advanced guard, in the rear of which was the body of Major Dade, and to the right that of Captain Frazer.

"These were all, doubtless, shot down at the first fire of the Indians, except perhaps Captain Frazer, who must have fallen very early in the fight. Those in the road and by the trees fell during the first attack. It was during the cessation of the fire that the little band still remaining, about thirty in number, threw up the triangular breastwork, which, from the haste with which it was constructed, was necessarily defective, and could not protect the men in the second attack."*

---

* For Alligator's account of the massacre, see Sprague's History of the Florida War, p. 90.

Osceola and his band arrived at the Wahoo Swamp that night, too late to participate in the fight, but in time to assist in the celebration of the victory.

It was not until some time afterwards that General Clinch learned the fate of Dade's command. It is said, however, that on the next day after the Dade massacre it was known among the negroes in St. Augustine that a terrible slaughter of white troops had taken place in the interior, the news, it is supposed, having been rapidly communicated by Indian runners through the country, and that the Indian negroes sent word to their relatives in St. Augustine.

The treacherous negro guide, Luis Pacheco, feigned to fall at the first fire, but joined the Indians at the earliest moment, and ever afterwards remained with and aided them, and was eventually sent to Arkansas, where his accomplishments seem to have been obscured.

This massacre astounded the country. No such event had ever before occurred in the annals of Indian warfare. That two entire companies of trained and disciplined soldiers, fully armed and in perfect order and equipment, well and bravely officered, with a field-piece at their command, in an open field and under the bright sun of a Florida sky, should be totally cut off and annihilated by a not very numerous band of half-naked savages, was without a parallel. Alligator says that he counted the whole Indian force, amounting to one hundred and eighty. Captain Hitchcock estimated, from the appearance of the ground afterwards, that there must have been three hundred and fifty. The true number will never be known; but, even supposing the latter estimate correct, it seems at first sight extraordinary that such a number could accomplish the entire destruction of a body of disciplined troops.

On the 1st of December, General Clinch heard of the murder of Charley Emathla, and at once called for volunteers, and by the 15th several companies from Nassau and Duval Counties joined General Call, with five hundred men from Middle Florida, at Newnansville. On their way to Fort Drane they encountered two small parties of Indians, and reached Fort Drane on the 24th of December, and formed a junction with General Clinch. As the volunteers were levied for only one month, the forces were put in motion for the Withlacoochee as soon as Colonel Fanning, with three companies of artillery from Fort King, could join them. These having arrived, the expedition reached the Withlacoochee on the 31st, and most of the troops had succeeded in crossing, when they were attacked by the Indians, who had anticipated their attempt to cross at the usual ford, and were prepared to dispute their passage at that point, where the advantages of position would have been greatly in their favor.

The Indians had spent the night of the 28th in a drunken carousal, and were perhaps on that account less watchful than usual. General Clinch had only a canoe to cross with, and some of the volunteers swam their horses over, but the larger number, under General Call, were still on the other side of the river when the attack commenced. The force which had crossed consisted of one hundred and ninety-five regulars and twenty-seven volunteers, and that of the Indians of two hundred and fifty, inclusive of thirty negroes, led by Osceola and Alligator. The Indians fought bravely, and the fortune of the day hung for some time in the balance; the Indians were protected by a heavy hammock and scrub, and poured a galling fire upon the troops, who charged twice up to the hammock and fell back, until at length General Clinch dismounted, addressed his men with much feeling, and ordered another charge, which resulted in the total rout of the enemy. The battle was fought within three miles of Osceola's town; and the Indians, fresh from their victory over Major Dade, fought with impetuosity and great perseverance. The Indian loss in the engagement, so far as known, was five killed and several wounded. The regulars under General Clinch lost four killed and twenty-five wounded, and the volunteers had fifteen wounded. General Clinch had a ball through his cap and another through his sleeve. The time of the volunteers being about to expire, General Clinch returned with his command to Fort Drane unmolested. The volunteers returned home, and General Clinch was left with but one hundred and fifty men to hold the important positions of Fort King, Fort Drane, and Micanopy, and to guard the wagon-trains which were requisite to supply his troops with provisions.

The settlements in the interior were at once broken up; and the inhabitants gathered in stockades or fled to the coast. Below St. Augustine, and in the neighborhood of New Smyrna, extensive sugar plantations had been opened. During the month of January, 1836, sixteen plantations, employing from one hundred to two hundred negroes, were entirely destroyed, with all their buildings and improvements. The country was desolated in every direction, and many of the settlers, men, women, and children, were ruthlessly massacred. The Indians made it literally a war to the knife. On the 17th of January, Major Putnam went to Tomoka in command of two companies of militia; they camped at Dunlawton, and were attacked by a superior force of Indians, under King Philip, and compelled to retreat. Seventeen of the volunteers were wounded, two mortally, and a son of Hon. Elias B. Gould fell into the hands of the Indians and was killed by them.

The public mind was thoroughly aroused, and volunteers came in rapidly from the adjoining States. General Clinch was authorized to call for and accept any amount of force he might require from South Carolina, Georgia, and Alabama.

General Gaines was on duty at New Orleans at this time, with a considerable force of regular troops at his command. Upon receiving information of the massacre of Major Dade's command, and a report that Fort Brooke, on Tampa Bay, was invested by a force of negroes and Indians, he deemed the emergency so grave that he ought, with the forces at his command, to proceed with all haste to the rescue, without awaiting the slow progress of official orders from Washington. He dispatched a messenger to General Clinch, informing him of his intention to leave at once for Fort Brooke with seven hundred men, and that he would be glad to co-operate with General Clinch for the prompt chastisement of the Indians.

General Gaines embarked at New Orleans on the 3d of February with a force of eleven hundred men, comprising six companies of the 4th Infantry, who were doubtless eager to avenge the loss of their comrades in Major Dade's command, and a regiment of Louisiana volunteers under command of General Persifer Smith. He reached Fort Brooke on the 10th, and on the 13th commenced a march across the country to Fort King. He had no means of transportation, and the men carried ten days' rations on their backs. On the 20th they reached the scene of the Dade massacre, and on the 22d of February arrived at Fort King, without having seen a hostile Indian, but not without having been watched and seen by them. At Fort King he found one company of artillery, with no surplus provisions beyond their own rations. General Clinch was at Fort Drane, equally unprovided, and General Gaines found himself far from any base of supplies, almost out of provisions.

With great chagrin, the generous and gallant soldier and his comrades concluded that no other course was left to them but to return to Fort Brooke, and, to give a fuller exhibition of his force, he concluded to take a return route considerably to the west of the one by which he had come up, having been assured by his guides that a ford could be found lower down the Withlacoochee. On the 27th, he reached this river, and, while searching for the ford, the Indians opened fire from the opposite bank. The river was here some thirty yards wide, deep and rapid. While trying to ascertain the depth of the water, Lieutenant Izard was mortally wounded. The crossing in face of the enemy was found impracticable. Finding a considerable body of Indians in front of him, General Gaines sent an express to General Clinch, desiring him to bring what force and provisions he could spare, and co-operate with him in an attack upon them. This General Clinch was unable to do, as he had been superseded in the command of the forces in Florida by General Scott, and was without provisions.

General Gaines proceeded to strengthen his position, while at the same time he prepared rafts for crossing the river. On the 29th, a vigorous attack was made upon the troops from all sides, which continued for two hours, during which one man was killed, and three officers and thirty of the men wounded. On the 30th, another express was sent to General Clinch, asking for provisions and a reinforcement. Upon the receipt of General Gaines's letter, inclosed to him by General Clinch, General Scott had written to the latter, expressing a considerable amount of pique against General Gaines, applying to him the term interloper, and saying, "even if you had sufficient stores and means of transportation, I should command you to send no subsistence to him, unless to prevent starvation." There seems to have been a strong personal dislike existing between

General Scott and General Gaines, which interfered with prompt relief being furnished to the latter.

General Clinch, however, on receipt of this second message of General Gaines, and learning the condition of his command, gathered some cattle, and, taking stores from his own plantation, went, with one hundred men, to his relief.

General Gaines was now closely besieged for several days; the rations were reduced to a pint of corn per day, and they began to consume their horses and dogs.

General Clinch reached their camp on the 6th of March, and on the 9th General Gaines turned over the command of his troops to General Clinch, who returned with them to Fort Drane on the 10th. A talk had been held between Captain Hitchcock, of General Gaines's staff, and Osceola, Jumper, and Alligator, on the day of General Clinch's arrival, in which they had consented to make peace if they could be allowed to remain south of the Withlacoochee.

General Scott had now assumed the command in Florida, and planned a campaign on paper, which he felt satisfied would close the war in a single season.

His plan was to form three wings, which were to move simultaneously from Volusia, on the St. John's River, Fort Drane, near Orange Lake, about the centre of the peninsula, and Tampa Bay, and to thus inclose the whole Indian force supposed to be about the forks of the Withlacoochee. Unfortunately, this distinguished military commander was not familiar with the nature of the country, or with the character of the foe against whom he had to contend. It was a very great mistake, as is now generally admitted, to supersede General Clinch, who was better calculated than any one else, at that time, to operate against the Indians, and who had achieved the only decided success which had been obtained.

General Scott's combinations were good only on paper; the delays and obstacles inseparable from movements in such a country met him at every step. Indians, who could slip through the lines in a single night, were not to be caught by a trilateral movement. The campaign was a failure, and operations closed by the 1st of June. This was unfortunate, as it left an impression, on the minds of the Indians, of the weakness of the government.

The wings of General Scott's movement had marched and countermarched between Fort King and Tampa, but, with the exception of a few skirmishes, nothing was accomplished.

During the summer of 1836, the regulars were ordered to summer quarters, and the volunteers returned home. General Clinch, disgusted with the treatment he had received at the hands of the War Department, resigned his commission and retired to his home at St. Mary's.

About the middle of March, Major McLemore had been ordered to the Suwanee, to procure a quantity of corn and proceed with it to the Withlacoochee River, for the use of the troops. He executed the order, and erected a small block-house, about fifteen miles up the river, and left Captain Halliman with a small party to defend it until General Scott should send for it. Major McLemore died within a few days after making his camp, and his detachment at the block-house was lost sight of. On the 12th of April, the Indians attacked them in large numbers, but were spiritedly repulsed. On the 3d of May, Captain Halliman was shot, and on the 15th and 24th heavy assaults were made and the roof of the block-house was burned off. The garrison were twenty-eight days subsisting on corn alone, and were finally rescued by sending down three men in a boat, who reported their situation, and a force was sent to relieve them.

The Indians pursued their predatory incursions, cutting off express-riders and butchering exposed families. In June they made an attack upon the post at Micanopy, some two hundred or more participating in the affair, but they were promptly met by Major Heileman, the gallant officer in command, and driven two miles. Major Heileman died shortly afterwards, from the effects of overexertion during the engagement.

In August, a sharp skirmish occurred at Fort Drane, between a force of one hundred and ten men, commanded by Major Pierce, and three hundred Indians, under command of Arpeika.

On the 1st of May, Judge Randall's plantation, east of Tallahassee, was attacked and negroes stolen, and on the 8th hostile Indians appeared near St. Mark's.

Fort King was abandoned about the last of May. The summer of 1836 was a very sickly season, and the troops suffered severely at all the posts. Fort Drane was especially unhealthy, and was ordered to be abandoned in July. A wagon-train, removing the stores from that point with a large escort, was attacked near Micanopy, and would probably have been captured but for the timely arrival of reinforcements.

All the settlements east of the St. John's, lying south of the Picolata Road, had been destroyed, and all those south of Black Creek and Newnansville had been broken up. In July, the Indians appeared on the St. John's River, at New Switzerland, and attacked the places of Colonel Hallows, Dr. Simmons, and Mr. Colt, and destroyed the buildings. They afterwards appeared in considerable force at the Travers plantation, at the mouth of Black Creek, and a sharp skirmish ensued with a detachment under Lieutenant Herbert.

About the last of August the post at Micanopy was

broken up, and the whole country between Newnansville and Tampa abandoned to the Indians, who found abundant supplies on the deserted plantations.

In September, the Johns family, seventeen miles west from Jacksonville, was attacked, Mr. Johns was killed, Mrs. Johns shot and scalped, and the house burned. A little later a large force of Indians approached Newnansville. Colonel Warren marched out to meet them upon the edge of San Felasco Hammock, with a force consisting of one hundred mounted volunteers, twenty-five citizens, and twenty-five United States regulars under Captain Tompkins, with a twenty-four-pound howitzer. After about two hours' fighting, the Indians retreated.

The command of the army in Florida now devolved upon General R. K. Call, of Florida. General Armstrong, with a command of twelve hundred Tennesseeans who had been operating in the Creek country, was ordered to report to General Call for duty in Florida. With these troops, one hundred and forty Florida militia, and one hundred and sixty regulars under Major Pierce, General Call began an offensive movement on the Withlacoochee in October, but, being prevented by high water from crossing, he fell back upon Fort Drane for supplies.

In November, General Call, reinforced by some regular troops and a regiment of Creek volunteers, advanced again to the Withlacoochee, and crossed and attacked an Indian encampment, which was broken up and the Indians routed. On the 18th, five hundred Tennesseeans attacked a considerable body of the enemy, posted strongly in a hammock. After two hours' hard fighting, the Indians fled, leaving twenty-five dead on the field. On the 20th, Lieutenant-Colonel Pierce, with a detachment of regulars, joined General Call.

The enemy being reported in large numbers in Wahoo

Swamp, an attack was made in that quarter, and an engagement ensued, lasting several hours. The Indians being protected by a creek and deep miry swamp, it was found impracticable to dislodge them, and the forces of General Call retired again to Fort Drane for supplies.

This affair ended military operations for the year 1836. The result of the year's campaign was well calculated to encourage the Indians. They had driven not only the citizens but the troops nearly out of the peninsula, and at its close held their ground in all quarters. They had clearly the advantage thus far.

In October, General Jesup reached Tampa, and in the latter part of November joined General Call at Volusia, with four hundred men, and, under instructions of the War Department, relieved that officer of the command of the army in Florida.

CHAPTER XXI.

Florida War, continued—General Jesup in Command—Indian Assault on Fort Mellon—Capitulation of Fort Dade—Flight of the Indians from Fort Brooke—Capture of King Philip, Coacoochee, and Osceola—Battle of Okechobee—Escape of Coacoochee—Surrender of Halleck-Hajo and others—Results of General Jesup's Operations—General Taylor appointed to the Command.

1836—1837.

GENERAL THOMAS S. JESUP, upon his assignment to the prosecution of the war in Florida, had the experience of his predecessors, Generals Scott and Call, to warn him against the perils of insufficient preparation and temporary and spasmodic movements. Eight thousand troops were placed at his disposal, and he prepared for a vigorous campaign during the winter months, when active movements could best be carried on.

The official reports of all the movements of troops during the previous year had based the want of successful pursuit upon the want of supplies. General Jesup moved forward with rapidity with mounted troops, both officers and men carrying their rations in their haversacks, the commanding general himself often carrying his own haversack. The stronghold of the Indians was in the neighborhood of the Withlacoochee, which they had successfully defended against every effort to dislodge them.

Colonel Foster was directed to move up from Tampa and approach the west side of the Withlacoochee, and to scour the hammocks and swamps, General Jesup himself entering the country lying between the forks of the river and the heart of the Wahoo Swamp. The Indians saw in these movements the indications of a new system of warfare, and that their fastnesses on the Withlacoochee were no longer tenable. The troops thoroughly explored the region, and found the habitations of the Indians but recently deserted; one solitary native was discovered and taken prisoner. A careful examination indicated that the Indians had removed to the southeast.

The term of service of the Tennessee troops, under General Armstrong, being about to expire, they were embarked for New Orleans. A strong post was established on the Withlacoochee, called Fort Dade, as a depot and post of observation in the region which had heretofore been the centre of the Indian settlements.

Having ascertained that the Indians had moved in the direction of the Everglades, General Jesup organized several detachments to make a vigorous pursuit. On the 23d of January, Colonel Canfield, with a detachment of Alabama and other troops, attacked Osarchee near Ahapopka Lake. The Indian chief and his son were killed, and several prisoners taken, but the main body escaped.

Numerous herds of cattle were found on the Thlo-thlo-pop-ka-hatchee Creek, and the Indians were discovered on the Hatchee-Lustee Creek, were attacked by the troops, and dispersed; their baggage and a number of their women and children were captured. The same evening another camp of Indians was dispersed. The troops then moved forward and took a strong position on Topelika Lake, and several hundred head of cattle were taken on the borders of that lake. An Indian prisoner was sent out to invite Abraham, the Interpreter, to come into the camp. Abraham shortly afterwards made his appearance, and after an interview with General Jesup, returned to the nation to induce the chiefs to enter into negotiations. On the 3d of February, Abraham returned, with Jumper, Alligator, and Hapatophe. The result of the conference was that the Indians expressed their desire to treat for peace, and agreed to meet General Jesup at Fort Dade, with the other chiefs, on the 6th of March, and that in the mean time all hostilities should cease.

With this understanding, General Jesup withdrew from further pursuit, and returned to Fort Dade.

A military post had been established at Fort Mellon, on the west side of Lake Monroe, in December, 1836, by Colonel Fanning. The post was occupied by two companies of artillery, a battalion of South Carolina volunteers, four companies of dragoons, under Colonel Harney, and a detachment of Creeks. The Indian spies had shortly before reported that there was but a small force at the fort, and King Philip and his son Coacoochee assembled about four hundred Seminoles and made an attack at daylight on the 8th of February, 1837. The Indians fought with great steadiness, against a superior force, for nearly three hours, and then retired. Fortunately, the post had received considerable reinforcements a day or two before the attack, the arrival of whom was unknown to the Indians. Captain Mellon, a veteran officer of the 2d Artillery, was killed; Lieutenant McLaughlin, and fourteen others, severely wounded. The Indian loss was said to be about twenty-five.

The Indians had encountered a succession of defeats, and were being driven from their fields and homes by a superior force. The season for planting was passing away, and they had no assurance of being able to obtain provisions in any quarter during the coming season. From conviction of its necessity on the part of some, and from policy on the part of others, it was agreed that the chiefs should comply with their agreement to meet General Jesup.

On the 6th of March, the Indians assembled in large numbers, with their chiefs, at Fort Dade, and entered into articles of capitulation. They agreed that they would cease hostilities, and withdraw south of the Hillsborough River, and stipulated that they would at once prepare to emigrate to the West, in the mean time leaving hostages in the hands of the government.

General Jesup agreed, on behalf of the United States, that the Seminoles and their *allies* who come in to emigrate to the West shall be secure in their lives and property, that their negroes, their bona fide property, should accompany them to the West, and that their cattle and ponies should be paid for by the United States.

The capitulation was signed by Jumper, Holatoochee, Hoeth Lee Mathlee, Taholoochee, and Cawaya.

A location about ten miles from Tampa was agreed upon as the place of rendezvous of the Indians, preparatory to embarkation.

By the middle of May a considerable number of the Indians had arrived at the rendezvous, and some twenty-five transports were in readiness to take them to Arkansas. They asked for more time, that others belonging to their families might come in and accompany them.

In the mean time, Osceola, Philip, Coacoochee, and Coe-Hajo, with a large number of Seminoles, gathered in the neighborhood of Fort Mellon, and drew rations from the government, preparing, as they said, to emigrate.

In consequence of the prevalence of sickness at Fort Mellon, that post was abandoned, and subsequently Volusia was evacuated from the same cause.

The war was considered at an end. Arrangements were made for withdrawing the troops to healthier localities.

The settlers prepared to reoccupy their abandoned homes, and others were ready to move into the country.

On the 2d of June, Osceola, at the head of two hundred Miccosukies, came to the camp of the Indians, near Tampa, and either forced or persuaded the whole number, upwards of seven hundred, to leave the camp and seek their fastnesses down towards the Everglades. All the hostages took flight with the rest, and Abraham, the Interpreter, was the only one who remained.

Various reasons for their flight were given. One was, that a report was spread among the Indians that when they were all embarked their throats were to be cut. Another, given by Osceola, was their fear of the smallpox, the measles having broken out among the soldiers at the fort.

At the time the troops left Fort Mellon, Colonel Harney said to Coacoochee that unless the Indians complied with the treaty the United States would exterminate them. The young chief replied that the Great Spirit might exterminate them, but the pale-faces could not, else why had they not done it before?

It is supposed by some, and probably by very many, that this treaty of capitulation, entered into by the Indians with General Jesup, was, from the outset, a mere ruse and device to gain time to plant their fields, and to delay operations against them until the warm season should, as in the previous year, force the troops to suspend their movements. This is, however, a supposition drawn from the event rather than from any evidence of prior intentions. The Indians, to the number of seven hundred, did come in, and could at any moment have been placed on the transports. Many of them, including Micanopy, their head-chief, were thoroughly satisfied that they could not withstand the power of the government of the United States. The younger chiefs, at the head of whom was Osceola, undoubtedly were treacherous, and anxious to defeat the emigration project, and their leader was reckless enough to be willing to abide the consequences, and he had influence enough to give currency and effect to the two absurd stories which have been mentioned. There was another influence at work which did much, undoubtedly, to induce the breaking of the stipulations of the Indians for removal. Many negroes had taken refuge with the Indians, and were now liable to be returned to their owners if the emigration should take place. They had, therefore, every motive to induce them to use their influence with the Indians to prevent the carrying out of the capitulation agreed upon.

General Jesup, on the 5th of April, 1837, issued his order No. 79, in which he says,—

"The commanding general has reason to believe that the interference of unprincipled white men with the negro property of the Seminole Indians, if not immediately checked, will prevent their emigration and lead to a renewal of the war. Responsible as he is for the peace and security of the country, he will not permit such interference under any pretense whatever; and he therefore orders that no white man, not in the service of the United States, be allowed to enter any part of the Territory between the St. John's River and the Gulf of Mexico, south of Fort Drane."

Many persons were desirous of identifying and reclaiming their slaves, and this order, which seemed to have both the purpose and effect of depriving them of the power of obtaining their property, was looked upon as arbitrary and oppressive.

When it was known that the Indians had fled from their camp at Tampa, great consternation prevailed through the country, and the planters, taught by former experience of their insecurity, abandoned their crops and sought refuge near the military posts.

In June, the Indians killed Captain Walton, the keeper of the light-ship on Carysfort Reef, and one of his men. About the same time, Captain Gilliland was murdered near Ichatuckny Spring.

General Jesup now determined to prosecute the campaign with effect as soon as the season would permit the resumption of active operations. Volunteers were called for from Georgia, Florida, Louisiana, Tennessee, Alabama, and Kentucky. On the 24th of October he issued a general order, in which he recites the success attending his previous operations in the field. He truly says, "When the army took the field in December, the enemy's strongholds were on Orange Lake, Ocklawaha, Withlacoochee, Aunutiliga Hammock; they are now south of Lake Monroe and Tampa Bay. The permanent results of the campaign are thirty Indians and negroes killed, and upwards of five hundred prisoners taken."

On the 4th of September, 1837, several negroes surrendered near Fort Peyton. In consequence of information obtained from them, General Hernandez, with the forces under his command, proceeded south, and captured two camps of Indians and negroes; among the Indians were several chiefs, one of the most important of whom was King Philip, called Emathla. Philip desired to send a message to his family, and an Indian having been sent returned with Coacoochee, known better as Wild Cat, a son of Philip, who offered to bring in many others. On the 17th of October, Wild Cat returned, and said that about one hundred Indians and as many negroes were on their way in. General Hernandez met them at Pellicier Creek, and directed them to encamp at Fort Peyton. On the 20th, Osceola and Coe-Hajo sent word they had camped near the fort, and desired to see General Hernandez. Upon the ground that these chiefs and Indians had all capitulated at Fort

Dade in March previous, and that Osceola had brought in his family to Fort Mellon and received rations for his band, General Jesup directed General Hernandez to make prisoners of them and bring them to St. Augustine. Osceola afterwards sought an interview with General Jesup, and told him that Micanopy and Jumper, with the greater part of the Seminoles, were ready to execute the treaty, and asked that messengers might be sent to them and to their own people.

On the 1st of December, 1837, General Jesup had under his command about nine thousand men, of whom one-half were regulars.*

The principal Indian force was on the Upper St. John's, except some roving bands through the peninsula. The troops under General Jesup were assigned to duty as follows: Colonel P. F. Smith, on the Calosahatchee, and to operate as far south as Cape Sable; General Taylor was directed to proceed from Tampa Bay eastwardly, and establish posts at the head of Pease Creek and on Lake Kissimee, and to the St. John's River and Lake Okechobee. General Taylor moved out from Tampa on the 14th of December with a force of about eleven hundred, and proceeded to the neighborhood of Lake Okechobee, where he found a large Indian force, occupying a dense hammock, and protected by a miry saw-grass pond in front of them. With great gallantry, and under great disadvantages of position, the troops charged the enemy, and, after a hard-fought battle, routed them, but at a heavy loss. Lieutenant-Colonel Thompson, Captain J. Van Swearingen, Lieutenant Francis Brooke, and Second-Lieutenant J. P. Center, of the 6th Infantry, also Colonel Gentry, of the Missouri Volunteers, and twenty-two privates were killed. Nine officers

---

* General Jesup's General Report, July 6, 1838.

and one hundred and two men were wounded. The Indians were commanded by Alligator, Arpeika, Coacoochee, and Halleck-Tustenuggee, and numbered about four hundred. Eleven Indians and one negro were killed, and nine wounded. The troops fell back after the battle to Tampa.

General Hernandez moved down with his force to Indian River and the head of the St. John's. The result of his operations was two Indians killed, and two hundred and ninety-seven Indians and negroes taken prisoners.

Brigadier-General Nelson operated along the coast of the Gulf, along the Suwanee River, and in Middle Florida. In the course of his operations he killed six Indians, and took fourteen prisoners. Colonel Snodgrass was assigned to the occupation of the country south of Black Creek and west of the St. John's, between that river and the Ocklawaha. He destroyed several Indian villages, and expelled the Indians from that region. Other officers were constantly moving with detachments, and scouring the country in all directions.

A Cherokee deputation, headed by John Ross, was sent into Florida to persuade the Seminoles to surrender. Their mission, according to General Jesup, was not only useless, but injurious, by the loss of valuable time and the suspension of active operations in the field. Coe-Hajo was sent out as a guide to the Cherokees, and returned with many of his people, accompanied by the Cherokees and the Seminole chiefs Micanopy, Cloud, Toskegee, and Nocase Yoholo, with fifteen or twenty of their followers. A council was held; the chiefs agreed to fulfill their treaty, and sent messengers to collect their people and bring them to camp. The Indians failed to come in, the few who had accompanied the chiefs silently withdrew, and the Indians again scattered.

The failure to complete these negotiations was attributed to the escape of Wild Cat from the fort at St. Augustine, with seventeen of his followers. This chief, with a considerable number of other Indians, had been confined within the old Spanish fort for security. They occupied a room on the west side of the fort, immediately adjoining the southwest bastion. A narrow embrasure gave light and air to the room. The embrasure was some twenty-five feet above the ditch or moat, which was dry at all times. Coacoochee conceived the idea of squeezing through this narrow aperture and descending into the moat, where he would find himself at once at liberty. The task was easily enough accomplished, and with very little risk. Once at liberty, he hastened to rejoin the Indians in the southern part of the peninsula, and, exasperated by the treatment he had received, used every influence to prevent the submission of the Seminoles. The active operations of the large body of troops had harassed the Indians greatly, and the difficulty of providing places of security for their women and children, and of transporting provisions for their sustenance in the winter season, had greatly discouraged them.

By establishing depots of supplies on the Upper St. John's and at strong posts between Tampa and Lake Monroe, General Eustis was enabled to penetrate the region lying on the northern margin of the Everglades, and many Indian settlements were broken up. General Taylor in the course of his operations captured and secured four hundred and eighty-four Indians and negroes. The battle of Okechobee was a hard-fought engagement, and reflected great credit upon the bravery of the troops, who marched through a deep morass against a foe concealed and protected from their fire; but it was a victory gained at a heavy cost, and the result, it would seem, might have been attained in an easier way. The comparatively slight loss inflicted on the Indians, and their ready escape, would naturally impress them with a consciousness of their great advantages in this kind of warfare. Okechobee was the last general fight in which the Indians engaged. They ever afterwards avoided all engagements, and trusted to the climate, the swamps and morasses, and the almost invincible natural obstacles of their country, to fight their battles for them.

During the summer, General Eustis and other officers urged upon General Jesup the propriety of closing the war, by allowing the Indians to remain within a small territory in the southern part of the peninsula. Colonel Twiggs afterwards, with other superior officers, called upon General Eustis, and urged upon him the same views. Anxious as they all were to get out of a region in which they experienced the most extreme hardships, without the compensation of even military glory or the excitement of success, it was very natural that they should see no objection to a peace on such terms as would relieve that part of the country which was habitable and desirable from this inconsiderable Indian tribe, and confine them to an almost insular location, where their presence would injure no one, leaving it to the government to decide, at some future period, when the neccesity existed for their removal. As they diminished in numbers, and retreated farther to the south, the more difficult became their pursuit.

In February, 1838, impressed with these views, General Jesup, at that time encamped near Jupiter Inlet, sent "a messenger to the Indians, to offer them peace," but determined, he says, "on no account to grant them the privilege of remaining in the country, unless the measure should be sanctioned by the general government."*

Halleck-Hajo and Toskegee came in and had a conference with General Jesup, and, after discussion, it was

---

* General Jesup's Report of July 6, 1838.

agreed that the Indians should come into camp near Fort Jupiter within ten days, and await the decision of the President whether they should remain in the country.*

A considerable number of Indians and negroes came in under this arrangement. General Jesup communicated to the War Department the propositions which had been made, and urged that the requisite permission should be given.

Secretary Poinsett replied, under date of March 1, 1838, saying that, however desirable such an arrangement might be, it could not be sanctioned, as it was the duty of the President to carry out the provisions of the treaty.† This communication reached General Jesup about the 20th of March, and, as he was satisfied that if the decision of the War Department was known to the Indians they would at once retire to the swamps, he called a council to be held on the 22d March, and, in the mean time, directed Colonel Twiggs to secure the Indians. Colonel Twiggs promptly executed the order, securing five hundred and thirteen Indians and one hundred and sixty-five negroes. Passac-Micco and fourteen others escaped capture.

The Indians and negroes secured at Jupiter were at once transferred, under a strong guard, to Tampa Bay. Those who had been previously secured at Fort Peyton, with Osceola (Powell), had been transferred to Fort Moultrie, in Charleston harbor.

It seems proper here to take some special notice of this distinguished leader of the Seminoles, whose name and reputation stand perhaps higher in public estimation than those of any other of his race. His true Indian name was As-se-se-ha-ho-lar, or Black Drink, but he was commonly called

---

* General Jesup's Report of July 6, 1838.
† Sprague, p. 201.

Osceola, or Powell. He belonged to a Creek tribe called Red Sticks, and was a half-breed. He removed to Florida with his mother when a child, and lived near Fort King. At the beginning of the Florida war he was about thirty-one years of age, of medium size, being about five feet eight inches in height, resolute and manly in his bearing, with a clear, frank, and engaging countenance. He was undoubtedly the master-spirit of the war, and by his firmness and audacity forced the nation into the war which a large majority were averse to engaging in, and either broke up every attempt at negotiations or prevented their fulfillment. He was to have been one of the leaders at Dade's massacre, but was detained at Fort King by his determination to gratify his revenge upon General Thompson. He participated in the battles at the ford of the Withlacoochee and Camp Izard, and led the attack upon Micanopy, where, with his force of less than two hundred and fifty men, within sight of the fort, he attacked upwards of one hundred regular troops in an open field, supported by a field-piece.

His capture by General Hernandez was due to his audacity and self-confidence. Bad faith, and a disregard of the usages of civilization, have been imputed to General Jesup on this occasion, Osceola having come in under a white flag to negotiate; but that officer contended that Osceola had broken his faith in reference to the Fort Dade capitulation, and was to be treated as an escaped prisoner.

From all that can be gathered of his character, Osceola was possessed of nobler traits than usually belong to his race. His manners were dignified and courteous, and upon the field he showed himself a brave and cautious leader. It is said that he instructed his people in their predatory excursions to spare the women and children. "It is not," said he, "upon them that we make war and draw the scalping-knife. It is upon men. Let us act like men."

Osceola has furnished to the poet, to the novelist, and to the lover of romance, a most attractive subject, and scarce any limit has been placed to the virtues attributed or the exploits imagined in connection with this renowned chief of the Seminoles. A poet has sung of him,—

> "His features are clothed with a warrior's pride,
> And he moves with a monarch's tread ;
> He smiles with joy, as the flash of steel
> Through the Everglades' grass is seen."

Upon his removal to Charleston he became dejected and low-spirited, and gradually pined away. All efforts to interest him in a Western home failed to arouse him, and in a few weeks he died of a broken heart, and was buried just outside of the principal gateway of Fort Moultrie, where his resting-place is inclosed and a monument erected.

Major Lauderdale, with a company of the 3d Artillery and two hundred Tennessee volunteers, explored the country south, and established a post at New River. Lieutenant-Colonel Bankhead, with an additional force, joined Major Lauderdale, entered the Everglades, and captured Pahase-Micco, a sub-chief of Micco, with a band of forty-seven persons, and went in pursuit of Arpeika and his followers. After wading through the mud and water for many miles, they found the Indians upon an island, but were unable to prevent their escape. Afterwards, Colonel Harney came up with Arpeika below Key Biscayne, and attacked him, but was unable to pursue him. General Jesup crossed from Fort Jupiter to Tampa Bay in April, 1837, to attack the Miccosukies and Tallahassees, near the mouth of the Withlacoochee, when the troops were ordered to the Cherokee country and General Jesup was relieved from the command.

This officer is entitled to great credit for the energy and perseverance with which he performed his duties. After he assumed command, there was no longer the complaint of a want of supplies, or the report of falling back in consequence of being short of rations. Within the year and a half during which he held command, the number of Indians and negroes altogether who surrendered or were taken amounted to nineteen hundred and seventy-eight, twenty-three of whom escaped. The number of Indians and negroes taken and killed by the different detachments of the army were equal to four hundred, making the whole number twenty-four hundred, of whom seven hundred were warriors,—considerably exceeding the entire estimated number of Indians in the country at the beginning of the war.

General Jesup also reported, what he believed to be true, but was only so in part, that the villages of the Indians had all been destroyed, and their cattle, horses, and other stock captured or destroyed, and that the small bands who remained dispersed over the Territory had nothing left but their rifles.*

The Indians who had been captured or had surrendered were now placed on transports, under charge of Lieutenant J. F. Reynolds, and removed west of Arkansas. Twelve hundred and twenty-nine constituted the first party, which emigrated in May, 1837. In June, another party of three hundred and thirty was sent to the same destination. Captain Stephenson was appointed their agent West.

On the 15th of May, 1837, General Jesup retired from the command in Florida, which then devolved upon General Zachary Taylor.

---

* Report of General Jesup to the War Department, Ex. Doc., 8th vol., 2d Sess., 25th Cong.

CHAPTER XXII.

Florida War, continued, under General Taylor —Removal of Apalachee Indians—General Macomb's Treaty with the Indians—Proclamation that the War was ended—Resumption of Hostilities—Massacre of Colonel Harney's Detachment—Tragical Fate of Mrs. Montgomery—The Cuba Bloodhounds—Expedition of Colonel Worth to Okechobee—Recapture of Coacoochee.

1838—1842.

THE first important action of General Taylor after assuming command was the removal of some two hundred and twenty Apalachee Indians from West Florida, in October, 1838. The winter campaign of 1838–39 was arranged by General Taylor by districting the country under separate commanders. Lieutenant-Colonel Green was left in Middle Florida; Colonel Twiggs, with about two regiments, was stationed between the Santa Fé River and the coast, and directed to occupy both sides of the St. John's River to Lake Monroe; Colonel Davenport, with six companies, was placed to look after the enemy between the Suwanee and Withlacoochee Rivers and along the Gulf coast; Major Loomis was to operate from Okechobee, south, in concert with General Floyd, commanding a force of mounted Georgians; and Colonel Cummings, with four companies of 3d Artillery, was to establish posts, twenty miles apart, between Tampa and Fort Mellon.

The winter of 1838–39 was spent by the troops in active service in the endeavor to hunt out from their hiding-places the small Indian bands scattered through the country, but with little success, as the Indians, by their better knowledge of the country, were enabled to avoid their pursuers. Occasionally their settlements were reached and broken up, but few of the Indians were seen.

During the operations of this campaign, one hundred and ninety-six Indians and negroes surrendered or were captured, and sent West.

The policy of the Indians was now, says General Taylor, to avoid giving battle to regular troops, even in single companies, while, at the same time, every opportunity was seized to wreak their vengeance on the unarmed inhabitants of the country. Moving by night, rapidly, in small squads, they were able to appear unexpectedly in remote parts of the country, their presence indicated only by their rifles and shrill yells as they approached at daylight the home of some unsuspecting settler. Murders were committed by the Indians within a few miles of Tallahassee and St. Augustine.

Discouraged at the failure of his efforts either to find the Indians or bring them to a stand, General Taylor adopted the plan of dividing the whole country into squares, and placing a block-house, with a small detachment, in each, a part of the number to be mounted. The officer commanding was to scout his district every alternate day, thoroughly examining the swamps and hammocks to see that they were clear of Indians. The merits of this plan were not tested, as it was never fully carried out. While the posts were being established, it was the misfortune of Florida to have Major-General Macomb sent out by the President "to make an arrangement with the Seminoles." General Macomb arrived at Fort King on the 20th of May, 1839, and runners were sent out to invite the Indian chiefs in to hold a grand council.

Halleck-Tustenuggee and Tiger-Tail were present, and Sam Jones sent Chitto-Tustenuggee as his representative. Halleck-Tustenuggee was the mouth-piece of the Indians, and said they were willing to enter into terms if they were not required to go to Arkansas.

An arrangement was entered into by General Macomb with the Indians, assigning them temporarily to a portion of the country below Pease Creek and Lake Okechobee; that they should have sixty days to remove within said limits, where they were to remain until further arrangements were made; and they were forbidden to pass out of such limits, and all other persons were forbidden to go within their boundary.

General Macomb reported to the Secretary of War that the Indians at the council, when he explained to them who he was, and dictated terms of peace, which they readily accepted, manifested great joy, "and they have since been dancing and singing, according to their fashion, in token of friendship and peace, in which many of our officers joined them, being satisfied of the sincerity of the respective parties."*

General Macomb, on the 18th of May, issued his general orders, announcing that

"The major-general commanding in chief has the satisfaction of announcing to the army in Florida, to the authorities of the Territory, and to the citizens generally, that he has this day terminated the war with the Seminole Indians by an agreement entered into with Chitto-Tustenuggee, etc."†

The termination of the war being thus so authoritatively announced, and the terms being so favorable to the Indians, conceding, as they did to them, the privilege of remaining in Florida, and being virtually a capitulation and surrender on the part of the United States of the point at issue,—

---

* General Macomb's Report of May 22d, 1839.
† Sprague, p. 228.

the question of emigration to the West,—the citizens were led to believe that the war had indeed been closed. Many prepared to return to their devastated fields, hoping to make at least a partial crop. All were glad to be relieved of the terror and apprehension of the last three years, and to escape from the restraint of their "forted" villages.

The month of June was quiet and undisturbed, and public confidence increased. General Macomb returned to Washington, and General Taylor resumed command. The season for active operations by the troops had passed, when, early in July, the Indians began hostilities in all parts of the country. Plantations were attacked, and the settlers forced to leave everything behind them. Express- and post-riders and travelers were shot down on the roads, and a feeling of general insecurity revived.

Colonel Harney had gone down to Charlotte Harbor to establish a trading-post for the Indians after they should have retired beyond Pease Creek. His detachment consisted of twenty-five men of the 2d Dragoons, with the store-keeper, Mr. Dalham, and Mr. Morgan, his clerk. They were encamped in the open pine barren near the Calosahatchee, about twenty miles from the mouth. At daybreak on the 22d of July they were attacked by some two hundred and fifty Indians, led by Chechika and Billy Bowlegs. Many were killed at the encampment; others ran to the river, and were shot in the water. Colonel Harney escaped in his shirt and drawers only, and swam to a fishing-smack lying down the river. Out of thirty men, eighteen were killed. The two negro interpreters, Sandy and Samson, were taken prisoners. Sandy was killed next day, and Samson kept prisoner for two years.

The Indians had, up to the time of the attack, professed to be very friendly, coming into camp every day, and talking with the men, professing to be entirely satisfied with the treaty.

Upon receipt of the intelligence of this attack, Lieutenant Hanson seized forty-six Seminoles, who had come in for provisions, and shipped them to Charleston.

This fiasco of a treaty made by General Macomb was due to the action of Congress, which had passed a resolution to that effect, and made an appropriation for that purpose. It was an unfortunate interference, and protracted the war, while it fruitlessly placed the government in a humiliating position.

The prosecution of the war became now extremely discouraging, and the end seemed further off than three years before. The Indians had become familiarized with the exhibition of military power, and had learned to contemn it. They found themselves at the close of four years still in possession of the country, and powerful for annoyance and to inflict revenge, and their ferocity seemed to increase with its exercise.

Governor Reid, in his message to the Legislature of Florida, in 1839, said,—

"The efforts of the general and territorial governments to quell the Indian disturbances which have prevailed through four years, have been unavailing. The close of the fifth year will find us struggling in a contest remarkable for magnanimity, forbearance, and credulity on the one side, and ferocity and bad faith on the other. We are waging a war with beasts of prey; the tactics that belong to civilized nations are but shackles and fetters in its prosecution; we must fight 'fire with fire;' the white man must, in a great measure, adopt the mode of warfare pursued by the red man, and we can only hope for success by continually harassing and pursuing the enemy. If we drive him from hammock to hammock, from swamp to swamp, and penetrate the recesses where his women and children are hidden; if, in self-defense, we show as little mercy to him as he has shown to us, the anxiety and surprise produced by such operations will not, it is believed, fail to produce prosperous results.

"It is high time that sickly sentimentality should cease. 'Lo, the poor Indian!' is the exclamation of the fanatic pseudo-philanthropist. 'Lo, the poor white man!' is the ejaculation which all will utter who have witnessed the inhuman butchery of women and children, and the massacres that have drenched the Territory in blood."

The citizens and troops had now become so exasperated against the Indians for their repeated massacres of the feeble and the unprotected that a feeling had grown up that they were deserving of extermination, and that any and every means should be used to hunt and capture or destroy them. The great difficulty in so wide an extent of country, abounding in thick hammocks, palmetto and scrubby lands, swamps, islands, and morasses, was to pursue them successfully.

In July, 1838, General Taylor forwarded to the War Department a communication he had received on the subject of procuring bloodhounds from Cuba, to a d the army in its operations against the Indians in Florida. General Taylor says, "I am decidedly in favor of the measure, and beg leave to urge it as the only means of ridding the country of the Indians, who are now broken up into small parties, that take shelter in swamps and hammocks as the army approaches, making it impossible for us to follow or overtake them without the aid of such auxiliaries. . . . I wish it distinctly understood that my object in employing dogs is only to ascertain where the Indians can be found, not to worry them."

An agent was sent to Cuba to procure bloodhounds, in December, 1839, and brought thirty-three, with five Spaniards to manage them, at a cost of about one hundred and fifty dollars for each hound. They did not answer the purpose, and they were soon discarded; but in the mean time the subject had been taken up in Congress, and a resolution of inquiry passed requiring a report from the Secretary of War, and the employment of these bloodhounds was used as political capital against Mr. Van Buren when a candidate for re-election as President.

There was a body of Spanish Indians inhabiting the lower part of the peninsula, who had not heretofore taken any part in the contest, but, finding the Seminoles driven down into their region, and probably urged by the savages, who seemed now to have acquired an insatiate thirst for blood, they attacked various settlements upon the islands along the coast, murdered wrecked seamen, and waged war against the fishermen who had frequented the coast for years. One of the most notable of these attacks was made, at Indian Key, upon the family of Dr. Perrine, a botanist of distinction, who was devoting himself to the cultivation of tropical plants. A large party of Indians attacked the settlement on the 7th of August, 1840, and plundered and then burned the houses. Mrs. Perrine and her children were saved by concealing themselves under a wharf. The doctor was massacred in the upper part of the house. The family got possession of a boat which the Indians were loading with plunder, and pushed off to a vessel in the harbor. Several others escaped to the same vessel.*

General Taylor, having now been in command for two years, asked to be relieved from the arduous position he had so faithfully filled. On the 6th of May, 1840, Brevet Brigadier-General W. R. Armistead, 3d Artillery, was assigned to the command.

---

* In Sprague's History, p. 244, will be found a very interesting account of the escape of the Perrine family.

Fruitless expeditions marched out and returned, and failed to find the enemy. The work of surprise and massacre still went on by invisible bands, who struck the blow and disappeared. The country was discouraged, the troops were disheartened, and the Indians remained unmolested. Instructions had been given to endeavor to procure amicable relations. An interview was obtained at one time with Halleck-Tustenuggee, through a Seminole delegation which had been brought from the West, but which accomplished nothing towards bringing matters into a more satisfactory state. Occasionally the Indians came in, professed friendship, said they were tired of the war, received subsistence, and then suddenly disappeared, having obtained all they came for.

On the 28th of December, 1840, Lieutenant Sherwood started from the military post at Micanopy, in company with Lieutenant N. Hopson, a sergeant, and ten privates of the 7th Infantry, to escort Mrs. Montgomery, the wife of Major Montgomery, to the military post at Wacahootee, ten miles distant. About four miles from Micanopy they were suddenly fired on by a large party of Indians, concealed in a hammock which skirted the road. Two privates were killed at the first fire. Lieutenant Sherwood determined to stand his ground, and requested Mrs. Montgomery to dismount and get into the wagon, where she would be less exposed. As she was dismounting, she was shot through the breast. Lieutenant Hopson returned to Micanopy for reinforcements. Lieutenant Sherwood and his men continued a gallant hand-to-hand fight, until they were overpowered by the greatly superior force of the Indians. The latter were led by Halleck-Tustenuggee and Cosa-Tustenuggee, and consisted of thirty warriors.

Cosa-Tustenuggee, fearing the consequences of this barbarous act, prepared to come in and surrender, when he encountered a detachment of dragoons, by whom his whole band, consisting of thirty-two warriors and sixty women and children, were brought in, and the party shortly after sent to Arkansas.*

This tragic event roused anew the indignation of the whole country at the manner in which this miserable war was being carried on, and there sprung up a universal demand to have it brought to a close and the Indians driven out. The War Department rescinded the instructions to the commander to urge the Indians to an amicable surrender, and directed him to prosecute the war. Congress, on the 1st of January, made an appropriation of one hundred thousand dollars for the benefit of such of the Indians as might be willing to surrender, and, on the 3d of March, appropriated upwards of one million of dollars for suppressing Indian hostilities in Florida.

The Indians were now occupying all parts of the Territory; some on the Ocklockonee, some near the Okefinokee Swamp, and some in their old hiding-places on Orange Lake and the Withlacoochee.

Lieutenant Alburtis was in command of Fort Russell, west of Pilatka, when a party headed by Halleck-Tustenuggee killed a corporal and approached the fort with yells of defiance. A spirited attack by Lieutenant Alburtis with some seventeen men only resulted in killing three Indians and wounding two.

Waxehadjo, who had been a leader in waylaying the express-riders and others, had killed the express from Fort Cross to Tampa Bay, and, after torture, had cut off the head of the unfortunate man and set it upright on the coals of his camp-fire, when a detachment of dragoons, with Captain Lloyd Beall, came up and drove him into a pond, where he was killed.

---

* Sprague, p. 249.

Billy Bowlegs, the Prophet, and Hospetarkee, Shiver and Shakes, were the head-men of a large party of Seminoles who occupied the country south of Pease Creek. In December, 1840, Colonel Harney, with a detachment of one hundred men, penetrated this hitherto-unexplored region in canoes, and created much alarm among the occupants of this almost inaccessible portion of the country. Chekika, the Spanish Indian chief, was overtaken by a detachment of troops and killed, and six of his companions captured and hung on the spot, and, it is said, their bodies were suspended from the trees.

This expedition, and the summary punishment inflicted by Colonel Harney, greatly intimidated the Indians, and they resorted to their old expedient of having a "talk" and expressing a strong desire for peace and amity. As their sincerity could only be tested by the result, their offers were accepted, and they came in and received clothing and subsistence, thus gaining time to plant their fields and devise new measures of security for their families. During the winter and spring, every day they could delay operations against them was important. In April, having accomplished their purposes, they again disappeared, leaving the baffled officers of the government to speculate once more on the uncertainty of Indian professions.

Major Belknap, stationed at Fort Fanning on the Suwanee, succeeded, during the month of March, 1840, in securing, and sending West, Echo-E-Mathlar, the Tallahassee chief, with sixty of his band.

During the early summer, the old artifice of professing to be tired of fighting and willing to emigrate was practiced successfully by small bands of Indians, who would come in with a tale of starvation and ask for subsistence for their families to enable them to reach the military posts. The anxiety of the officers of the government to get them in, made them hopeful and desirous of availing themselves of every offer of surrender, and induced them to extend the time and allow still further subsistence. Thus, by cunningly devised stories and well-invented excuses, they drew their subsistence from the government until they were able to dispense with it and the season was too late to operate against them.

The Territory was divided into seven military districts, extending from Black Creek to Sarasota, each under the charge of a district commander. Five years had elapsed, and still the Indians remained, and the government was in the position of almost a suppliant for peace. The efforts of the troops against the Indians were evaded by the exercise of the utmost caution and cunning. With the sagacity and thorough wood-craft of natives of the forest, while the white soldier was plodding his weary way dependent upon guides or the compass for a knowledge of his route, the Indian stopped behind some clump of bushes or peered forth from some leafy covert and saw his pursuers pass by, and then stole back to attack some point in the rear of the pursuing troops, which had been left unprotected. Ill success brought, naturally, criticism and wholesale censure. Those who knew least were wisest in such matters, and had always a plan which, if adopted, would infallibly succeed. Constant changes of plans, of officers, and of troops, made matters worse. An uncertain policy, holding out the olive-branch at one time, and fire and sword at another, alternately coaxing and threatening, gave to the Indians a feeling of distrust mingled with contempt. They thought that they had been deceived by fair words and false professions, and they used the same means to further their own purposes.

In January, 1841, offensive operations were resumed. Colonel William J. Worth, of the 8th Infantry, had been placed in command of the district of which Tampa was the headquarters, and about the 1st of February a battalion of the 8th Infantry, under General Worth, moved out to the Kissimee. The country was found overflowed in all directions. Believing that Coacoochee, the most active and enterprising of the Indian chiefs, was in that region, and that some arrangement might be made through him, a messenger was sent to find and, if possible, bring him in. A few days afterwards, he visited the camp, arrayed in a gorgeous theatrical costume obtained a few months previously when he had attacked a company of actors on the Picolata Road six miles from St. Augustine, several of whom were killed and their theatrical wardrobe became a valuable booty to the handsome young Indian chief.

At this interview with General Worth he agreed to consult his followers and other chiefs, and return in ten days. On the tenth day he returned, regretting that he could not collect his people, but wished to see General Armistead at Tampa Bay, to appoint a day when he would have his people assembled. On the 22d of March, he came to Fort Brooke and met General Armistead, when it was agreed that he would bring his band in to Fort Pierce, on Indian River. During April and May he came in frequently to Fort Pierce, expressing great anxiety to emigrate, but saying that the movements of the troops had caused his people to scatter and conceal themselves, and he had great difficulty in finding them. He said a council was to be held at Lake Okechobee, where he would meet Arpeika, Billy Bowlegs, and Hospetarkee, and he would endeavor to induce them to consent to emigrate. From the caution and sobriety evinced by him, and the large requisitions he made for whisky and provisions, Major Childs, commanding at Fort Pierce, became satisfied that Wild Cat was carrying on a deceptive game, and advised his seizure, and orders were issued for that purpose.

A band of Indians on the Ocklockonee River, in Middle Florida, kept all that portion of the Territory in continual alarm, and although nearly a regiment of regular troops occupied the country, their commanding officer reported, in April, that he was unable to find or capture them. Another band lurked in and around the Okefinokee Swamp, and disturbed all that region of country.

One of the most active and treacherous of the remaining chiefs, Halleck-Tustenuggee, occupied the country around the Withlacoochee and Ocklawaha. He sent in his sub-chiefs to Major Plympton with a bundle of sticks, representing that he was gathering his people in order to emigrate, and asking for provisions, which being at length refused, he threw off the mask and left in his trail sixty sticks, representing his band, painted with blood.

Colonel Davenport, commanding at Sarasota, on the 26th of April reported an entire failure in the attempted negotiations with the Indians, and that they had all gone back to the woods, and gave a very hostile reception to the messengers sent to urge their return.

The close of the season of active operations left matters in very little better condition than at the same period in the previous year. General Armistead, in May, 1841, asked to be relieved of the command in Florida. The result of his operations during the previous year was the surrender or capture of four hundred and fifty Indians, of whom one hundred and twenty were warriors. A delegation of friendly Indians had been brought from Arkansas to use their influence in persuading the remaining Seminoles to emigrate. They were instructed to give a favorable account of the country assigned to the Indians west of Arkansas, and to use every inducement to obtain their surrender. It was doubted whether they did not accomplish more harm than good. General William J. Worth was now assigned to the command, making the eighth commander sent out to close the war. No better choice could have been made than that of the distinguished officer who so well earned the distinctive title assigned to him by universal consent,—the *gallant* Worth.

No more unpromising field for distinction could have been found than Florida presented at the period when General Worth was assigned to the command. As the number of Indians had been reduced, their tactics had been changed. They no longer presented themselves, as at first, to contest the passage of troops in the open field. They now found that by subdividing into small squads they could distract the attention of the troops, and, by the smallness of their number, find ready concealment and elude pursuit. They had become accustomed to the mode of conducting military operations, and knew that with the approach of the summer heats they would remain unmolested. Far down in the Everglades there were islands never trodden by the foot of the white man, where they could place their families in security and plant their crops in peace. From these fastnesses they could sally forth upon long expeditions for murder and rapine; acquainted with coverts to which they might readily fly in all parts of the country, able to support themselves upon the abundant game, they possessed an unlimited power of doing mischief, and were almost as unapproachable as the birds in the air. Where they had been, was easily ascertained by the bodies of the slain victims and the ashes of destroyed homes, but where they were, it was a matter of impossibility to more than conjecture. And when other means of support failed, or it was desirable to check a too active movement in the direction of their camps, they had the convenient resort of a friendly talk and peaceful overtures, accompanied with an abundant supply of whisky and rations.

The officer now in command comprehended fully the task before him. He had seen, in the failures of his predecessors, the results of going into summer quarters one-half of the year, and the cessation of hostilities during peace negotiations occupying much of the remaining portion. He had been assigned to the command on 31st May, a period of the year when it was usual to go into summer quarters. General Worth at once inaugurated a different policy. The force at his disposal was about five thousand men in all, but of these over one thousand were unfit for duty. He at once organized his force in the most effective manner, and prepared for a continuous campaign, irrespective of the season; and the simple injunction, "Find the enemy, capture or exterminate," was to govern the commanders in their operations. General Worth established his headquarters at Fort King. Early in June a detachment of troops penetrated the swamps surrounding Lake Fanee Suffeekee, with the hope of surprising Halleck-Tustenuggee, but, after a severe night march, they found his camp deserted.

On the 15th of June, Major Childs, commanding at Fort Pierce, acting under the orders he had received from General Armistead, secured Coacoochee, his brother, a brother of King Philip, together with thirteen warriors and three negroes who came in to his post. They were immediately sent off to Arkansas. General Worth being advised of this capture, and of their being shipped West, sent one of his officers to New Orleans to intercept the vessel on which they had been sent, in order to bring back Coacoochee, whom he desired to make use of in his ulterior operations. Major Capers, the officer sent, intercepted the vessel, Coacoochee expressing the greatest pleasure at being taken back to Florida, and promising to bring in his whole band.

A simultaneous movement was ordered to take place in each district, for the purpose of breaking up any camps which the Indians might have formed, destroying their crops and stores wherever they might be found. Boat detachments ascended the Withlacoochee, found several fields of growing crops, and destroyed them. Every swamp and hammock between the Atlantic and Gulf coasts was visited, and the band of Halleck-Tustenuggee routed out of the Wahoo Swamp. Many fields were found in the hammocks and islands of the Charl-Apopka country, with huts, palmetto sheds, and corn-cribs. Tiger-Tail had a large field upon one of these islands, which was his reliance for the ensuing year, and from a tree in the hammock he witnessed its entire destruction by the troops. Several fields were destroyed on the Suwanee and in Wacasassa Hammock.

The operations of the army were harassing and destructive to the Indians, and they were driven to make use of every expedient to escape pursuit and capture by the troops, who were scouting in every direction. The last of June they held a council to consult upon their situation. They determined not to surrender, but to put to death any messenger, whether white, Indian, or negro, who dared to come within their reach. They agreed to keep together for mutual protection, and had scouts out to report the number and approach of troops.

The detachments thus engaged in scouring the country continued in the field twenty-five days. The number engaged was about six hundred, and about twenty-five per cent. were sent to the hospitals. The thermometer averaged 86°; and, considering the heat and exposure, the experiment satisfactorily demonstrated the ability of the troops to operate in the summer. In the course of their movements they destroyed thirty-five fields and one hundred and eighty huts or sheds.

The inhabitants were invited to return to their homes, and inducements of subsistence and protection were offered them if they would do so.

CHAPTER XXIII.

Florida War, continued, under Command of General Worth—Interview between General Worth and Coacoochee at Tampa Bay—Surrender of Coacoochee's Band—Active Operations of General Worth in the Everglades — Surrender of various Bands — Close of the Florida War.

GENERAL WORTH, having been informed that Coacoochee had arrived at Tampa, proceeded to that point to hold an interview with him. The Indian chief and his companions were on board a transport in the harbor, and held in irons to prevent the hope or possibility of escape.

On the morning of the 4th of July the interview took place on the transport. The stately and soldier-like presence of the commanding general was enhanced by the presence of his staff in full uniform. Nothing was omitted to give impressiveness to the scene. After the general had arrived, and his party had been seated, Coacoochee and his companions came forward, heavily ironed, and moving with difficulty, and sat down on the deck. General Worth rose, and, taking the young chief by the hand, said, "Coacoochee, I take you by the hand as a warrior, a brave man; you have fought long, and with a true and strong heart, for your country. I take your hand with feelings of pride; you love your country as we do; it is sacred to you; the ashes of your country are dear to you and the Seminole; these feelings have caused much bloodshed, distress, horrid murders; it is time now the Indian felt the power of the white man. Like the oak, you may bear up for many years against strong winds; the time must come when it will fall. This time has arrived. You have withstood the blasts of five winters, and the storms of thunder, lightning, and wind of five summers; the branches have fallen, and the tree, burnt at the roots, is prostrate.

"Coacoochee, I am your friend; so is your Great Father at Washington. What I say to you is true. My tongue is not forked like a snake's. My word is for the happiness of the red man. You are a great warrior; the Indians throughout the country look to you as a leader; by your counsels they have been governed. This war has lasted five years; much blood has been shed,—much innocent blood. You have made your hands and the ground red with the blood of women and children. This war must now end. You are the man to do it; you must and shall accomplish it. I sent for you that through the exertions of yourself and your men you might induce your entire band to emigrate. I wish you to state how many days it will require to effect an interview with the Indians in the woods. You can select three or five of these men to carry your talk; name the time, it shall be granted; but I tell you, as I wish your relatives and friends told, that unless they fulfill your demands, yourself and these warriors now seated before us shall be hung to the yards of this vessel when the sun sets on the day appointed, with the irons upon your hands and feet. I tell you this that we may well understand each other. I do not wish to frighten you; you are too brave a man for that; but I say what I mean, and I will do it. It is for the benefit of the white and red man. *The war must end, and you must end it!*"

Silence pervaded the company as the general closed. Coacoochee rose, and replied, in a subdued tone,—

"I was once a boy; then I saw the white man afar off.

I hunted in these woods first with a bow and arrow, then with a rifle. I saw the white man, and was told he was my enemy. I could not shoot him as I would a wolf or bear; yet like these he came upon me; horses, cattle, and fields he took from me. He said he was my friend; he abused our women and children, and told us to go from the land. Still he gave me his hand in friendship; we took it; while taking it he had a snake in the other; his tongue was forked; he lied and stung us. I asked but for a small piece of these lands, enough to plant and live upon, far south, a spot where I could place the ashes of my kindred; a spot only sufficient upon which I could lay my wife and child. This was not granted me. I was put in prison. I escaped. I have been again taken; you have brought me back; I am here. I feel the irons in my heart. I have listened to your talk. You and your officers have taken us by the hand in friendship. I thank you for bringing me back. I can now see my warriors, my women and children; the Great Spirit thanks you; the heart of the poor Indian thanks you. We know but little; we have no books which tell all things; but we have the Great Spirit, moon, and stars; these told me last night you would be our friend. I give you my word; it is the word of a warrior, a chief, a brave; it is the word of Coacoochee. It is true I have fought like a man; so have my warriors; but the whites are too strong for us. I wish now to have my band around me and go to Arkansas. You say I *must* end the war! Look at these irons! Can I go to my warriors? Coacoochee chained! No; do not ask me to see them. I never wish to tread upon my land unless I am free. If I can go to them *unchained*, they will follow me in; but I fear they will not obey me when I talk to them in irons. They will say my heart is weak, I am afraid. Could I go free, they will surrender and emigrate."

General Worth, in reply, told him distinctly that he could not go, nor would his irons be taken off until his entire band had surrendered, but that he might select three or five of the prisoners, who should be liberated, and permitted to carry his *talk;* they should be granted thirty, forty, or fifty days if necessary. He concluded by saying,

"I say to you again, and for the last time, that unless the band acquiesce promptly with your wishes, to your last wish, the sun, as it goes down on the last day appointed for their appearance, will shine upon the bodies of each of you hanging in the wind."

Coacoochee, after consultation, selected five of his companions to bear his message. After reciting his past services and claims upon his band, he concluded:

"My feet are chained, but the head and heart of Coacoochee reach you. The great white chief (Po-car-ger) will be kind to us. He says when my band comes in I shall again walk my land free, with my band around me. He has given you forty days to do this business in: if you want more, say so; I will ask for more; if not, be true to the time. Take these sticks; here are thirty-nine, one for each day; *this*, much larger than the rest, with blood upon it, is the fortieth. When the others are thrown away, and this only remains, say to my people that with the setting sun Coacoochee hangs like a dog, with none but white men to hear his last words. Come, then; come by the stars, as I have led you to battle. Come, for the voice of Coacoochee speaks to you."

The five messengers were relieved of their irons, and went on their embassy. As time passed, the utmost anxiety was felt by all for the return of the messengers. Old Micco accompanied them, and in ten days returned with six warriors and a number of women and children. They continued to arrive in small parties, when, on the last of the month, all had come in, numbering seventy-eight warriors, sixty-four women, and forty-seven children,—one hundred and eighty-nine in all.

When Coacoochee was told that his people had all come in, he seemed greatly relieved. "Take off my irons," he said, "that I may once more meet my warriors like a man." His irons being taken off, he proceeded to the shore; three ostrich plumes hung from his turban, his breast was covered with silver ornaments, his colored frock and red leggings, a red sash around his waist, containing a scalping-knife, completed his costume. On arriving on shore he gave a shrill whoop, passed on to headquarters and saluted General Worth, then, turning to the crowd, said,—

"Warriors, Coacoochee speaks to you! You have listened to my word and taken it; I thank you. The Great Spirit speaks in our councils. The rifle is hid, and the white and red man are friends. I have given my word for you; then let my word be true. I am done. By our council-fire I will say more."

General Worth, by this sagacious use of Coacoochee, had accomplished the first part of his plan,—the securing of this warlike and troublesome band, numbering some two hundred in all.

Coacoochee was by no means the great warrior his vanity led him to estimate himself. He was vain, bold, and cunning. General Worth had operated upon his weak point by treating him as a great chief. The general now proposed to make still further use of him by procuring his services in bringing in the other bands, which he thought might more easily and certainly be brought to surrender by negotiation than by hostile pursuit. Coacoochee himself having surrendered, he desired to increase his influence at the West by carrying with him a larger force, and readily consented to use his influence in inducing the rest to emigrate. At his instance, the active operations of the army were to some degree suspended.

Detachments, however, continued to operate on the frontier, and scouting-parties were patrolling the country. In August a detachment under Captain Gwynn established a post on Pease Creek, twenty miles above its mouth. Shortly afterwards Sole-Micco, accompanied by two other men and twenty women and children, came into the post for protection, being closely pursued by a party of the Prophet's band from the Big Cypress Swamp.

In this swamp had now gathered a large number of desperate characters from all the tribes, and runaways from the Creeks in Georgia. The influence of the Prophet, himself a runaway Creek, was supreme. Micco had been sent out from Sarasota to carry a talk to some of the chiefs, but was in peril of his life, and took the first opportunity to escape, bringing in his mother and other relatives. He was able to give important information as to the location and designs of the Indians in that quarter.

Coacoochee had a brother, Otulkee, whom he was anxious to reach and have come in to go West with him. He proposed that his younger brother should go down to Pease Creek with an Indian woman, who was to carry a talk to Arpeika and Billy Bowlegs. This messenger, after an absence of ten days, returned to the post on Pease Creek, bringing with him Otulkee and five others. Otulkee brought a message from Hospetarkee that he was coming to see Coacoochee. General Worth arrived about that time at Pease Creek with Coacoochee, who, learning that Hospetarkee was in camp near there, went out to find him, and succeeded in getting him to come into camp with eighteen of his followers to have a talk. General Worth appointed the talk on board a transport in the river, and, being satisfied that the old chief did not intend to surrender, he secured him and his warriors. Messengers were sent to procure the coming in of the remainder of his band, with the women and children, who, some weeks afterwards, came in at Punta Rossa, and joined Hospetarkee at Fort Brooke.

In September an embassy arrived from Tiger-Tail and his brother, expressing themselves anxious for peace. A party of fifteen warriors, belonging to Halleck-Tustenuggee, was captured, and another party of fifteen belonging to various bands. Communication was opened with several chiefs, and Coacoochee and Aleck Hajo, a sub-chief, who had been captured, used their influence to bring in others. The negro interpreter Sampson, who had been captured at the attack on Colonel Harney on Carlosahatchee, now came in, having made his escape from the Prophet's band, and gave important information.

In October, at the solicitation of Hospetarkee and Coacoochee, their bands were sent to Arkansas with others who were at Tampa. The number sent was two hundred and eleven.

Alligator, one of the leading chiefs who had been sent by General Jesup to Arkansas, had been sent for to use his influence with Tiger-Tail and Halleck-Tustenuggee, and had an interview with Tiger-Tail shortly after his arrival. During the month of October, thirty of Halleck-Tustenuggee's band came in, and a portion of Tiger-Tail's.

A combined land and naval expedition, under Captain Burke of the army, and Lieutenant McLaughlin of the navy, was made through the Everglades in October. No Indians were captured, but a very thorough scout was made. It was now determined by General Worth to organize a large force and penetrate the southern part of the peninsula by land and in boats, and to attack the stronghold of the Indians in the Big Cypress, where Ar-

29*

peika and the Prophet held supreme command. A large naval expedition was to accompany the movement. The examination of the hiding-places of the Indians was thorough and complete. The troops marched through swamps, deep in mud and water; their boats penetrated every creek and landed upon every island. The Indians, apprised of their presence, fled towards the coast and were seldom seen; extensive fields were found and destroyed, and every hut and shelter burned. The Indians now saw that no hiding-place was secure, and that, with a vigilant and energetic commander like General Worth to deal with, they were to encounter war in a different form from that which they had previously experienced. They had hitherto considered their homes in the Big Cypress and in the islands of the Everglades inaccessible, and they went on the warpath when it suited their convenience, noiselessly stole upon the unsuspecting traveler, or the isolated family of the settler, and, scattering death and devastation, gathered up their plunder and regained their coverts in security. There was for the savage a horrible fascination in a life like this, and the young Indian lads, who had grown up to manhood during the conflict, hardly knew what a peaceful existence meant. A state of warfare had become habitual. The older warriors clearly perceived now that this state of affairs could not last, and that they must make terms with their foe. Their fields devastated, flying for their lives to new hiding-places, powder and ball becoming too scarce to be used for hunting, and fearful that the sound of their rifles would betray their location, this unceasing prosecution of hostilities began to tell upon and discourage them.

The following graphic summary of the Big Cypress expedition is appended to a long and interesting diary kept by an officer. "Thus ended the Big Cypress campaign, like all others. Drove the Indians out, broke them up, taught them we could go where they could; men and officers worn down; two months in water; plunder on our backs; hard times; trust they are soon to end. . . . Indians asking for peace in all quarters. The only reward we ask is the ending of the Florida War."*

In connection with the expedition entering the Everglades from the Gulf, orders were given to Major Wade, commanding at Fort Lauderdale, on the southeastern part of the Atlantic coast of Florida, to scout for any Indians who might be driven out in that direction from the interior. He succeeded in finding two villages, and captured fifty-five Indians and killed eight, destroying twenty canoes, and all their fields and huts.

While these active measures were going on to reach the main body of the Indians in the Everglades, the small parties lying out in different parts of the country continued to commit murders and evade pursuit. A considerable party was concealed on the Esteen-hatchee and adjacent hammocks, consisting mainly of Creeks under Halpater-Tustenuggee. Another band, headed by Octiarche, were in the Gulf Hammocks, near the Wacasassa.

On the 20th of December, 1841, the majority of the men in the Mandarin settlement, on the east side of the St. John's, about twelve miles from Jacksonville, went out on a general hunt. During their absence, a party of seventeen Indians, belonging to Halleck-Tustenuggee's band, attacked the settlement and killed two men, two women, and a child, and burned the houses. As this attack was made in one of the most thickly settled parts of the country, it created universal fear and consternation. The Indians were traced to the hiding-place of Tustenuggee, on Dunn's Lake.

---

* Lieutenant C. R. Gates's Journal, Sprague, 370.

Major Belknap succeeded in opening negotiations with some of the sub-chiefs of Bowlegs and Sam Jones in the neighborhood of Lake Istokpoga, and secured sixty-seven of their followers, including thirty-two young warriors.

On the 5th of February, 1842, two hundred and thirty Indians were shipped from Tampa to Arkansas, and on the 10th of April one hundred more were sent to the same destination.

General Worth now determined to make a final effort to secure Halleck-Tustenuggee and his band. This cunning and vindictive chief had eluded every effort which had been made to capture him, and laughed to scorn all the messages received from friendly Indians advising his surrender. He was a complete master of wood-craft, and could conceal his tracks, or so arrange them as to mislead those engaged in the pursuit. He had baffled every detachment sent after him, and the commanding general now took command in person. Tustenuggee was finally brought to bay in April, 1842, in the Pilaklikaha Swamp, and his hiding-place surrounded. The troops charged the hammock with great gallantry, and received the fire of the Indians, who discharged their rifles rapidly, but soon broke into small parties and escaped, leaving one killed, two wounded, and one prisoner, the loss of the troops being about the same.

The troops were thus again baffled in their expectation of capturing this noted chief. They had, however, captured his father-in-law, Osane-Micco (the King of the Lakes), through whom a talk was sent to Tustenuggee, and who shortly afterwards influenced the chief to come in to hold a talk with General Worth. General Worth appointed the time for another talk with him at Fort King. Taking advantage of the absence of their chief, Colonel Garland succeeded in getting the entire band to attend a feast, and secured the whole party, and the chief was also secured by General Worth. The capture of the one Indian in the first instance thus resulted, by the sagacious use of this means of communication, in getting possession of the entire party, consisting of thirty-two warriors and thirty-eight women and children. This was one of the most important steps towards bringing the war to a close. This band had done more to keep up the general alarm, and disturb the settlements, than all the others.

The band of Creeks and outlaws still occupied the swamps west of the Suwanee. A large detachment took the field, and made a thorough scout through every part of this region where they were likely to be found. Their fields and settlements were visited and destroyed, and two Indians were killed, and two squaws and three children were captured. To revenge this pursuit, Halpatter-Tustenuggee, with a war-party, crossed the Suwanee River, attacked a settler's family near Newnansville, killing a woman and three children, and burned the house. They then turned south, and fired upon a detachment of troops near Blue Peter Pond, west of Wacahootee, killing two soldiers, and, being sharply pursued, joined Octiarche in Wacasassa Hammock.

In February, 1842, General Worth had addressed a communication to the War Department, submitting a statement of the number of Indians remaining in Florida, which, from the best sources of information he could obtain, amounted to one hundred and twelve warriors and one hundred and eighty-nine women and children, and suggesting that, with such an insignificant number to deal with, the government might now safely close the war by allowing such of them as chose to remain within certain limits below Pease Creek to have the privilege of doing so as a temporary arrangement; that being confined within limits far distant from the white settlements, with a knowledge of their own weakness, they would remain quiet and inoffensive.

This proposal was not at first approved, but subsequently, in a message to Congress, of May 10, 1842, President Tyler approved of General Worth's suggestions, and orders were issued accordingly.

On the 14th of July, Halleck-Tustenuggee, forty warriors, and eighty women and children were embarked for Arkansas.

On the 14th of August, 1842, General Worth issued his General Order, No. 28, announcing that hostilities with the Indians in Florida had ceased, and designating the limits assigned for the temporary occupation of the Indians, being from the mouth of Pease Creek to the fork of the southern branch, thence to the head of Lake Istokpoga, thence down to the Kissimee, thence to Lake Okechobee, and down through the Everglades to Shark River, and along the coast to the place of beginning.

A part of General Worth's policy had been to reoccupy the habitable part of the country with settlers, who, with block-houses to resort to in case of need, should hold an armed occupation. This plan was successfully carried out, and over three hundred settlers with their families were located.

On the 17th of August, General Worth turned over the command in Florida, and proceeded to Washington, in pursuance of orders of the War Department. Upon his arrival, he was conducted by the Secretary of War to the President, who expressed his appreciation, and that of the country, of the fidelity with which all grades of the army had discharged their duty in Florida, and handed him the commission of a brevet brigadier-general, conferred by the Senate of the United States, in consideration "of gallantry and highly-distinguished services as commander of the forces in the war against the Florida Indians."

The headquarters of the army had been established at Cedar Keys, and negotiations were going on, when the intelligence was brought to Colonel Vose that, on the 11th of August, a band of ten Indians had attacked the settlement at San Pedro, in Madison County, and killed two citizens. Colonel Bailey raised a party, and immediately went in pursuit, overtook the Indians and killed two and wounded five of their number. This event, occurring in the midst of a populous country, just at the time when General Worth had issued his announcement that hostilities had ceased, caused much anxiety, and induced many persons to censure or distrust the step which had been taken to close the war.

Public opinion in Florida, acting upon the authorities at Washington, caused the War Department to issue instructions, on the 22d of September, to Colonel Vose, directing him to muster into service a militia force, and push vigorously for the capture and punishment of the enemy.

Colonel Vose suspended the execution of these orders, explaining to the War Department the true condition of affairs.

On the 4th and 5th of October, a violent gale caused an unprecedented tidal wave and high water at Cedar Keys, destroying all the government stores, and nearly submerging the whole island.

On the 1st of November, General Worth, under orders of the War Department, resumed command in Florida.

Octiarche and Tiger-Tail had been for a long time carrying on a negotiation with the commanding officer for surrender and emigration. These negotiations had been accompanied with requisitions for subsistence and whisky, but new excuses for delay were constantly made. Finding that Octiarche would probably be involved in difficulties with Billy Bowlegs, who now claimed to be the head-chief of the Seminoles, General Worth directed that he and his followers should be secured when they next came into Fort Brooke. Shortly afterwards, Tiger-Tail and those remaining with him were captured and brought in.

The Indians remaining on the Oklockonee with Pascoffer, still remained out. Colonel Hitchcock went out with a detachment to operate against them, and, by his energetic and vigilant pursuit, compelled the surrender of that chief and his entire band, numbering fifty-nine, twenty-nine of whom were warriors. Middle and West Florida were, by this surrender of Pascoffer, entirely relieved of Indians, and the surrender of Tustenuggee, Octiarche, and Tiger-Tail had removed nearly all from the central and northern parts of East Florida. These Indians were now all sent to New Orleans, and thence to Arkansas.

No other Indians now remained in the Territory, except those under Arpeika and Bowlegs, who were within the limits assigned them south of Pease Creek, and there was no longer any apprehension of difficulty, and, by common consent, it was admitted that the credit of finally closing the Florida War was attributable to the rare combination of qualifications for this work exhibited by the gallant Worth. Skillful alike in military combinations and in negotiation, he was never outwitted or overreached. His operations were conducted with great economy of life and treasure, and in the space of little more than a year he solved the problem which had so perplexed his predecessors and embarrassed the government. Like other commanders, he was at times severely criticised by those who were unable to comprehend, or were ignorant of, his plans; but at this day only a sentiment of profound respect and admiration exists for the memory of the able and chivalrous general who could win laurels upon so unpromising a

HISTORY OF FLORIDA.

field as that presented in Florida, and who earned a nation's gratitude on the plains of Mexico.

In November, 1843, General Worth estimated the whole number of Indians remaining in Florida as follows: of warriors, Seminoles, forty-two; Miccosukies, thirty-three; Creeks, ten; Tallahassees, ten; ninety-five warriors in all, and, including women and children, three hundred in all, under Holatter-Micco as head-chief, and Assinwar and Otulko-Thlocko, the Prophet, sub-chiefs. In 1845, Captain Sprague, who had been specially in charge of the Indian department in Florida, estimated the total number at three hundred and sixty. Sam Jones (Arpeika) was only a sub-chief; he was then reputed to be ninety-two years of age.

The Florida War may be said to have commenced with the massacre of Major Dade's command, on the 28th of December, 1835, and closed, by official proclamation, on the 14th of August, 1842, having lasted nearly seven years. It was generally said to have cost the United States forty millions of dollars, which, before our recent contest, was considered an immense sum of money. Captain (now General) Sprague, in his valuable work, states the expenditures at upwards of nineteen millions.

The number of troops, of all descriptions, employed during the several years was as follows:

Nov. 30, 1836.	General Jesup commanding,		. . .	4220
" " 1837.	" " "		. . .	8866
" " 1838.	" Taylor "		. . .	3471
1839.	" " "		. . .	3814
1840.	" Armistead "		. . .	6034
1841.	" Worth "		. . .	3801

The number of deaths among the regular troops during the war amounted to an aggregate of fourteen hundred and sixty-six, of whom the very large number of two hundred and fifteen were officers.

On two subsequent occasions there were difficulties with the Indians, caused by their coming in conflict with white settlers outside of their boundaries. After a brief campaign of State troops, they were driven back within their limits.

An inconsiderable number of Indians still inhabit the more southerly portion of the peninsula, peacefully supporting themselves by hunting and fishing.

HISTORY OF FLORIDA.

INDEX.

----, Abraham 278 304-305 307
ADAMS, John 223
ALAMINOS, 13 23 Anton de 19
ALBERT, 97 Capt 95-97
ALBURTIS, Lt 326
ALEXANDER VI, Pope 15
AMBRISTER, 267
ANDRE, 231
ARBUTHNOT, 267
ARCHDALE, Gov 171
ARMISTEAD, Gen 329-330 332 349 W R 324
ARMSTRONG, Gen 301 304
ASHLEY, Col 254-255
ATKINSON, George 255
AUNON, Father 161
AVILES, Pedro Menendez 131
BADAZOZ, Father 161
BAILEY, Col 347
BALBOA, 13
BANKHEAD, Lt-Col 316
BARNWELL, Col 179
BARROWS, Mr 182 Mrs 181
BARTRAM, William 242 272
BASANIER, M 130
BASINGER, Lt 290-291 W E 289

BASSET, Sailing-Master 265
BAYLEY, 201
BEALL, Lloyd 326
BEE, Joseph 230
BELKNAP, Maj 327 344
BERESFORD, Richard 230
BERWICK, John 230
BIENVILLE, De 183-184
BLAKE, Edward 230
BORDEAUX, D 230
BOWLES, 246-248 William Augustus 246
BRE, De 146 Peter de 146
BROADNAX, Lt 258
BROOKE, Francis 310
BROWN, Col 224
BRY, De 58 99 104 128
BRYANT, Lt 194
BUDD, John 230
BURDETT, Charles 242
BURGUIGNON, Nicolas 56
BURKE, Capt 341
BUSH, Joanna 13
CABOT, 14 28 Sebastian 13
CABRERA, Juan Marquez 164 166
CALDERON, Capt 79
CALL, Gen 294 301-303 R K 301
CALLAVA, Gov 268

HISTORY OF FLORIDA.

CAMPBELL, Comm 254 Gen 236
CANFIELD, Col 304
CAPELLES, Juan 163
CAPERS, Maj 332
CARAVALLO, 32
CARDROSS, Lord 166
CARLETON, Guy 231
CASTILLO, 45 Alonzo 42 Capt 38 41
CENTER, J P 310
CHALEUX, Nicholas 119
CHAMPMESLIN, Desnade de 186
CHARLEMAGNE, 94
CHARLES II, 165 King of Spain 168
CHARLES IX, King of France 93 128
CHESTER, Gov 219
CHILDS, Maj 329 332
CLARK, 291 Archibald 255 Rawson 291
CLARKE, 250 Charles W 255 Elijah 249 Geo I F 260 George I F 255
CLINCH, Col 260 263-264 266 284 Duncan L 263 282 Gen 284-287 289 293-299
COCKRANE, Robert 230
COLIGNY, 93 98
COLT, Mr 300
COLUMBUS, 14
CONEY, de 291
COPPINGER, Gov 268
CORDOVA, 13
CORONADO, 77
CORONDELET, Gov 249
CORPA, Father 161
CORTEZ, 23 27 29-30 37 Hernan 29
CRAIG, William 255
CRIPPS, J S 230
CROUCH, H V 230
CUDWORTH, Benjamin 230
CUMMINGS, Col 318
CUNIGA, Gov 175 Jos 173
D'ARLAC, 98
D'AVILAS, Pedro Arias 50
D'ERLACH, 129
D'ESTAING, 229
D'IBERVILLE, 168
D'OTTIGNI, 98
DADE, F L 289 Francis L 288 Maj 288-289 292 295-296
DALHAM, Mr 321
DANIEL, Col 173-174
DARRELL, Edward 230
DAVENPORT, Col 318 330
DAVILA, Father 162-163
DAVIS, Capt 156 John 165
DEAGUILAR, Jose 198
DEAHUMADA, Pedro 78
DEAILA, 166
DEALAMINOS, Anton 19
DEALAS, Hernando 164
DEALVARADO, Luis Muscoza 68 77
DEARRIOLA, Andres 168
DEAYALA, Juan 182-183
DEAYLLON, 13 20-23 25-27 Lucas Vasquez 20
DEBASTRO, Fra Luis Cancer 78

DEBENAVIDES, Antonio
    183
DEBETATA, Fra Gregorio 78
DECALDIVAR, Juan 77
DECANCER, Luis 79
DECERON, 87 Juan 87
DECHASTELLAN, Adm 93
DECORDOVA, Fernandez 19
DEFERIA, Pedro 89
DEGALLEGOS, Baltazar 68
DEGALVEZ, 228-229
    Bernardo 229 236
DEGARAY, 19-20 Francisco
    19
DELAVEGA, Garcilasso 73
DELEON, 17 Juan Ponce 14
    22 Louis 24 Ponce 13 15-
    16 18 23-24 28
DELUNA, 83 86-87 90 93 167
    Tristan 77 81-82 89-91
DEMENENDEZ, Pedro 91
DEMONTEANO, Manuel
    192
DENARVAEZ, 39 74
    Pamphilo 46 Panfilo 29
    41 50
DEPENALOSA, Fra Diego 78
DEPORCALLO, Vasco 52
DEREBELLADO, Diego 164
DERIBERA, Jose Primo 182
DESALACAR, Juan Hita 164
DESALINAS, Gregorio 182
DESALIS, Alonzo 41
DESAMANO, Julian 78
DESOLIS, 122-123
DESOTO, 24 47 51-53 55-58
    61-66 68 71 73-77 82 90
    167 Fernando

DESOTO (Cont.) 68
    Hernando 50 Isabella 65-
    66
DESSAUSSURE, Daniel 230
DETORRES, Lauseano 168
DEVACA, 32 34 40 43-46 77
    90 Alvar Nunez Cabeca
    47 Cabeca 29 38 42 45 47-
    48 50 69 88 Cabeza 46
DEVEREUX, Col 237-238
DEVICENTE, Juan 136
DEVILLAFANE, Angel 89
DEVILLAREAL, Gonzalez
    120
DIAZ, Bernal 19
DICKSON, Lt-Gov 229
DOMINGO, Father 89
DORANTES, 45 Andreas 42
    Capt 38 41
DRAKE, 160-161 Francis 56
    156 159-160
DRAYTON, Chief-Justice
    242 Mr 223 William 219
    222
DUNCAN, William 216
DUNMORE, Lord 246
DUSTAN, 181
DUVAL, W P 274 William P
    270
EDWARDS, John 230
EGMONT, Lord 219
ELLIOT, Mr 215
ELLSWORTH, H L 280
ELPHINSTONE, Capt 225
ENRIQUEZ, 38 41
ESQUIVEL, 40
ESTEVANICO, 45
ESTRADA, Col 255

EUSTIS, Gen 312-313
FANNING, Col 294 305
FANSHAW, Capt 193
FERGUSON, Thomas 230
FERNANDEZ, Alonzo 52
  Alvarez 46
FERNANDO, Don 46
FISH, Mr 215
FLAGG, George 230
FLOYD, Gen 318
FORBES, 215 John 242 Mr 215
FORT, Capt 257-258
FOSTER, Col 303
FRANCISCO, 25
FRAZER, Capt 290 292 N 242 U S 289
FUENTES, 78-79
FUSER, Col 225-227
GADSDEN, A C 230 Gen 230 James 274 278
GAINES, Gen 263 291 296-298
GALVEZ, 236
GARCIA, 264 Comm 265 Fra Juan 78
GARDINER, S 289 Capt 290
GARLAND, Col 344
GATLIN, Dr 290 J S 289
GENTRY, Col 310
GERARD, Mr 215
GIBBS, Wm Hazel 230
GIDDINGS, Mr 280
GILLILAND, Capt 309
GOMEZ, Luis 201
GOULD, Elias B 295
GOURGUES, de 130 143-156 Dominic de 142-144

GRAHAM, Maj 226
GRANT, Gen 219 Gov 215 222 James 214 242
GRANVILLE, Lord 219
GREEN, Lt-Col 318
GRINBALL, Thomas 230
GUERLACHE, 97
GWINNETT, Pres 224
GWYNN, Capt 340
HAKLUYT, 48
HALL, George A 230 Thomas 230 William 230
HALLIMAN, Capt 299
HALLOWS, Col 300
HALY, Nicolas 56
HANCOCK, John 223
HANSON, Lt 322
HARNEY, Col 305 307 316 321 327 341
HARRIS, 271 Gen 260
HAWKE, Lord 219
HAWKINS, John 106-107 115
HEILEMAN, Maj 300
HENDERSON, Lt 290 R 289
HENRY, Mr 215
HENRY VII, King of England 13
HENRY VIII, King of England 159 210
HERBERT, Lt 300
HERNANDEZ, Gen 309-311 315
HEYWARD, Thomas Jr 230
HILLSBOROUGH, Lord 219
HITCHCOCK, Capt 291 293 298 Col 348
HOLMES, Isaac 230

HISTORY OF FLORIDA. 355

HOPSON, N 325
HOUSTON, Gov 226
HOWE, Gen 226
HUGER, Mr 215
HUMPHREYS, Capt 258 Col 274 277 G 275 Gad 273
HUTSON, Richard 230
INDIAN, Aequera 101 Aleck Hajo 341 Alexander Mcgillivray 245 Alligator 285 290 292-294 298 305 311 341 Allimicany 102 Allimicany Paracoussi 101 Anacharagua 101 Anitagua 101 Arpeika 300 311 316 329 340-342 348-349 As-se-se-ha-holar 314 Assinwar 349 Ays 139 Billy Bowlegs 321 327 329 340 348 Black Dirt 285 Black Drink 314 Bowlegs 258-259 272 348 Cadecha 101 Calany 101 Cawaya 306 Charley Emathla 283 286 293 Chechika 321 Chief Bowlegs 257 Chief Charley Emathla 278 283 Chief Chekika 327 Chief Cloud 311 Chief Coi-hadjo 278 Chief Fuch-lus-to-had-jo 278 Chief Helicopali 147 Chief Hicks 275 Chief Hirrihigua 53 Chief Holati Emathla 278 Chief Jumper 278-279 Chief King Philip 309

INDIAN (Cont.) Chief Lafarka 263 Chief Mcgillivray 249 Chief Micanopy 307 311 Chief Mucoso 55 101 Chief Nocase Yoholo 311 Chief Olata Utina 106 Chief Olocatora 146 Chief Osceola 307 Chief Payne 257 Chief Pennyman 247 Chief Prophet Francis 267 Chief Sam Jones 278 Chief Satourioura 137 146 Chief Secoffee 271 Chief Toskegee 311 Chief Vitachuco 57 Chief Ya-ha-had-jo 278 Chilili 101 Chitto-tustenuggee 319-320 Coacoochee 303 306-307 309 311-312 318 329 332 335-341 Coava 139 Coe-hajo 306 309 311 Cosa-tustenuggee 325 Echo-e-mathlar 327 Eclanan 101 Emathla 309 Enacoppe 101 Halleckhajo 303 313 Hallecktustenuggee 311 319 325-326 330 332-333 341 344 346 Halpatertustenuggee 343 Halpatter-tustenuggee 345 Hapatophe 305 Hirrihigua 54-55 Hoeth Lee Mathlee 306 Holatoochee 306 Holattermicco 349 Hospetarkee 327 329 340-341

INDIAN (Cont.) Jumper 285
298 305-306 310 Katehahaigo 264 King of
Atimiaca 176 King Payne
247 258 King Philip 295
303 305 Macaya 139
Mcgillivray 247 249
Micanopy 285 290 295
310 315 Micco 316 340
Mucoso 55 101 Octiarche
345 347-348 Old Micco
338 Olocatora 147 Osanemicco 344 Osceola 283
285-289 293-294 298 303
306-307 309-310 314-316
Otima 139 Otulkee 340
Otulko-thlocko 349
Pahase-micco 316
Pascoffer 348 Passacmicco 314 Payne 258-259
272 Philip 306 309 Powell
315 Sam Jones 285 319
349 Satourioura 139-140
146 Secoffee 271 Shakes
327 Shiver 327 Solemicco 340 Taholoochee
306 Te Deum 120 The
Prophet 327 340 342 349
Tiger-tail 319 341 347-
348 Tomoka 295 Toskegee
313 Tustenuggee 348
Waxehadjo 326 Wild Cat
309 311 329
ISAACS, Capt 264 Col 230
IZARD, Capt 315 Lt 297 Mr
215
JACKSON, Gen 260-262 266-
268 271 284 Pres 282

JESUP, Gen 302-311 313-317
341 349 Thomas S 303
JOHNS, 301 Mr 301 Mrs 301
JOHNSTONE, William 230
JONES, 196-197 Noble
Wimberley 230
KINDELAN, Gov 257
KINGSLEY, Mr 259
Zephaniah 255
LACAILLE, 126-127
LAGRANGE, Capt 121
LASALLE, 167-168 de 167
LAUDERDALE, Maj 316
LAUDONNIERE, 92 98-100
103-104 106-108 111 117-
120 130 146 Capt 99 103
Rene De 98
LAURENS, Mr 215
LAVAL, Maj 262
LAVEGA, 57
LECLERC, 97
LEE, William 230
LEFEBVRE, 178
LEMOYNE, 121 127
LENT, John 181
LEWIS, John 230
LINCOLN, 229
LOFTHOUSE, Capt 224
LOGAN, William 230
LOOMIS, Lt 264 Maj 318
Sailing-Master 263
LOPEZ, Don Jose 254 Jose
254
LOUIS XIV, King of France
168
LUFFBOROUGH,
Midshipman 264
LUIS, Don 157 Fra 79

LUSHINGTON, Richard 230
MACOMB, Gen 319-322 Maj-Gen 319
MALDONADO, 65 Francisco 64
MANIGAULT, Mr 215
MANREQUEZ, Gov 261
MARCOS, Francis 80
MARIGNY, De 153
MARTINEZ, Father 138
MASSEY, William 230
MATTHEWS, 271 Gen 252 254 256
MCCREA, Miss 181
MCCREADY, Edward 230
MCGILLIVRAY, Lachlan 245
MCGIRTH, 248 Daniel 247
MCINTOSH, 197 Capt 193 195-196 198 228 Gen 250-251 John 250 John H 254 Maj 264-265 Mr 228 Rory 225-226 228-229
MCKAY, 197 Capt 195-196
MCKEE, John 252
MCLAUGHLIN, Lt 305 341
MCLEMORE, Maj 299
MELLON, Capt 305
MENDOZA, 77 Chaplain 153
MENENDEZ, 111-116 118-130 132-141 149-150 152-153 155-159 161 166 169-170 188 Carlos 139 Carolina 164 Francisco 188 Marquis de 158 Pedro 131 164
METAMORAS, Gov 183-184 Juan Pedro 182
MEXIA, 176 Juan 176-177

MIDDLETON, Arthur 230 Gov 188
MIRUELO, 13 31 Diego 19
MITCHELL, Gov 256-257 260
MONCRIEF, Capt 225
MONTEANO, 198 200-206 208 Gov 198-199 206
MONTGOMERY, Col 222 Mrs 318 325
MONTLUC, 144
MOORE, 175-176 Col 177 Gov 171-175 178
MORALES, Pedro 56
MORGAN, Mr 321
MORGUES, Jacques 104-105
MORRISON, 229 Mr 229
MORTON, 166
MOUATT, John 230
MOULTRIE, Alexander 230 Gen 222 Gov 215 222-223 244 James 242 Lt-Gov 222 242 Maj 219
MOWBRAY, Capt 226
MUDGE, Lt 290 R R 289
MUHLENBERG, Maj 264-265
MUNOZ, 79 Juan 78
MURRAY, Mr 215
NAIRN, T 179
NAPOLEON III, 94
NARVAEZ, 29-31 33 35-36 38 40-42 46 51 53-54 92 167
NEGRO, Samson 321 341 Sandy 321
NELSON, Brig-Gen 311
NEUFVILLE, John 230

NEWMAN, 258-259 Col 257
NICHOLS, 266 Col 262
NORTH, Edward 230
O'NEIL, Gov 248
OGILVIE, Maj 214
OGLETHORPE, 190-194 199-208 Gen 191 199
ORANTES, 46
ORTIZ, 54-55 Juan 42 53 56 65 101
OSWALD, Mr 215 220 Richard 220
OTTIGNY, 127
OVANDO, 14
PACHECO, Antonio 288 Luis 293
PALAZIR, Gov 209
PALMER, 194 Col 189 194-198
PARDO, 139 Juan 139
PARKER, Joseph 230
PEARCE, Capt 193
PEDRO, Don 182
PENALOSA, 78-79 Capt 38 41-42
PERRINE, Dr 324 Mrs 324
PETERS, Christopher 230
PHAGAN, John 277-278 Maj 277-278 280 282
PHILIP, King of Spain 152-153
PHILIP II, King of Spain 112 131
PIERCE, Lt-Col 301 Maj 300-301
PINCKNEY, Mr 215
PINKNEY, Gen 260
PIUS V, 131

PIZARRO, 51
PLYMPTON, Maj 330
POCAHONTAS, 54
POINSETT, Secretary 314
POMPIERRE, 127
PORCALLO, 56
POSTELL, Benjamin 230
POYAS, John Ernest 230
PREVOST, Gen 229 Maj 226 228
PRINCE, 257
PRIOLEAU, Samuel 230
PUTNAM, Maj 295
QUESADA, 250 Gov 250
REAIS, J L 289 Lt 290
REED, Lt 258
REID, Gov 322
REYNOLDS, J F 317
RIBAUT, 91-92 94-98 100 111 115-117 120-121 124-129 143 152 Capt 111 130 Jean 93 95 130
RIBERA, Jose 188
RIDGLEY, Lt 255
RODRIGUEZ, Father 161
ROGERS, Mr 288
ROLLE, Dennis 220 Lord 220 Mr 235
ROMANS, Bernard 242
ROSS, John 311
RUTHERFORD, Gen 230
RUTLEDGE, Edward 230 Hugh 230
SAINT GERMAIN, Lord 231
SANSOM, John 230
SAVAGE, Thomas 230
SCHERMERHORN, J F 280
SCOTT, Gen 297-299 303

SEGUI, Bernardo 274
SEGURA, Father 157-158
SHERWOOD, Lt 325
SIMMONS, Dr 300 William H 270
SIMMS, W Gilmore 63
SINGLETON, Thomas 230
SKINNER, Capt 227
SLAVE, Lewis 288 Tom 228-229
SMITH, Buckingham 163 169 Col 255-257 Constantine 287 Josiah 230 P F 310 Persifer 296
SNODGRASS, Col 311
SOLANA, 236 Adm 236
SPRAGUE, Capt 279 349
STARK, William 242
STEPHENSON, Capt 317
STEVANICO, 42
STOKES, Montfort 280
SUAREZ, Juan 38 41
SWEARINGEN, J Van 310
TAYLOR, Capt 264-265 Gen 303 310 312 318-319 321 323-324 349 Zachary 317
TELLEZ, Capt 38 41
THOMAS, 291
THOMPSON, Gen 282-289 315 James Hampden 230
TIMOTHY, Peter 230
TODD, John 230
TOMPKINS, Capt 301
TOMPSON, Lt-Col 310
TONYN, Gov 223 232 Patrick 231
TOOMER, Anthony 230

TOWNSHEND, Capt 193
TURNBULL, Andrew 216 242 Dr 216 220 222 243
TWIGGS, Col 313-314 318 Gen 249
TYLER, Pres 346
VACQUIEUX, 153
VAN BUREN, Mr 324
VANDERDUSSEN, Col 192 194 202
VELASCOLA, Fra 162
VELASQUEZ, Gov 37
VERAZZANO, 13 Juan 27
VITACHUCO, 58
VOSE, Colonel 347
WADE, Major 343
WAKEFIELD, James 230
WALLER, Benjamin 230
WALTON, Capt 309 Mr 215
WARREN, Capt 193 Col 301
WEYMAN, Edward 230
WHITE, 251
WILKINSON, Morton 230
WILLIAM, King of England 168
WILLIAMS, 181 John Lee 270 Llewellyn 286 Lt 256-257 Major 286
WILSON, 291
WOODBINE, 266
WORTH, Col 318 Gen 329 331-332 335 338-342 344-349 William J 328 331
WRIGHT, Capt 201
YONGE, Mr 221
ZESPEDEZ, Gov 239

www.ingramcontent.com/pod-product-compliance
Lightning Source LLC
Chambersburg PA
CBHW070227230426
43664CB00014B/2236